IGWEBUIKE:

AN AFRICAN COMPLEMENTARY PHILOSOPHICAL FRAMEWORK

Ikechukwu Anthony KANU

authorHOUSE®

AuthorHouse™ UK
1663 Liberty Drive
Bloomington, IN 47403 USA
www.authorhouse.co.uk
Phone: UK TFN: 0800 0148641 (Toll Free inside the UK)
         UK Local: (02) 0369 56322 (+44 20 3695 6322 from outside the UK)

Published by AuthorHouse 06/17/2022

ISBN: 978-1-6655-9969-6 (sc)
ISBN: 978-1-6655-9968-9 (e)

In Memory
of
Sir Emmanuel Nwafor Kanu, KSJI
An Igwebuike Philosopher

CONTENTS

INTRODUCTION

Igwebuike is essentially a transcendent complementary comprehensive systematic effort to understand the structure and dynamics of reality ultimately for the purpose of giving honest answers to fundamental questions or opinions to questions that arise within the arena of asking questions and questioning answers, selfless enlightenment and furthering of human happiness. In this search for truth, *Igwebuike*, within an integrated systematic framework, strives beyond all forms of particularities, peculiarities, paradoxes and contradictions and espouses the path of complementation, therefore, showing how realities can relate to one another in a mutually harmonized non-absolutistic mode.

This piece studies the dimensions of *Igwebuike*, which include its place within the theater of being, and its literal and linguistic meanings. It also searches for the basis of inter-subjectivity in the African worldview conceptualized in *Igwebuike* philosophy, and this it locates in *Chi*. The next two papers study aspects of Plutarch's ethical-political thought in comparison with the *Igwebuike* philosophy and employed *Igwebuike* as an ontological toolbox that forms the trajectory system of the Igbo-African world. There are further inquiries on the relationship between *Igwebuike* and the liberation and ethics.

There is also a study of the relationship between *Igwebuike* ideology and the "I – Thou" philosophy of Martin Buber, which the author avers are both geared towards an authentic human existence. It further inquires into the possibility of the *Igwebuike* principle of complementarity advancing interreligious dialogue and modern efforts towards conflict resolution. There is also a discourse on the relationship between *Igwebuike* as a philosophy and leadership.

This piece remains a major contribution to the corpus of literature on *Igwebuike* philosophy. I, therefore, introduce this piece to all lovers of African philosophy, religion and culture.

THE DIMENSIONS OF IGWEBUIKE PHILOSOPHY

Ikechukwu Anthony KANU
Department of Philosophy and Religious Studies
Tansian University Umunya, Anambra State
ikee_mario@yahoo.com

EXECUTIVE SUMMARY

This paper has studied the dimensions of Igwebuike. As a unifying concept of African thought, especially, Igwebuike is understood as that aspect concerning the human person's conception of the spiritual and material universe in which they live. It is an explanatory theory or principle that interprets the puzzle of our complex relationship with the non-corporal world and human social life, that is, the major social institutions that ensure social continuity and group identity, and further underpins the epistemological manifestations of the human person's universe. This piece has studied the dimensions of Igwebuike, which include its place within the theater of being, and its literal and linguistic meanings. It also focused on the anthropological and epistemological foundations of Igwebuike, and also its ontological and cosmological foundations. This work, although it has studied the linguistic and literal senses of Igwebuike, goes further by focusing on the philosophical dimension of the concept. The method of inquiry employed for the purpose of this research is the Igwebuike complementary approach.

Keywords: *Igwebuike*, Linguistic, Literal, Ontological, Epistemological, Anthropological

INTRODUCTION

Igwebuike, essentially, is a transcendent complementary comprehensive systematic quest to penetrate the structure and dynamics of reality ultimately for the purpose of giving honest answers to fundamental questions or opinions to questions, for selfless enlightenment and furthering of human happiness. In this search for truth, *Igwebuike,* within an integrated systematic framework, strives beyond all forms of paradoxes and contradictions and espouses the path of complementation, therefore, showing how realities can relate to one another in a mutually harmonized non-absolutistic mode. Thus, *Igwebuike* explores methods and principles for the mediation, coalescing and comprehension of the different units of reality:

1

ideal and real, universal and particular, progressive and conservative, necessary and contingent, transcendent and immanent, essential and inessential and other units of reality within the same framework. It treats all units, fragments or components of reality, no matter how minute, as units and combinations, or missing links that are necessary for the conceptualization of reality as a whole.

The above notwithstanding, this piece will study the dimensions of *Igwebuike* philosophy. This would include its understanding within the theater of being, and the literal and linguistic settings. It will further focus on the anthropological and epistemological foundations of *Igwebuike,* and also its ontological and cosmological foundations.

IGWEBUIKE IN THE THEATRE OF BEING

'To be' in Igbo ontology is *idi.* The operative word in *Idi* (to be) is *di* (be), and it comes from the word *odi* (it is), which is the third person of the singular *idi.* It means 'to exist' or 'to be'. It is an adjective and can be suffixed to anything to show that it exists. For instance, *Okwute di* (stone exists), *Nkita di* (dog exists), *Kanu di* (Kanu exists), *Uwa di* (the world exists). Although every reality has a force, not all realities have the same amount of force. The variety of the degree of forces is at the base of the categorization of being, and thus, the hierarchy of forces (Kanu 2017a). In the hierarchy of forces, those with a greater force come first, with God at the apex as the source of all force (Kanu, 2017b). In Igbo-African ontology, reality is subsumed into the following categories: *Muo* (Spirit), *Madu* (Human Being), *Anu* (Animal), *Ihe* (Thing), *Ebe* (Place), *Oge* (Time) and *Uzo* (Manner, Modality or Style of being). Everything is in relation to the other, except the creator (Kanu, 2017c). As subjects in the horizon of perception and realization of their existential ends, beings depend on each other for their temporal flourishing. The dependence here is a positive dialectics, resulting from their physical and spiritual limitations. Human beings are not ontological creators of themselves; they are essentially limited, and their existence and action, in the midst of communication, are limited by time, place, perception and knowledge. Their being is existentially complementary (Kanu, 2017d&e). Hence, they are, naturally, candidates for company and co-operations. This modality of being is what *Igwebuike* conceptualizes.

IGWEBUIKE IN ITS LITERAL AND LINGUISTIC SETTING

Igwe bu ike is an Igbo proverb and also a typical Igbo name. Igbo proverbs and names are among the major traditional vessels where African philosophy, religion and culture have continued to be preserved. Mbiti (1970) writes that: "It is in proverbs that we find the remains of the oldest forms of African religious and philosophical wisdom" (p.89). They contain the wisdom and experience of the African people, usually of several ages gathered and summed up in one expression. Proverbs spring from the people and represent the voice of the people and also express the interpretation of their beliefs, principles of life and conduct. It express the moral attitudes of a given culture, and reflect the hopes, achievements and failings of a people (Kanu, 2018). This is to say that beyond the linguistic expression lies a deeper meaning, that is, the spirit of the letter. It is at the philosophical level that *Igwebuike* is understood as providing an ontological horizon that presents being as that which possesses a relational character of mutual relations (Kanu, 2016c).

The expression, *Igwebuike,* is a combination of three Igbo words. It can be understood as a word or a sentence: as a word, it is written as *Igwebuike*, and as a sentence, it is written as, *Igwe bu ike,* with the component words enjoying some independence in terms of space. Literally, *Igwe* is a noun which means number or multitude, usually a large number or population. The number or population in perspective are entities with ontological identities and significances; however, it is part of an existential order in which every entity is in relation to the other. *Bu* is a verb, which means *is*. *Ike* is a noun, which means *strength* or *power* (Kanu 2016a&b). *Igwe, bu* and *Ike* put together, means 'number is strength' or 'number is power' (Kanu, 2017f). However, beyond the literal sense of *Igwebuike,* it means *otu obi* (one heart and one soul) – *cor unum et anima una.*

This is anchored on the fact that the universe in which the human person lives is a world of probabilities. An Igbo proverb says: "If a thing remains one, then nothing remains". This is because the power or strength generated by a person is not strong enough to withstand the existential gamble of life, as the chances of being overcome are on the high side; thus, the need for an existential backing. There is also an African proverb that says: "While going to the toilet in the morning, ensure that you carry two sticks". The sticks are used for cleaning oneself after using the convenience. But because there is always the high probability of the stick falling into the pit, it is always advisable to take a second stick, just in case. With two sticks, one has a greater assurance of cleaning oneself up after using the toilet; the higher the number, the greater the preparedness towards minimizing the casualty of life. The second stick is also necessary in case of a second coming or remainder of the output. In a metaphoric sense, it is used within the Igbo linguistic setting to refer to relational engagement in the world, accomplished in solidarity and complementarity, and the powerful and insurmountable force therein (Kanu, 2017g). The closest words to it in English are complementarity, solidarity and harmony.

ANTHROPOLOGICAL AND EPISTEMOLOGICAL FOUNDATIONS OF *IGWEBUIKE*

Igwebuike has anthropological and epistemological foundations, which are based on the nature of the human brain which functions in an inclusive manner for the realization of holistic knowledge. A cursory glance at the human brain reveals different sections which could be described as circles. Below is a diagram to explain the different sections of the brain and what they represent.

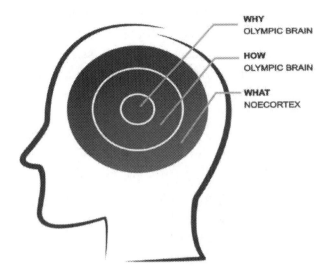

A DIAGRAM SHOWING THE DIMENSIONS OF THE HUMAN BRAIN

The human brain has the Olympic dimension, referred to as Olympic brain, and the Noecortex dimension, also referred to as the Noecortex brain. The Olympic brain has two sections, which include the inner and outer Olympic brain. Thus, the three circles of the brain are the Inner Olympic Brain, the Outer Olympic Brain and the Noecortex Brain. These different parts of the brain concern themselves with different questions that arise in human relationships: the questions of WHY, HOW and WHAT. While the Inner Olympic Brain responds to the question of WHY, the Outer Olympic Brain responds to the question of HOW, and the Noecortex Brain responds to the question of WHAT (Kanu, 2017c).

For knowledge to be holistic and translate into action for transformation, it must be based on an understanding of the WHAT, HOW and WHY questions about reality. For a leader to be effective, the led need to know what they do, how to do what they do, and why they do what they do. The absence of any of these strangles followership. In advertisements, most organizations only explain what they do, how they do what they do, without explaining why they do it. This explains why many organizations fail. This is based on the fact that people patronize you because of why you do what you do, and not only because of what or how you do it. The question of WHY speaks of your uniqueness and the newness you are bringing into the system. It is at the WHY Level that you find: feelings, loyalty, trust, decision making and human behaviour. For a comprehensive understanding, they must complement one another. The connection of complementarity to the human brain explains the epistemological and anthropological foundations of *Igwebuike*.

ONTOLOGICAL FOUNDATIONS OF *IGWEBUIKE*

The mutual relations and complementarity that *Igwebuike* conceptualizes is are anchored on the following basic human conditions (Njoku 2015):

a. The world in which we live is one in which we encounter several needs, however, with very little resources to take care of the needs. This limitation calls for the mobilization of other forces outside of the self, a social fellowship for the satisfaction of particular needs.

b. Nature has placed in us the alikeness for fellowship. This is based on the fact that we were created by God in His own image and likeness.

c. Although we are equal essentially, we have different gifts and abilities. What I may be able to do, another may not be able to do, meaning that my relationship with the other completes what is lacking in me.

d. Collaboration with the other is ground for becoming, as everything takes a bit of another to make itself. It is a ground for staying alive and transforming the universe.

Human fellowship and cooperation is a reality that is rooted in the human nature, and to keep away from relating is to place a limitation on our being. It is, therefore, a unit of order inscribed in the human nature for survival. The more a person relates, the more he/she lives out his/her or her being to the full. Mutual cooperation and fellowship in the society increases protection, assistance, etc. Being in the company of the other reduces the burden that nature imposes on a person as an individual.

COSMOLOGICAL FOUNDATIONS OF *IGWEBUIKE*

Igwebuike is a cosmological idea enshrined in the African cosmos that shapes the African cultural, religious and social activities. It is a universe of particularities where every creature as an independent entity must negotiate another's existential highway for mutual survival. It is a dependent, interdependent and combinational universe. Negotiation is very important in the African universe because it is a world that one shares with the other in an atmosphere of inter-subjective relations (Kanu, 2018). These inter-subjective relations only play out without chaos when the individual is able to skillfully bridge his/her interiority with the individuality of the other.

The African universe has physical and spiritual dimensions. In the spirit realm, God represents the Chief Being, and sits at the apex of power. In the physical world, human beings dominate, occupying the central position in the scheme of God's creation. The structure of the African universe can be illustrated in three levels: the sky, the earth and the underworld. The sky is where God *Chukwu* or *Chineke* and angels reside; the earth, where human beings, animals, natural resources, some devils and some physical observable realities abide; and the underworld, where ancestors and some bad spirits live (Kanu, 2013). These worlds interact in spite of their peculiarities, and persist because of a healthy inter-subjective relation. There is really no wall between the physical and spiritual worlds, between the visible and invisible, the sacred and profane, as there is a cooperate existence of reality. Thus, certain elements can move from one structure to another to commune with other elements. In this interaction, human beings commune with God, the divinities, the ancestors and vice versa.

CONCLUSION

From the foregoing, *Igwebuike* is employed as a unifying concept of African thought, especially, that aspect concerning the human person's conception of the spiritual and material universe in which he/she lives. It is an explanatory theory or principle that interprets the puzzle of our complex relationship with the non-corporal world and the human social life; that is, major social institutions that ensure social continuity and group identity, and further underpins the epistemological manifestations of the human person's universe. This piece has studied the dimensions of *Igwebuike*. These dimensions include its place within the theatre of being, and its literal and linguistic meanings. It also focused on the anthropological and epistemological foundations of *Igwebuike*, including its ontological and cosmological foundations. Although this work included the study of the linguistic and literal senses of *Igwebuike*, it goes beyond that in its focusing on the philosophical dimension of the concept.

REFERENCES

Kanu, A. I. (2016a). *Igwebuike* as a trend in African philosophy. *IGWEBUIKE: An African Journal of Arts and Humanities. 2. 1.* 97-101.

Kanu, A. I. (2017c). *Igwebuike* as an Igbo-African philosophy of inclusive leadership. *Igwebuike: An African Journal of Arts and Humanities.* Vol. 3 No 7. pp. 165-183.

Kanu, A. I. (2017d). *Igwebuike* philosophy and the issue of national development. *Igwebuike: An African Journal of Arts and Humanities.* Vol. 3 No 6. pp. 16-50.

Kanu, A. I. (2017f). *Igwebuike* as an Igbo-African Ethic of Reciprocity. *IGWEBUIKE: An African Journal of Arts and Humanities. 3. 2. pp.* 153-160.

Kanu, I. A. (2013). African Identity and the Emergence of Globalization. *American International Journal of Contemporary Research.* Vol. 3. No. 6. pp. 34-42.

Kanu, I. A. (2016a). *Igwebuike* as the consummate foundation of African Bioethical principles. *An African journal of Arts and Humanities* Vol.2 No1 June, pp.23-40.

Kanu, I. A. (2016b) *Igwebuike* as an Expressive Modality of Being in African ontology. *Journal of Environmental and Construction Management. 6. 3.* pp.12-21.

Kanu, I. A. (2017). *Igwebuike* as an Igbo-African Philosophy for Christian-Muslim Relations in Northern Nigeria. In Mahmoud Misaeli (Ed.). *Spirituality and Global Ethics* (pp. 300-310). United Kingdom: Cambridge Scholars.

Kanu, I. A. (2017). *Igwebuike* as an Igbo-African Philosophy for the Protection of the Environment. *Nightingale International Journal of Humanities and Social Sciences.* Vol. 3. No. 4. pp. 28-38.

Kanu, I. A. (2017). *Igwebuike* as the Hermeneutic of Individuality and Communality in African Ontology. *NAJOP: Nasara Journal of Philosophy.* Vol. 2. No. 1. pp. 162-179.

Kanu, I. A. (2017a). *Igwebuike* and Question of Superiority in the Scientific Community of Knowledge. *Igwebuike: An African Journal of Arts and Humanities.* Vol.3 No1. pp. 131-138.

Kanu, I. A. (2017b). *Igwebuike* as a Complementary Approach to the Issue of Girl-Child Education. *Nightingale International Journal of Contemporary Education and Research.* Vol. 3. No. 6. pp. 11-17.

Kanu, I. A. (2018). *Igwe Bu Ike* as an Igbo-African Hermeneutics of National Development. *Igbo Studies Review. No. 6.* pp. 59-83.

Kanu, I. A. (2018). Igwebuike as an African Integrative and Progressive Anthropology. *NAJOP: Nasara Journal of Philosophy.* Vol. 2. No. 1. pp. 151-161.

Kanu, I. A. (2012). The problem of being in metaphysics. *African Research Review: An International Multi-Disciplinary Journal.* Vol.6. No.2. April. pp. 113-122.

Kanu, I. A. (2012). The problem of personal identity in metaphysics. *International Journal of Arts and Humanities.* Vol.1. No.2. pp.1-13.

Kanu, I. A. (2012a). The concept of life and person in African anthropology. In E. Ezenweke and I. A. Kanu (Eds.). *Issues in African traditional religion and philosophy* (pp. 61-71). Nigeria: Augustinian.

Kanu, I. A. (2012b). Towards an Igbo Christology. In E. Ezenweke and I. A. Kanu (Eds.). *Issues in African traditional religion and philosophy* (pp. 75-98). Nigeria: Augustinian.

Kanu, I. A. (2013). African identity and the emergence of globalization. *American International Journal of Contemporary Research.* Vol. 3. No. 6. pp. 34-42.

Kanu, I. A. (2013). Globalisation, globalism and African philosophy. C. Umezinwa (Ed.). *African philosophy: A pragmatic approach to African probems* (pp. 151-165). Germany: Lambert.

Kanu, I. A. (2013). On the sources of African philosophy. *Filosofia Theoretica: Journal of African Philosophy, Culture and Religion, Vol. 2. No. 1.* pp. 337-356.

Kanu, I. A. (2013). The dimensions of African cosmology. *Filosofia Theoretica: Journal of African Philosophy, Culture and Religion, Vol. 2. No. 2.* pp. 533-555.

Kanu, I. A. (2014). A historiography of African philosophy. *Global Journal for Research Analysis. Volume. 3. Issue. 8.* pp. 188-190.

Kanu, I. A. (2014). Being and the categories of being in Igbo philosophy. *African Journal of Humanities. Volume 1. Issue 1.* pp. 144-159.

Mbiti, J. S. (1970). *African religions and philosophy.* Nairobi: East African Educational Publishers.

Njoku, F. O. C. (2015). *The philosophical grid of Igbo socio-political ontology: Ibu anyi danda.* 147th Inaugural Lecture of the University of Nigeria, Nsukka.

SEMIOTIC INTERPRETATION AND THE IGWEBUIKE IDENTITY: AN ANTIDOTE FOR INTERPERSONAL MISUNDERSTANDING

Dozie Iwuh, OSA
Department of Philosophy
Augustinian Institute Makurdi
Benue State
registered501@gmail.com

EXECUTIVE SUMMARY

That which is validly true about our human existence and all that pertains to it is the reality of communication. It is communication that breeds human interrelationships, a rapport, assuring us that we are not isolated in the world, but have access to other human persons like us. The communication that is spoken of here cannot be limited to just the verbal type, if we do that, we would be registering a stereotype. Communication also pertains to the non-verbal, the non-visible (the supposedly telepathic means of communication), etc. Yet, what is to be maintained is that whether it is verbal or non-verbal, visible or non-visible, communication is mediated through the use of signs. Language is what can be defined as an oral/worded/lettered, yet mental (This is because before ever a word is uttered, it is first constructed in the mind, whether it be consciously or unconsciously. More to that, people think or construct their line of thought in tandem with the language they speak.) representation of signs. This goes to indicate that, even though there is the external world, the human person, in his own subjective worldview (which is internal), is able to make contact with the external world, by means of sign inter-rapport. That is to say that he understands the signs that are external to him and is able to relate to the external world also by means of signs. The external world that is being spoken of here also pertains to the other human person that is not "I", but the "YOU". The individual mediates the external world, by means of signs received and perceived (The focus of this piece is between the "I" and the "YOU."). There is no means of really understanding what lies in the depths of the mind of the other person, the "You". The "I" can only decipher according to those signs that have been let out by the "You". It should be noted that misunderstandings arise when the signs given by the "I" is not properly deciphered by the "You". Misunderstandings have been the bane of the human existence, causing strife, suspicion, conflicts, divisions, etc. The Igwebuike ideology proffers what its name signifies, namely "togetherness", arising on the wings of a better understanding amongst persons. Yet, this would not be the case when there is a failure to rightly understand and decode those signs that are received, with the reciprocal giving of the right signs as well. Semiosis, which considers the meaning of signs, can also prove to be very vital in the ensuring of the "togetherness" which the Igwebuike stands for. Igwebuike itself is a sign, one that communicates to us and that needs to be semiotically interpreted, to make sense of what it proffers, namely "ensuring a communal existence of the humanity." Yet, it seems as if the issue of misunderstanding will always remain with the human person. This is because there is a near impossibility of decoding what is the in the mind of the other. That is to say that the mental state of the other person remains his exclusive hub, unless such a one allows another in, via the unleashing of signs. The other side of the coin is the right way in which such mental state should be conveyed to the other. This piece will be dedicated to the rightful appreciation of the sign Igwebuike communicates.

Keywords: Igwebuike, Kanu Ikechukwu Anthony, Semiotics, Semiosis, Human Person, Igwebuike, Social Interaction.

WHAT IS SEMIOTICS?

Semiotics is properly referred as the science of signs and developed out of the need of physicians of the western world to understand the interactive pattern between the body and the mind within certain cultural domains.[1] It is the study of signs and symbols as elements of communicative behaviour, the analysis of systems of communication, as language, gestures or clothing. At its most fundamental level, semiotics is the study of how meaning is made. Even if we endorse the fact that it studies signs, this is to be taken on a broad spectrum of the meaning of a sign: that is to say, sign as that which communicates a meaning beyond itself. We call signs all and only those things which represent something other than themselves, and we have found that this can occur only when and insofar as the "other" is represented to or for some other still.[2] For example, a Rose may represent naturally a flower (plant), or it may indicate love or passion. At the most basic level, human beings interpret signs as they communicate with one another. Meaning derivation from signs denotes that which is proper to the animal (even brutes, what has now come to be referred to as zoosemiosis[3]). Nonetheless, "Semiotics", however, as a term, has become conventionalized as the generally accepted term to label the study of signs in their distinctive action.[4]

"Semiotics" as an English word comes to us from a kind of bastard Greek coinage made by John Locke in the *Essay concerning Humane Understanding* that he published in 1690, where, at the conclusion of his book, he proposed *semiotike* as the one-word equivalent of the English

---

[1]   T.A. Sebeok, *An Introduction to Semiotics*, University of Toronto Press Incorporated, 1994, xi.

[2]   J. Deely, *On 'Semiotics' as Naming the doctrine of Signs*, in Semiotica vol 152, 2004, 75-139.

[3]   There are other areas of semiosis added to the zoosemiosis, they include, anthroposemiosis and phytosemiosis, all these pertain to a larger area of study known as biosemiosis.

[4]   J. Deely, *On 'Semiotics' as Naming the doctrine of Signs.*

expression, "doctrine of signs".[5] This term, as it appears in Locke, according to J. Deely, is malformed. Deely remarked that, according to the applicable requirements of Greek grammar, the term should have had an epsilon separating the *mu* from the *iota*, as in *semɛiotike*. This is not apparent. Furthermore, in his reasoning, one cannot say that this malformation be dismissed as a printer's error; for, in every subsequent edition of the *Essay* prepared by Locke prior to his being overtaken by the boundary of time and made a definitively *past* author, the original malformation is meticulously maintained.[6] J. Deely notes:

Now it is interesting that "semiotics" is not a straight transliteration of Locke's Greek malformation. What *is* a straight transliteration of the Greek malformation Locke introduced, however, is the Latin term "*semiotica*", which no Latin author ever used. So the term, a Greek malformation in Locke's *Essay*, is in effect a neologism in Latin transliteration, but it means in English "the doctrine of signs", according to the only definition Locke provided in his original introduction of and comment upon the term. The reason that this detour through the Latin transliteration of Locke's Greek malformation is interesting is because "*semiotica*" as Latin neologism would be a neuter plural name that could only be translated into English as "semiotics". Professional linguists have been careful to point out that there is in English a class of "-ics" words which do not conform to the usual rule that an English noun is made plural by adding an "s" to its ending. By this reckoning, "semiotics" is not the plural form of "semiotic". Nonetheless, "semiotics" is the direct English transliteration of the Latin "*semiotica*", which in turn is the direct transliteration of the Greek malformation Locke introduced into the closing chapter of his *Essay*. So a Latin, rather than a Greek, background proves etymologically decisive for sign and semiotics alike as contemporary notions, despite Locke's conscious choice of the Greek root (*sem-*) for the notion of "natural sign" (*semeion*) in his one-word summation or name (*semiotike*) for the doctrine of signs.[7]

The phenomenon that distinguishes life forms from inanimate objects is semiosis. This can be defined simply as the instinctive capacity of all living organisms to produce and understand signs. A sign is any physical form that has been imagined or made externally (through some physical medium) to stand for an object, event, feeling, etc., known as a referent, or for a class of similar (or related) objects, events, feelings, etc., known as a referential domain. In human life, signs serve many functions. They allow people to recognize patterns in things; they act as predictive guides or plans for taking actions; they serve as exemplars of specific kinds of phenomena; and the list could go on and on. The English word 'cat' for example, is an example of a particular kind of human sign - known as verbal- which stands for a referent that can be described as a 'carnivorous mammal with a tail, whiskers and retractile claws. Each species

---

[5]   J. Deely, The Red book. The Beginning of PostModern Times or Charles Sanders Peirce and The Recovery of *Signum*, in the Metaphyiscal Club for the University of Helsinki, Finland, 2000, 1-79. We ought to note that even though John Locke had translated this word semiotike from the greek, to mean semiotics, it was 50 years earlier thoroughly studied by John Poinsot, unknown to Locke.

[6]   Ibid.

[7]   ibid.

produces and understands certain kinds of specific signs for which it has been programmed by its biology. These can range from simple bodily signals to advanced symbolic structures such as words. Signs allow each species to

(1) Signal its existence,
(2) Communicate messages within the species, and
(3) Model incoming information from the external world.

Semiotics is the science that studies these functions. The goal of this opening chapter is to introduce several basic notions for the formal study of semiosis.[8]

The primary objective of semiotics is to understand both a species' capacity to make and understand signs and, in the case of the human species, the knowledge-making activity this capacity allows human beings to carry out. The former is known, as mentioned above, as semiosis, while the latter activity is known as representation. Representation is a deliberate use of signs to probe, classify, and hence know the world. Semiosis is the biological capacity itself that underlies the production and comprehension of signs, from simple physiological signals to those that reveal a highly complex symbolism.[9] Human intellectual and social life is based on the production, use and exchange of signs and representations. When we gesture, talk, write, read, watch a TV program, listen to music, look at a painting, etc. we are engaged in sign-based representational behaviour. Representation has endowed the human species with the ability to cope effectively with the crucial aspects of existence - knowing, behaving purposefully, planning, socializing and communicating. However, since representational activities vary from culture to culture, the signs people use on a daily basis constitute a mediating template in the worldview they come to have.[10]

Semiotics considers both verbal and non-verbal signs, enabling a community of communication between and amongst biological species.

VERBAL AND NON-VERBAL SIGNS

According to Semiology, there are six types of verbal signs, which include:

1. Symptom: the symptom is a reflex of anatomical structure. Animals with widely divergent anatomies will manifest virtually no symptomatology in common. It is interesting to note, by the way, that the term symptom is often extended metaphorically

---

[8]   T.A. Sebeok, *Signs. An Introduction to Semiotics 2nd ed*, University of Toronto Press Incorporated, Toronto, 2001, 3.

[9]   Ibid, 8.

[10]   Ibid.

to refer to intellectual, emotional and social phenomena that result from causes that are perceived to be analogous to physical processes.

2. Signal: All animals are endowed with the capacity to use and respond to species-specific signals for survival. Birds, for instance, are born prepared to produce a particular type of coo, and no amount of exposure to the songs of other species, or the absence of their own, has any effect on their cooing.

3. Icon: An icon is a sign that is made to resemble, simulate or reproduce its referent in some way. Photographs may be iconic signs because they can be seen to reproduce their referents in a visual way. Onomatopoeic words are also iconic signs because they simulate their referents in an acoustic way.

4. Index: An index is a sign that refers to something or someone, in terms of its existence or location in time or space, or in relation to something or someone else. Smoke is an index of fire, pointing out where the fire is; a cough is an index of a cold; and so on. The most typical manifestation of indexicality is the pointing index finger, which humans the world over use instinctively to point out and locate things, people and events in the world.

5. Symbol: A symbol is a sign that stands for its referent in an arbitrary, conventional way. Most semioticians agree that symbolicity is what sets human representation apart from that of all other species, allowing the human species to reflect upon the world separately from stimulus-response situations. Words in general are symbolic signs. But any signifier - object, sound, figure, etc. - can be symbolic. A cross figure can stand for the concept 'Christianity'; a V-sign made with the index and middle fingers can stand symbolically for the concept 'victory' ; white is a colour that can be symbolic of 'cleanliness,' 'purity,' or 'innocence,' but dark can be a symbol of 'uncleanness,' 'impurity,' or 'corruption'; and the list could go on and on. These symbols are all established by social convention.'

6. Name: This is an identifier sign assigned to the member of a species in various ways, as we shall see subsequently, that sets the specific member off from the others. A human name is a sign that identifies the person in terms of such variables as ethnicity and gender. Added names (surnames, nicknames, etc.) further refine the 'identity referent' of the name.[11]

Another form of sign conveying is by non-verbal communication. Non-verbal communication takes place within an organism or between two or more organisms. Within an organism, participators in communicative acts may involve - as message sources or destinations or both - on rising integration levels, cellular organelles, cells, tissues, organs, and organ systems. In addition, basic features of the whole biological organization, conducted non-verbally in the *milieu interieur*, include protein synthesis, metabolism, hormone activity, transmission of nervous impulses, and so forth.[12] Homo sapiens are capable of communicating, simultaneously

---

[11] Ibid, 9-11.
[12] Ibid, 12

or in turn, by both non-verbal and verbal means. The expression 'by verbal means' is equivalent to some such expression as 'by means of speech,' or 'by means of script,' or 'by means of a sign language' (e.g., for use in a deaf group), that are, each, manifestations of any prerequisite natural language with which human beings are singularly endowed. However, not all humans are literate or can even speak: infants normally do develop a capacity for speaking, but only gradually; some adults never acquire speech; and others lose speech as a result of some trauma (e.g., a stroke) or in consequence of aging. Such conditions, notwithstanding, humans lacking a capacity to verbalize - speak, write, or sign - can, as a rule, continue to communicate non-verbally.[13]

These two modes of signature can also stand in as the two modes of communication in the human person.

UNDERSTANDING THE CONCEPT OF *"IGWEBUIKE"*

Igwebuike is the heart of African thought and, in fact, the modality of being in African philosophy. It is taken from the Igbo language, and is a composite word made up of three dimensions. Therefore, it can be employed as a word or used as a sentence: as a word, it is written as *Igwebuike*, and as a sentence, it is written as, *Igwe bu ike,* with the component words enjoying some independence in terms of space. The three words involve: *Igwe* is a noun which means number or population, usually a huge number or population. *Bu* is a verb, which means *is. Ike* is another verb, which means *strength* or *power.* Thus, put together, it means 'number is strength' or 'number is power', that is, when human beings come together in solidarity and complementarity, they are powerful or can constitute an insurmountable force.[14] *Igwebuike*

---

[13] Ibid, 11-12.

[14] A.I. Kanu, *Igwebuike As A Trend In African Philosophy* In Igwebuike: An African Journal of Arts and Humanities Vol. 2, No. 1, 2016, 97-101. Kanu, Ikechukwu Anthony. *Igwebuike and the Logic (Nka) of African Philosophy,* 14. Kanu, I. A. (2018). *Igwe Bu Ike* as an Igbo-African hermeneutics of national development. *Igbo Studies Review. No. 6.* pp. 59-83. Kanu, I. A. (2018). *Igwebuike* as an African integrative and progressive anthropology. *NAJOP: Nasara Journal of Philosophy.* Vol. 2. No. 1. pp. 151-161. Kanu, I. A. (2018). New Africanism: *Igwebuike* as a philosophical Attribute of Africa in portraying the Image of Life. In Mahmoud Misaeli, Sanni Yaya and Rico Sneller (Eds.). *African Perspectives on Global on Global Development* (pp. 92-103). United Kingdom: Cambridge Scholars Publishing. Kanu, I. A. (2019). Collaboration within the ecology of mission: An African cultural perspective. *The Catholic Voyage: African Journal of Consecrated Life.* Vol. 15. pp. 125-149. Kanu, I. A. (2019). *Igwebuike* research methodology: A new trend for scientific and wholistic investigation. *IGWEBUIKE: An African Journal of Arts and Humanities (IAAJAH). 5. 4.* pp. *95-105.* Kanu, I. A. (2019). *Igwebuikeconomics*: The Igbo apprenticeship for wealth creation. *IGWEBUIKE: An African Journal of Arts and Humanities (IAAJAH). 5. 4.* pp. *56-70.* Kanu, I. A. (2019). *Igwebuikecracy*: The Igbo-African participatory cocio-political system of governance. *TOLLE LEGE: An Augustinian Journal of the Philosophy and Theology. 1. 1.* pp. 34-45. Kanu, I. A. (2019). On the origin and principles of *Igwebuike* philosophy. *International Journal of Religion and Human Relations.* Vol. 11. No. 1. pp. 159-176. Kanu, I. A. (2019b). An *Igwebuike* approach to the study of African traditional naming ceremony and baptism. *International Journal of Religion and Human Relations.* Vol. 11. No. 1. pp. 25-50. Kanu, I. A. (2017). *Igwebuike* as an Igbo-African philosophy for Christian-Muslim relations in Northern Nigeria. In Mahmoud Misaeli (Ed.). *Spirituality and*

is anchored on the African worldview, which is characterized by a common origin, common world-view, common language, shared culture, shared race, colour and habits, common historical experience and a common destiny.[15] Life is a life of *sharedness,* one in which another is part thereof. It is a relationship, though, of separate and separated entities or individuals but with a joining of the same whole.[16] Philosophically, according to A.I. Kanu, *Igwebuike* points to the complementary nature of reality and is not limited to the Igbo world, it is a universal philosophy that is the incarnation and confirmation of the universal relevance of solidarity and complementarity.[17] The richness of this philosophy pointing to the complementarity and solidarity of reality also has much relevance in a meaning- laden reality. What is being said is that the reality that confronts the human person is a reality that is teeming with meaning. Thus, it is worthy of note to insist that this philosophical term, although of Igbo origin, has universal implications. A.I. Kanu succinctly touches on this point as he says

> Negotiation is very important in the African universe because it is a world that one shares with the other in an atmosphere of inter-subjective relations. This intersubjective relations only plays out without chaos when the individual is able to skillfully bridge his or her interiority with the individuality of the other.[18]

Global Ethics (pp. 300-310). United Kingdom: Cambridge Scholars. Kanu, I. A. (2017). *Igwebuike* as an Igbo-African philosophy for the protection of the environment. *Nightingale International Journal of Humanities and Social Sciences.* Vol. 3. No. 4. pp. 28-38.

15 A.I. Kanu, *Igwebuike As An Igbo-African Ethic Of Reciprocity,* in Igwebuike: An African Journal of Arts and Humanities Vol. 3 No 2, March 2017, 153-160.

16 A.I. Kanu, *Igwebuike as an Igbo-African Philosophy of Education,* A paper presented at the International Conference on Law, Education and Humanities. 25th -26th November 2015 University of Paris, France.

17 A.I. Kanu, *On the Origin and Principles of the Igwebuike Philosophy,* in Journal of Religion and Human Relations, Volume 11 No. 1, 2019, 159-176. Kanu, I. A. (2017). *Igwebuike* as the hermeneutic of individuality and communality in African ontology. *NAJOP: Nasara Journal of Philosophy.* Vol. 2. No. 1. pp. 162-179. Kanu, I. A. (2017a). *Igwebuike* and question of superiority in the scientific community of knowledge. *Igwebuike: An African Journal of Arts and Humanities.* Vol.3 No1. pp. 131-138. Kanu, I. A. (2017a). *Igwebuike as a philosophical attribute of Africa in portraying the image of life.* A paper presented at the 2017 Oracle of Wisdom International Conference by the Department of Philosophy, Tansian University, Umunya, Anambra State, 27-29 April. Kanu, I. A. (2017b). *Igwebuike* as a complementary approach to the issue of girl-child education. *Nightingale International Journal of Contemporary Education and Research.* Vol. 3. No. 6. pp. 11-17. Kanu, I. A. (2017b). *Igwebuike* as a wholistic response to the problem of evil and human suffering. *Igwebuike: An African Journal of Arts and Humanities.* Vol. 3 No 2, March. Kanu, I. A. (2017e). *Igwebuike* as an Igbo-African modality of peace and conflict resolution. *Journal of African Traditional Religion and Philosophy Scholars. Vol. 1. No. 1. pp. 31-40.* Kanu, I. A. (2017g). *Igwebuike* and the logic (Nka) of African philosophy. *Igwebuike: An African Journal of Arts and Humanities.* 3. 1. pp. 1-13. Kanu, I. A. (2017h). *Igwebuike* philosophy and human rights violation in Africa. *IGWEBUIKE: An African Journal of Arts and Humanities.* Vol. 3. No. 7. pp. 117-136. Kanu, I. A. (2017i). *Igwebuike* as a hermeneutic of personal autonomy in African ontology. *Journal of African Traditional Religion and Philosophy Scholars. Vol. 2. No. 1. pp. 14-22.*

18 Ibid.

Can there be negotiations, without an in-depth grasp of the terms of negotiations? Can humans engage in any meaningful discourse, pertaining to ways and means to forge ahead in the bond of solidarity, when misunderstanding looms large? Can we as humans complement one another, in the absence of true brotherhood soldered on the ground rules of a rich understanding of each person's individuality? This is where semiotics (or Semiosis) meets with the *Igwebuike*.

IGWEBUIKE IN THE LIGHT OF SEMIOSIS: PART ONE

The *Igwebuike* philosophy is grounded on certain principles that have their roots in African proverbs and idioms. It should be said that communication in the African verse, before the dawn of the colonial rulers, was by means of idioms, proverbs and the likes. According to J.J Dyikuk,

> Communication in the traditional Igbo societies was by the means of idioms, proverbs, and figures of speech...Without idioms, proverbs, and figures of speech, conversation would be bland and distasteful. It is only infants and little children that speak in plain language.[19]

While the major reference in the aforementioned quotation is to the Igbo traditional society, it should be noted that such means of communication cut across the entirety of the African traditional society. As earlier noted, the *Igwebuike* is grounded on certain principles having their roots in the African proverbs and idioms, a few of these proverbs and idioms include:

a. A person is a person because of other people.
b. Sticks in a bundle cannot be broken.
c. When spiders unite they can tie up a lion.
d. If one finger tries to pick up something from the ground, it cannot.
e. Behind an able man there are always other able men.
f. It takes a village to raise a child.
g. If you want to go fast, go alone, if you want to go far, go together.
h. I am because we are, and since we are, therefore, I am
i. If a lizard stays off from the foot of a tree, it would be caught.
j. A tree does not make a forest.
k. If two or more people urinate in the same place at the same time, it would produce more foam.
l. When a bird builds its nest, it uses the feathers of other birds.
m. One person is not the whole world.
n. It is by taking a goat around that you are able to sell it.[20]

---

[19] J.J. Dyikuk, *The Intersection Of Communication In Igwebuike And trado-Rural Media: A Critical Evaluation*, in Journal of African Studies and Sustainable Development Vol. 2 No 3, 2019, 175-192.

[20] A.I. Kanu, *On the Origin and Principles of the Igwebuike Philosophy*.

There is a seeming thread that cuts across the above-mentioned proverbs, namely "TOGETHERNESS". The *Igwebuike* ideology that is borne on the wings of these proverbs express a sign, a sign that should be well elaborated in semiotic terms.

At this point, we need to really understand what a sign is, because inherent in every aspect of communication is the penchant to understand what is being communicated or signaled from the "signaler" to the one who is communicated to or signaled. In other words, in communication, there is a back and forth movement of signs. This back and forth movement of signs is conveyed verbally and non-verbally by words and actions. A word is the sign of some "thing"[21] which can be understood by the hearer when pronounced by the speaker.[22] According to Augustine, a sign is something that shows itself to the senses and something other than itself to the mind.[23] He repeats this further in his *De Doctrina Christiana*, where he says,

> a sign is a thing which, over and above the impression it makes on the senses, cause something else to come into the mind as a consequence of itself, just as when we see a footprint, we conclude that an animal whose footprint this is has passed by; and when we see smoke, we know that there is fire beneath; and when we hear the voice of a living man, we think of the feeling in his mind and when the trumpet sounds, soldiers know that they are to advance or retreat or do whatever else the state of the battle requires.[24]

Augustine gives two distinct types of signs, namely; the natural and the conventional signs.

> Natural signs are those which, apart from any intention or desire of using them as signs, do yet lead to the knowledge of something else, as for example, smoke when it indicates fire. For it is not from any intention of making it a sign that it is so, but through attention to experience we come to know that fire is beneath, even when nothing but smoke can be seen. And the footprints of an animal passing by belong to this class of signs. And the countenance of an angry or sorrowful man indicates the feeling in his mind, independently of his will; and in the same way every other emotion of the mind is betrayed by the tell-tale countenance, even though we do nothing with the intention of making it known.[25]

As pertaining to *signa naturalia*, no mental state is induced when such signs arise in our consciousness:, that is to say that we do not enter into any mental state when we become aware of such signs. For instance, when we think of some natural or cultural entity, like a tree, or a

---

[21] A thing according to Augustine, in his *De Dialetica*, V, «is whatever is felt (sensed) or understood or 'latet' (is hidden, inapprenhensible)"

[22] Augustine, *De Dialetica*, V. «uniuscuisuque rei signum, quod ab audiente possit intellgi, a loquente prolatum.»

[23] Ibid. «Signum est quod se ipsum sensui et praeter se aliquid animo ostendit."

[24] Augustine, *De Doctrina Christiana*, II, i,1.

[25] Augustine, *De Doctrina Christiana*, II, i, 2.

flag, we are not aware of any "mental state" as such. Rather, we are aware of a tree or a flag,[26] just that. Conventional signs are those which living beings mutually exchange for the purpose of showing the feelings of their minds or their perceptions, or their thoughts.[27] In other words, conventional signs are the exclusive reserve of the human beings. These are articulate signs that reflect the mindset, thought pattern, emotional state, and mood of the one who is talking or speaking. The hearer is able to perceive directly and understand wholesomely what the speaker is saying. In conventional signs, *signa data*, mental states are induced. Augustine continues,

> Nor is there any reason for giving a sign except the desire of drawing for the conveying into another's mind what the giver of the sign has in his own mind. We wish then to consider and discuss this class of signs so far as men are concerned with it... the beasts, too, have certain signs among themselves by which they make known the desires of their mind. For when the poultry-cock has discovered food, he signals with his voice for the hen to run to him, and the dove by cooing calls his mate, or is called by her in turn...[28]

According to a medieval Thomisitic commentator, John Poinsot, there are two things that concur to constitute the general rationale of a sign. The first is the rationale of something manifestative or representative. The second is an order to another, specifically, on the one hand, to the thing which is represented (which must be other than the sign, for nothing is a sign of itself nor signifies itself), and, on the other hand, to the cognitive power to which the sign manifests and represents the thing distinct from itself.[29] To the division of the sign, he notes:

> There are twofold division of the sign formal and instrumental signs... but insofar as signs are ordered to something signified, they are divided according to the cause of that ordering into natural and stipulative and customary. A formal sign is the formal awareness which represents of itself, not by means of another. An instrumental sign is one that represents something other than itself from a pre-existing cognition of itself as an object, as the footprint of an ox represents an ox. And this definition is usually given for signs generally. A natural sign is one that represents from the nature of a thing, independently of any stipulation and custom whatever, and so it represents the same for all, as smoke signifies a fire burning. A stipulated sign is one that represents something owing to an imposition by the will of a community, like the

---

[26] J.N. Deely, *Cognition from a Semiotic Point of View*, in Semiotics 1981, J.N. Deely-M.D. Lenhart (eds), Plenum Press, New York, 1983, 23.

[27] Augustine, *De Doctrina Christiana*, II, ii, 3.

[28] Ibid.

[29] John Poinsot, *Tractatus De Signis*, Part one, bk 1, q.1i, 646a9-41, University of California Press Berkeley, Los Angeles, California, 1985.

linguistic expression "man." A customary sign is one that represents from use alone without any public imposition, as napkins upon the table signify a meal.[30]

What should be said here is that, in the thought pattern of John Poinsot, also known as John of St Thomas, there are two categories of signs. There is the sign that is ordered according to power and that which is ordered according to something signified. As regards that which is ordered according to power, the sign can either be the formal or the instrumental. And for that which is ordered according to something signified, it is divided into the natural, stipulative and the customary sign.

In the light of the explication given by John Poinsot, we can situate *Igwebuike as a stipulative sign, one that represents something owing to an imposition by the will of the community*.[31] This implies that a stipulative sign is one that is knowable not immediately but mediately by means of another. The knowledge of *Igwebuike* is mediated upon the principles on which it stands.

In line with the Aristotelian categories of the substance and nine accidents, A Sign resides in the level of a relation. This relation, according to John Poinsot, is not a transcendental one, according to the way of being, but is an ontological one, that is according to the way the relation has being.[32] While it stands that to represent another is indeed required for a sign, a sign does not consist in this alone; for a sign adds something beyond representing, and formally bespeaks of representing another deficiently, or dependency upon the very thing signified, and by substituting in the capacity of that thing. And thus, a sign respects a significate, not as something purely self- manifested and self-illuminated, but as the principal knowable and the measure of the sign, something in whose place the sign is surrogated and whose vicegerent the sign is in bringing that knowable thing to a cognitive power.[33] A vivid example is in the case of smoke that signifies fire. As an ontological relation, a sign is not formally a relation but is the foundation of a relation. John Poinsot, notes,

> Therefore a sign does not formally consist in a relation, but in the fundament (foundation) of a relation. The major premise follows from the definition of sign. If a sign is "that which represents something to a knowing power," then it is accordingly something leading the power to an object signified.[34]

The foundation of a sign is seen in its propensity to move the cognizing power, or arouse in such mind, that to which it points to. It is to this that John Poinsot refers to the sign as a mover or an arouser, because it belongs to the capacity of arousing or moving.[35]

---

[30] John Poinsot, *Tractatus De Signis*, Part one, Chapter II, 9b34-10a26.

[31] Ibid.

[32] Ibid, Part one, bk 1, q.1i 647a16-b26.

[33] Ibid.

[34] ibid, 650b20-651a14.

[35] Ibid, 652a14-b16

Igwebuike as a stipulative sign bears the major mark of a sign, namely; that it is the foundation of a relation. It is for this that we say that a stipulated sign moves (acts) by reason of the imposition, not as knowable immediately and by reason of itself, but mediately and through another, just as any other unreal beings; and thus, we say, presupposing that its knowability is got by borrowing, a stipulated sign takes on the rationale of something moving and representing, just as it also takes on the rationale of something knowable.[36]

IGWEBUIKE IN THE LIGHT OF SEMIOSIS: PART TWO

As already noted there are principles on which *Igwebuike* is founded, and these include:

1. The principle of identity
2. The principle of hierarchy
3. The principle of contrariety
4. The principle of unity[37]

Yet, *Igwebuike* is anchored on an Igbo-centric African worldview, which, according to Iroegbu, is characterized by a common origin, common world-view, common language, shared culture, shared race, colour and habits, common historical experience and a common destiny. It is a complementary philosophy which understands life as a shared reality.[38] It indicates literally 'number is strength' or 'number is power;' that is, when human beings come together in solidarity and complementarity, they are powerful or can constitute an insurmountable force.[39] Its English equivalent is 'complementarity'. At this level, no task is beyond their collective capability. It is a concept that was employed by African traditional philosophers of the complementary school of thought to discuss the nature of the observed African reality.[40] *Igwebuike* rests on the African principles of solidarity and complementarity. It argues that 'to be' is to live in solidarity and complementarity, and to live outside the parameters of solidarity and complementarity is to suffer alienation. 'To be' is 'to be with the other', in a community of beings. This is based on the African philosophy of community, which is the underlying principle and unity of African Traditional Religions and philosophical experience.[41] According to B.I. Ekwulu:

---

[36] Ibid, 653b29-654a40

[37] A.I. Kanu, *On the Origin and Principles of the Igwebuike Philosophy.*

[38] A.I. Kanu, *Igwebuike As An Igbo-African Ethic Of Reciprocity*, in Igwebuike. An African Journal of Arts and Humanities Vol. 3 No 2, March 2017, 153-160.

[39] A.I. Kanu, *Igwebuike as a trend in African philosophy* in Igwebuike. An African Journal of Arts and Humanities, 2. 1. 2016, 97-101.

[40] A.I. Kanu, *Igwebuike as an Igbo-African hermeneutic of globalization* in Igwebuike: An African Journal of Arts and Humanities. 2. 1. 2016, 1-7.

[41] A.I. Kanu, *Igwebuike as a trend in African philosophy* in Igwebuike.

> If the other is my part or a piece of me, it means that I need him for me to be complete, for me to be what I really am. The other completes rather than diminishes me. His language and culture make my own stand out and at the same time, they enrich and complement my own. In the presence of his language and culture, the riches and poverty of my language and culture become clear and I see that his own and my own when put together form a richer whole when compared to any of them in isolation.[42]

It is a sign that indicates a move towards the other, the "YOU", for the sake of existential thriving of the self, the "I". This is the bedrock of *Igwebuike*. The implication of this is the rich complementarity that the *Igwebuike* philosophy brings to bear on S the broader spectrum of philosophy. It indicates how much of the "other" is in the "I", or better put, how much of you is contained in me, and me in you.[43] Ekwulu opines further that the self is not only completed in relating with the other, but that it attains self-realization in the other:

> I realize myself in the other because it is in the 'Thou-ness' of the Thou that my 'Is-ness' is realized. I am 'I' because you are 'You'. Without Thou there is no I. We are 'We' because they are 'They', and without 'They', there is no 'We'.[44]

It is within this being-laden context, which is life as sharedness, that all questions of meaning can be handled adequately and fully within the context of mutual complementarity of all possible relations.[45] According to Kanu, from the foregoing, this explains why the Igbo would refer to the 'Other' as *Ibe*, which means 'a piece of' or 'a part of', as in *ibe anu* (a piece of meat) or *ibe ede* (a piece of cocoyam). The Igbo would, therefore, refer to the 'other person' as *ibe* m, which means 'my piece' or *mmadu ibe* m (my fellow human being). This is the concept also employed in reference to relationships and reciprocity: love one another (*hunu ibe unu n'anya*); help one another (*nyere nu ibe unu aka*); respect one another (*sopuru nu ibe unu*), etc. Since, the 'other' refers to my own piece; it would, therefore, mean that to love the other is to love oneself, to help the other is to help oneself and to respect the other is to respect oneself.[46] Put in another way, to hate the other is to hate oneself, to refuse help to the other is to refuse help to oneself and to disrespect the other is to disrespect oneself.[47]

---

[42] B.I. Ekwulu, *Igbo concept of Ibe (the other) as a philosophical solution to the ethnic conflicts in African countries* in B. I. Ekwulu (Ed.), philosophical reflections on African issues, Enugu Publications, Delta, 2010, 183-192

[43] D. Iwuh OSA, *Action Understanding Is Not Entirely Neutral It Is Existential, It Is Igwebuike*, in IGWEBUIKE: An African Journal of Arts and Humanities Vol. 5 No 6, September 2019, 51-70.

[44] B.I. Ekwulu, *Igbo concept of Ibe (the other) as a philosophical solution to the ethnic conflicts in African countries.*

[45] I.I. Asouzu, Ibuanyidanda. New complementary ontology. Beyond world immanentism, ethnocentric reduction and impositions, Lit Verlag Publications, Munster, 2007, 252-253.

[46] A.I. Kanu, *Igwebuike As An Igbo-African Ethic Of Reciprocity.*

[47] D. Iwuh OSA, *Action Understanding Is Not Entirely Neutral It Is Existential, It Is Igwebuike.*

This complementarity that is the crux of the *Igwebuike* is that which is being given out as a sign or symbol that ought to be understood. It is a concept that is existential and ontological, arising from a culture and a people that have assimilated within themselves the importance of standing together and working together. It does not negate the reality of individuality; it rather pays a lot of tributaries to it by means of emphasis, as seen in the principle of identity (which is one of the principles, albeit the first principle, of the *Igwebuike*). As to the human individuality, it also endorses the fact of contraries, in life, in reality (physical and spiritual), in the mindset of persons, etc. That is to say that, in just as we would find contraries in reality and in every aspect that surrounds the human person, there is also bound to be contraries in thought patterns in each individual. This also emphasizes the individuality in persons. It supports and aligns itself with the principle of hierarchy, which appreciates the fact that in reality, although the physical is separated from the spiritual, yet there seems to be a communication between both, a communication of forces; the spiritual stands as a force higher than that of the physical. Yet in the singular reality of the spiritual, there is a gradation of powers, a diversity of forces, inherent in all these is the presence of contraries, all working together for the furtherance of one cause, namely existence. This is also visible in the physical realm. Nonetheless, there is a united working of each person, force or power, in a united front (the principle of unity), for the sake of existence. According to I.M. Onyeocha, "the African conceives of reality in terms of a universe of forces that are linked together, and are in constant interplay with one another".[48] This is because what is pertinent to *Igwebuike* is not that the branch grows out of the tree; it is that the branch remains connected to the tree, sharing one life force. It knows the tree as much as the tree knows it.[49] *Igwebuike* understands every individual reality as part and completion of the whole, and thus, there is a unity in the midst of diversity. *Igwebuike* presents being as that which possesses a relational character of mutual relations.[50]

As a stipulative sign, what does Igwebuike indicate? From the aforementioned, we have seen solidarity; we have also seen complementarity and we earlier saw togetherness. And all these are aimed towards one end, namely, Existence. The beauty of the human existence is seen not in isolation, but in interaction; it is not seen in a solipsistic reality, but in a shared reality; it is not seen in "I" alone, but in "YOU and I".

FINAL REMARKS

A cursory look at the work of John Poinsot, also known as John of St Thomas, will reveal that his definition and understanding of signs have no special affinity with the real or the unreal, being equally at home in signifying either. That is to say that signs can be equally and conveniently used to explain both the real and the unreal, the abstract and the concrete. Again, signs are necessarily mind-dependent, for it is the function of a sign as such to represent, not to

---

[48] I.M. Onyeocha, Africa's idea about the nature of reality in Maryland Studies. 3. 5., 2006, 89-105.

[49] D. Iwuh OSA, *Action Understanding Is Not Entirely Neutral It Is Existential, It Is Igwebuike.*

[50] A.I. Kanu, *On the Origin and Principles of the Igwebuike Philosophy.*

explain. It follows that to some extent, signs can take on a life of their own. Sign thus, is a being in its own right, as our words do, becoming relatively mind-independent as they are embedded in our culture by linguistic habit. Words, that are internally and externally representations of signs, are cultural signs; thus, to translate them is to bridge cultures, bringing one way of life into contact with another. *Igwebuike* philosophy has arisen from the Igbo people with their own culture, mode of thinking and operation. But, it is philosophy that has far-reaching implications. The *Igwebuike* sign is one that does not seek to explain what it stands for; it only seeks to represent or indicate what it refers to, namely; complementarity, solidarity and togetherness. As already noted, it is a sign that shows how much of the "I" resides in the "YOU", and how the "YOU" and the "I" complement each other. It represents how much can be achieved when human persons graft together, working for a well-defined purpose. In his *Magna Moralia*, Aristotle defined the friend as a second self, "For the friend is as we assert a second self".[51] There are far-reaching implications to this Aristotelian mode of thinking, one of which is this: Since this friend is a second self, it stands affirmative that knowledge of the self, can also be attained by focusing on the friend, the second self. Even though Aristotle downsized this relationship to existing between friends, that is, friends of character (friends of virtue, in the thought of Aristotle, are rare, because people of this kind are few.[52]), we can in the thought pattern of the *Igwebuike* extend this beyond the confines of the friends of character. *Igwebuike* maintains that we are all born out of one thread. It is to this effect that "I" find myself in "YOU", as much as "YOU" find yourself in "Me". As rare as it might seem to be, the friendship of virtue was never rare to the African, for it has always been a part of the African. We might allude here that the friendship of this sort (friendship of virtue) in the present time, for the African, is rare; *Igwebuike* calls out to us all, telling us to retrace our steps, to find out who we truly are. In *Igwebuike*, the strength of the other is my strength; the glory of the other is my glory; the positives of the other and her concomitant negatives are mine. I live for the other, just as the other lives for me. It is a reality founded on the friendship of virtue, thus making it an existential reality that ought to stand the test of time.[53]

BIBLIOGRAPHY

Aristotle, *Magna Moralia*, Bk II, I2i2b20-I2i3a23, Translated by G. Stock, Clarendon Press, Oxford, 1908.

Aristotle, *Nicomachean Ethics* 1156b31-32.

---

[51] Aristotle, *Magna Moralia*, Bk II, I2i2b20-I2i3a23, Translated by G. Stock, Clarendon Press, Oxford, 1908.
[52] Aristotle, *Nicomachean Ethics* 1156b31-32.
[53] D. Iwuh OSA, *Aristotle's Concept Of Friendship And The Igwebuike Philosophy* in Igwebuike: An African Journal of Arts and Humanities Vol. 5 No 7, September 2019, 46-57.

B.I. Ekwulu, *Igbo concept of Ibe (the other) as a philosophical solution to the ethnic conflicts in African countries* in B. I. Ekwulu (Ed.), philosophical reflections on African issues, Enugu Publications, Delta, 2010.

D. Iwuh OSA, *Action Understanding Is Not Entirely Neutral It Is Existential, It Is Igwebuike*, in IGWEBUIKE: An African Journal of Arts and Humanities Vol. 5 No 6, September 2019.

D. Iwuh OSA, *Aristotle's Concept Of Friendship And The Igwebuike Philosophy* in Igwebuike: An African Journal of Arts and Humanities Vol. 5 No 7, September 2019.

I. A. Kanu, *Igwebuike As An Igbo-African Ethic Of Reciprocity*, in Igwebuike: An African Journal of Arts and Humanities Vol. 3 No 2, March 2017.

I. A. Kanu, *Igwebuike as an Igbo-African hermeneutic of globalization* in Igwebuike: An African Journal of Arts and Humanities. 2. 1. 2016.

I. A. Kanu, *Igwebuike as an Igbo-African Philosophy of Education*, A paper presented at the International Conference on Law, Education and Humanities. 25th -26th November 2015 University of Paris, France.

I. A. Kanu, *On the Origin and Principles of the Igwebuike Philosophy*, in Journal of Religion and Human Relations, Volume 11 No. 1, 2019.

I. A. Kanu, *Igwebuike As A Trend In African Philosophy* In Igwebuike: An African Journal of Arts and Humanities Vol. 2, No. 1, 2016.

I. A. Kanu. (2019b). An *Igwebuike* approach to the study of African traditional naming ceremony and baptism. *International Journal of Religion and Human Relations*. Vol. 11. No. 1. pp. 25-50.

I. A. Kanu. *Igwe Bu Ike* as an Igbo-African hermeneutics of national development. *Igbo Studies Review. No. 6.* pp. 59-83. 2018

I. A. Kanu. *Igwebuike* and question of superiority in the scientific community of knowledge. *Igwebuike: An African Journal of Arts and Humanities.* Vol.3 No1. pp. 131-138. 2017

I. A. Kanu. *Igwebuike* and the logic (Nka) of African philosophy. *Igwebuike: An African Journal of Arts and Humanities.* 3. 1. pp. 1-13. 2017

I. A. Kanu. *Igwebuike* as a complementary approach to the issue of girl-child education. *Nightingale International Journal of Contemporary Education and Research.* Vol. 3. No. 6. pp. 11-17. 2017

I. A. Kanu. *Igwebuike* as a wholistic response to the problem of evil and human suffering. *Igwebuike: An African Journal of Arts and Humanities.* Vol. 3 No 2, March. 2017

I. A. Kanu. *Igwebuike* as an African integrative and progressive anthropology. *NAJOP: Nasara Journal of Philosophy.* Vol. 2. No. 1. pp. 151-161. 2018

I. A. Kanu. Igwebuike as an Igbo-African Hermeneutic of Globalization. *Igwebuike: An African Journal of Arts and Humanities,* Vol. 2 no. 1 2016:1-6.

I. A. Kanu. *Igwebuike* as an Igbo-African modality of peace and conflict resolution. *Journal of African Traditional Religion and Philosophy Scholars. Vol. 1. No. 1. pp. 31-40.* 2017

I. A. Kanu. *Igwebuike* as an Igbo-African philosophy for Christian-Muslim relations in Northern Nigeria. In Mahmoud Misaeli (Ed.). *Spirituality and Global Ethics* (pp. 300-310). United Kingdom: Cambridge Scholars. 2017

I. A. Kanu. *Igwebuike* as an Igbo-African philosophy for the protection of the environment. *Nightingale International Journal of Humanities and Social Sciences.* Vol. 3. No. 4. pp. 28-38. 2017

I. A. Kanu. *Igwebuike* as the hermeneutic of individuality and communality in African ontology. *NAJOP: Nasara Journal of Philosophy.* Vol. 2. No. 1. pp. 162-179. 2017

I. A. Kanu. *Igwebuike* philosophy and human rights violation in Africa. *IGWEBUIKE: An African Journal of Arts and Humanities.* Vol. 3. No. 7. pp. 117-136. 2017

I. A. Kanu. *Igwebuike* research methodology: A new trend for scientific and wholistic investigation. *IGWEBUIKE: An African Journal of Arts and Humanities* (IAAJAH). *5. 4.* pp. *95-105.* 2019

I. A. Kanu. *Igwebuikeconomics*: The Igbo apprenticeship for wealth creation. *IGWEBUIKE: An African Journal of Arts and Humanities* (IAAJAH). *5. 4.* pp. *56-70.* 2019

I. A. Kanu. *Igwebuikecracy*: The Igbo-African participatory cocio-political system of governance. *TOLLE LEGE: An Augustinian Journal of the Philosophy and Theology. 1. 1.* pp. 34-45. 2018

I. A. Kanu. New Africanism: *Igwebuike* as a philosophical Attribute of Africa in portraying the Image of Life. In Mahmoud Misaeli, Sanni Yaya and Rico Sneller (Eds.). *African Perspectives on Global on Global Development* (pp. 92-103). United Kingdom: Cambridge Scholars Publishing. 2018

I.I. Asouzu, Ibuanyidanda. New complementary ontology. Beyond world immanentism, ethnocentric reduction and impositions, Lit Verlag Publications, Munster, 2007.

I.M. Onyeocha, Africa's idea about the nature of reality in Maryland Studies. 3. 5., 2006.

J. Deely, *Cognition from a Semiotic Point of View*, in Semiotics 1981, J.N. Deely-M.D. Lenhart (eds), Plenum Press, New York, 1983.

J. Deely, *On 'Semiotics' as Naming the doctrine of Signs*, in Semiotica vol 152, 2004.

J. Deely, The Red book. The Beginning of PostModern Times or Charles Sanders Peirce and The Recovery of *Signum*, in the Metaphyiscal Club for the University of Helsinki, Finland, 2000.

J.J. Dyikuk, *The Intersection Of Communication In Igwebuike And trado-Rural Media: A Critical Evaluation*, in Journal of African Studies and Sustainable Development Vol. 2 No 3, 2019.

John Poinsot, *Tractatus De Signis*, Part one, bk 1, q.1i, 646a9-41, University of California Press Berkeley, Los Angeles, California, 1985.

T.A. Sebeok, *An Introduction to Semiotics*, University of Toronto Press Incorporated, 1994, xi.

T.A. Sebeok, *Signs. An Introduction to Semiotics 2ⁿᵈ ed*, University of Toronto Press Incorporated, Toronto, 2001, 3.

CHI: IN SEARCH FOR AN EXPLANATORY PRINCIPLE FOR THE INTERRELATEDNESS OF IGWEBUIKE PHILOSOPHY

Ikechukwu Anthony, KANU
Department of Philosophy and Religious Studies
Tansian University, Umunya
Anambra State
ikee_mario@yahoo.com

EXECUTIVE SUMMARY

This work is a search for the basis of intersubjectivity in the African worldview conceptualized in Igwebuike philosophy. This piece found the basis of intersubjectivity of the African reality in Chi, which carries a variety of meanings among the Igbo-African people. However, the nuance of Chi that is employed here is that which understands it as the divinity in every human person or the spark of the divine in created things. It understands Chi as the thumb print or mark of Chukwu in each and every one of us that places the other in a special place in relation to the self. This piece revealed that although Chi is a religious reality, it is conservative of the social institutions of the Igbo-African people. If I and the other have the thumb print of the same Chukwu, the spark of the Supreme Being, it then means that we relate in a special way that goes deeper than our individualities. This work, therefore, argued that our rootedness in Chukwu through Chi is what makes the other a part of me. To treat the other in a way that is undeserving of the divine mark in him or her not only affects the person(s), but the ontological structure to which I also belong and, thus, myself. The importance of Chi in this study is that the belief in Chi is as universal to the Igbo-speaking people as the belief in Chukwu, and it is a fundamental and outstanding characteristic of Igbo social structure and collective temperament. For the purpose of this study, the Igwebuike holistic approach of inquiry was adopted. Chi provides a central and satisfying framework for the understanding of the interrelatedness and individuality of the Igbo-African reality.

Keywords: Chi, Igwebuike, Philosophy, Intersubjectivity, Igbo-African, Explanatory Principle

INTRODUCTION

There are several spiritual and corporal elements in Igbo-African world that are central to the Igbo-African belief and actions. *Chi* is one of these elements, and occupies a very important place in the understanding of the Igbo-speakingAfrican people. It remains one of those elements that the Igbo employ to explain or picture the world around them. No wonder, Chukwukere (1980) avers that:

> The ideas, assumptions, beliefs and actions relating to the metaphysical conception point to its centrality in Igbo worldview and philosophy in general. Of particular interest here are the Igbo people's notions and expressions concerning human personality and the very broad theory of causation (p. 1).

Chi, therefore, is at the heart of the puzzle of human origin, social life and the principles of operations of social institutions that ensure continuity and group or individual identity. The operation of relations within the Igbo-African world, within the context of *Chi*, points to the reality that relationship in the Igbo world is both with and between the corporal and in-corporal worlds. It is this connection of *Chi* with relationships within the Igbo world that makes it a fundamental element in the understanding of the dynamics of inter-subjectivity in *Igwebuike* philosophy, as Igwebuike philosophy is a philosophy of interrelatedness, inter-subjectivity, complementarity and solidarity.

This work argues that *Chi* is the foundation or basis for the interaction or relationships in the Igbo-African universe. And its importance in this study is deepened by the fact that the belief in *Chi* is as universal to the Igbo-speaking people as the belief in *Chukwu*. This piece will, therefore, study the concept of *Chi* and its understandings in Igbo thought. This would be followed by a sociological interpretation of the concept, *Chi*, guided by the focal interest of this paper, which is the search for the fundamental and outstanding base of the Igbo social structure and collective temperament.

THEORETICAL FRAMEWORK

Durkheim (1915) posits that: "The first systems of representations with which men have pictured to themselves the world and themselves were of religious origin. There is no religion that is not a cosmology at the same time that it is a speculation upon divine things"(p. 21). In this, Durkheim argues for a very strong relationship between religious truths or perspectives and social life of people, that is, for an eminently social character of religion.

The germ of Durkheim's theory is that the religious beliefs and practices of people reflect their social structure. This perspective, notwithstanding, Evans-Pritchard (1956) and Goody (1961) have argued further on this theory that not all aspects of religion are tightly bound to social organizations. Some aspects can only be loosely linked and, thus, operate as semi-independent variables.

It is within this context that *Chi,* which is a religious reality or element, is employed to understand the foundations of the Igbo-African social or relational character of reality. In this sense, *Chi* becomes a religious symbol with accumulated meanings or intentions which sometimes contradict one another. And as a symbol, within the context of hermeneutics, it expresses a meaning or meanings, however, with a basic meaning always connected. It is in this regard that etymologically, an understanding of hermeneutics suggests a sacred origin, being derived from the Greek word "hermeneia," which is related to the name of the god, Hermes, and the verb, "hermeneuein", which means: to express/expression; to explain/explanation and to translate/ translation. All the three shades of meaning are rendered in English by - to interpret/interpretation, which, in general, means "bring to understanding" (Kanu, 2015). Thus, Oguejiofor (2009) holds that:

> Hermeneutics involves bringing an inner meaning into the open. It entails making explicit what is implicit. It is thus a quest for meaning, one's own meaning in one's life, society and milieu- in short, in the totality of one's universe, which could be said to be constituted by one's cultural symbols. (p. 80).

As a theory of interpretation, it goes back to ancient Greek philosophy, when Plato employed the term to differentiate between religious knowledge, that which has been revealed, and *Sophia*, which is knowledge of truth-value of utterance. During the Medieval and Renaissance ages, it emerged in relation to the scriptures, precisely, its interpretation. During this period, Gadamer (1976), Heidegger (1978) and Dilthey (1996) observe that Saint Augustine introduced the universal claim of hermeneutics and argue that interpretation of Scripture involves a deeper, existential level of self-understanding. These, notwithstanding, within the context of this study, *Chi* as a religious symbol expresses profound meanings about the spiritual world which helps in the interpretation of realities in the human world.

CHI IN IGBO-AFRICAN WORLDVIEW

There are various dimensions to the use of the concept of *Chi* by the Igbo. It is in this regard that Green (1947) writes that: "It is difficult to know what the real Igbo significance of the word is" (p. 30). Achebe (1975), recognizing the subtle analytical possibilities of the concept of *Chi* which is thrown open by the fundamental abstract notions of Igbo cosmology and theology, avers that its real meaning might never be revealed, and thus, he raises questions about the concept of *Chi* without proffering answers to them, knowing full well the implications of such a response.

> The exact relationship between the Supreme God (*Chukwu*), the sun and *Chi* in Igbo cosmology will probably never be (and perhaps was intended not to be) revealed. But if *Chukwu* means literally Great *Chi*, one is tempted to borrow the words of Christian dogma and speak of *Chi* as being of the same 'substance' and 'proceedings' from *Chukwu*. Or is *Chi* an infinitesimal manifestation of *Chukwu*'s infinite essence given to each of us separately… or does *Chukwu* have a separate existence as ruler over a community of *Chi*…? (p. 11)

Achebe's position points to the fact that the concept of *Chi* is as elusive as it is enigmatic. Thus, Nwodo (2004) avers that the elusiveness and enigma involved is attributable to the fact that the concept is metaphysical in the sense of being a non-material reality. From the foregoing, it is obvious that scholars are yet unable to reach a consensus on what *Chi* actually means for the Igbo people and what its relationship with the Supreme Being exactly is. It is in this regard that this piece would discuss the different understandings of *Chi* in Igbo ontology.

a. Chi as the Divine Aspect of Man

Some African thinkers have interpreted *Chi* as the divine aspect of man or a spark of *Chukwu* in man. It is a spiritual being or force that every Igbo-African is believed to possess within or outside of himself/herself. This explains why it is spoken of in the possessive sense like: *Chim* (my *Chi*), *Chigi* (your *Chi*), *Chiya* (his/her *Chi*), *Chi anyi* (our *Chi*), an Igbo interjection for surprise *Chim o* (My God), etc. This also explains why every Igbo who gets married, in most instances, establishes their own *Chi* symbol for the simple reason that it is personal. It is within this context that Ilogu (1974) avers that *Chukwu* has assigned to each human person at birth a portion of divinity referred to as *Chi*. This implies that each individual has a portion of the great God. It is also within this context that Nwodo (2004) argues that *Chi* is a divine person possessed of intellect and will.

b. *Chi* as Being

Abanuka (2004) understands *Chi* as being, as opposed to non-being. He argues that as being, it has three different aspects that are nonetheless related. *Chi* is first of all the principle of identity. In this regard, *Chi* performs the metaphysical function of making a particular thing what it is other than other things, that is, one with itself and consistent with itself. Second, *Chi* makes each thing unique. Thus, Ojike (1955) and Ekennia (2003) present *Chi* as a unique life force, which each person possesses as a principle of individuation. This implies that no two persons have the same *Chi* and that no person is replaceable. This can be spoken of in terms of the principle of authenticity. Third, *Chi* as a principle of subsidiarity, meaning that *Chi* is a generative or causal principle; this is understood in terms of exercising influence over things.

c. *Chi* as our Other Identity

This perspective is linked to the understanding of *Chi* as a spark of the divine in man. This position is noticed in Achebe (1975) who understands a person's *Chi* as his other identity in spirit-land - his spirit being complementing his terrestrial human being; this is based on the perspective that nothing can stand alone, there must be another thing standing beside it. In this case, the *Chi* shadows the physical aspect of our being on earth and in fact remains a more powerful aspect of us as its influence is high. This other part of us in the spirit-land is not in opposition with our identity here in the world but complements it. *Chi* as the source of identity could be understood better from the practice of the Igbo who plant a special tree in their compound like the *ogilisi* or *oha* or make a small clay pot, filled with sand with three sticks cut from a special plant thrust jointly into the sand, and preserved as the personal *Chi* of individuals which cannot be a symbol of the *Chi* of any other person. No wonder, once the person dies, his/her *Chi* is removed. These representations are usually kept in a special place, with an altar built around it for the offering of sacrifice.

d. *Chi* as Guardian Angel

In *Things Fall Apart,* Achebe (1958) presents the Igbo *Chi* as guardian angel. When Okonkwo, the protagonist of the novel, shot at Ekwefi (one of his wives) and missed, Chielo said: "Your *Chi* is very much awake my friend". In another scene, when Abame was attacked by the avenging band of white men, Obierika described the incident, thus: "Everybody was killed, except the old and the sick who were at home and a handful of men and women whose *Chi* were wide awake and brought them out of that market". As such, a person's *Chi* could be asleep or awake, expressed in the particular event in a person's life. When a bad thing happens, its said that the person's *Chi* is asleep, and when something good happens, it is said that a person's *Chi* is awake. There were other times that a *Chi* was considered good or bad. When a good thing happens to a person, it is said that he has a good *Chi* and when something bad happens, it is said that the person has a bad *Chi*.

e. *Chi* as the Determiner of Destiny

Describing *Chi* as a spark of the divine in man, Okere (1971) posits that it is through the gift of the *Chi* that the Supreme God determines the destiny of each person. Once the Supreme has determined a person's destiny through his *Chi*, it cannot be changed. In *Things Fall Apart*, Achebe (1958) describes Okonkwo as "a man whose *Chi* said nay despite his own affirmation". It is in this regard that one can understand Okonkwo's tragic fate as the result of a problematic *chi*—a thought that occurs to Okonkwo at several points in the novel. It was the belief at the time, as Achebe narrates in Chapter 14, a "man could not rise beyond the destiny of his *chi*." However, there is another understanding of *Chi* that conflicts with this definition.

In Chapter 4, the narrator relates, according to an Igbo proverb, that "when a man says yes his *chi* says yes also." According to this understanding, individuals can alter their destinies. In this case, Okonkwo seems either more or less responsible for his own tragic death. This, notwithstanding, the first definition explains why the Igbo would say that:

a. No matter how many divinities sit to plot a man's ruin, if his *Chi* does not affirm it, their plans will come to nothing.
b. Even water gets stuck inbetween the teeth of the person with a bad *Chi*.
c. The antelope learns to climb the day the person with a bad *Chi* goes hunting.
d. A person whose efforts at improving his fortunes are frustrated by his *Chi* should be absolved from blame.
e. A person with a bad *Chi* cut down an Iroko tree, but it got suspended on a spear grass.

It is in this regard that Nwodo (2004) avers that the *Chi* in Igbo cosmology enforces throughout an individual's life the spoken bond into which he willingly enters at his creation. For instance, Unoka, the Father of Okonkwo in *Things Fall Apart*, is said to have a bad *chi* because evil fortune followed him to his death. Ekwefi, Okonkwo's second wife, is also said to have a bad *chi* because she has given birth to many children, but only one has survived. Also, Okonkwo, exiled from the clan and disappointed that his son has joined forces with the white missionaries, also blames his *Chi*, believing that his *Chi* is not made for great things.

Okoro (2008) explains this further through the spectrum of Igbo application of *Chi*. When the Igbo says: *Chi m*, it mean 'my fate', 'my destiny', 'my portion'. In another case, *Chi ojo*, mean 'bad fate', 'bad destiny'. In this latter sense, *Chi* becomes destiny itself, rather than just the determiner of destiny.

CHI AS A BASIS FOR *IGWEBUIKE* PHILOSOPHY OF INTERRELATEDNESS

Igwebuike is a unifying concept of African thought, especially that aspect concerning the human person's conception of the spiritual and material universe in which he/she lives. It is an explanatory theory or principle that interprets the puzzle of our complex relationship with the non-corporal world and the human social life, that is, major social institutions that ensure social continuity and group identity, and further underpins the epistemological manifestations of the human person's universe (Kanu, 2016a;2017a). Taken from its etymology from the Igbo words (*Igwe*: number; *bu*: is; *Ike*: power), literally meaning that 'number is power', it points to a philosophical nuance of 'one heart and one mind', a spirit of complementarity, solidarity and interrelatedness that characterizes the African reality (Kanu, 2014;2015;2016b; 2017b). The basic question being attended to in this section of this work is: hat is the basis of this inter-subjectivity, interrelatedness, solidarity or complementarity of reality within the African universe? It is within this context that this piece argues that *Chi* is the basis of this complementarity or inter-subjectivity or interrelatedness of reality in the African universe.

Igwebuike, as a perspective, holds that, in spite of the contrariety of reality, there is something common to everything. It understands every individual reality as part and completion of the whole, and thus, there is a unity in the midst of diversity (Kanu, 2017c; 2018; 2019). Although *Chi* provides for the individuation, identity and contrariety of being, it is also the basis for the unity of being. How is this possible? *Chi,* being a 'thumb print' of *Chukwu* in all that He has made, provides a reason for the unity of being, and a basis for interaction and collaboration. Thus, the strong individualistic strain, which *Chi* provides in the theory of personality, does not contradict the emphasis on the overriding value of unity in diverse human situations. *Chi,* therefore, is not only a basis for identity in Igbo ontology; it is also a basis for unity - a common gift or platform for communal relations. This is evident in the way that the Igbo greet one another within the context of the word, *Chi: Ibo Chi,* a greeting that reflects a rhetorical, informative and questioning expectancy reports from the individuals that are in this relational (greetings) exchange; *Isa Chi,* a greeting that reflects also the same rhetorical, informative and questioning expectancy reports from both individuals engaged in the same relational exchange; *Ifo Chi,* a greeting that reflects the same rhetorical, informative and questioning expectancy from the dialoging individuals.

The nuance of *Chi,* employed in this work to drive the understanding of the unity of reality, is that which understands it as the divinity in every human person or the spark of the divine in created things. It is this *Chi,* which is a thumb print or mark of *Chukwu* in each and every one of us that places the other in a special place in relation to the self. If I and the other have the thumb print of the same *Chukwu,* the spark of the Supreme being, it then means that we relate in a special way that goes deeper than our individualities. Our rootedness in *Chukwu* is what makes the other a part of me. To treat the other in a way that is undeserving of the divine mark in him/her not only affects the persons but the ontological structure to which I also belong, and, therefore, myself as well.

CONCLUSION

This work has studied the concept of *Chi* and its implications for inter-subjectivity in the African universe. The concept of *Chi* has been used in various capacities by the Igbo; first, in the capacity of the Supreme Being, and as a guardian angel or a spiritual being or force which every person possess, among other perspectives. Its essence lies in the commonest everyday expression of the word, *Chi;* verbally, in possessive singular adjectival form: *Chim* (my *Chi*), *Chigi* (your *Chi*), *Chiya* (his/her *Chi*), *Chi anyi* (our *Chi*), an Igbo interjection for surprise *Chim o* (My God) or a common curse among the Igbo *Chi ne'ke kpo gi oku* (May God burn you). However, the concept of *Chi* that has helped in determining the basis of inter-subjectivity in the African universe is the understanding of Chi as a spark or portion of the Supreme Being in each and every human person. This creates a ground for relationships or connection between beings, and explains the necessity of solidarity and complementarity in the African universe.

Worthy of note is that, while the concept of *Chi* helps in explaining the basis of relationships or inter-subjectivity in the African universe, it also serves as a foundation of the Igbo-African philosopher's intellectual effort to make sense of the bewildering diversities of the human personality, experiences and cosmic phenomena, and, thus, an explanation for the dominant individualizing principle in the Igbo social order. While *Chi* provides an explanation for the interrelatedness of reality and the individuation of reality at the same time, it can be said to be a theory both of causation and human personality in the wider context of the Igbo-African cosmology. Thus, it serves as a framework within which the Igbo-Africans can boldly speculate, interpret or understand the world around them.

REFERENCES

Abanuka, B. (2004). *Philosophy and the Igbo World*. Enugu: Snaap Press.

Achebe, C. (1975). Morning yet on creation day: Essays. Heinemann African Writers.

Adibe, Gregory E. (2009). *Igbo Issues: Values, Chi, Akala aka, Ikenga, Magic, Agwu and Manipulation of Divinities*. Onitsha: Mid-Field Publishers.

Chukwukere, I. (1980). Chi in traditional Igbo religious thought: A key interpretative concept. A paper presented at the Workshop on the Foundations of Igbo Civilization. May 20-22, Institute of African Studies, University of Nigeria.

Dilthey, W. (1996). *Hermeneutics and the study of history*. Eds. Rudolf A. Makkreel and Frithjof Rodi. Princeton. New Jersey: Princeton University Press.

Durkheim, E. (1965). The elementary forms of the religious life. London: George Allen and Unwin Ltd

Ekennia, J. (2003). *Bio-Medical Ethics*. Owerri: Barloz Publishers.

Evans-Pritchard, E. E. (1956). *Theories of primitive religion*. Oxford: University of Oxford Press.

Gadamer, H. (1976). *Philosophical hermeneutics*. Trans. David E. Linge. Berkeley: University of California Press.

Goody, J. (1961). Religion and ritual: The definitional problem. *The British Journal of Sociology. Vol. 12. No. 2. Pp. 142-161.*

Green, M. M. (1947). *Igbo village affairs: Chiefly with reference to the village of Umbueke Agbaja*. Britain: Taylor and Francis.

Heidegger, M. (1978). *Gesamtausgabe.* Frankfurt am Main: Vittorio Klostermann

Ilogu, Edmund (1974). *Christianity and Igbo Culture.* New York: Nok Publishers.

Kanu, I. A. (2014). *Igwebuikology* as an Igbo-African philosophy for Catholic-Pentecostal relations. *Jos Studies. 22. pp.*87-98.

Kanu, I. A. (2015a). *African philosophy: An ontologico-existential hermeneutic approach to classical and contemporary issues.* Nigeria: Augustinian Publications.

Kanu, I. A. (2015b). *Igwebuike as an ontological precondition for African ethics.* International Conference of the Society for Research and Academic Excellence. University of Nigeria, Nsukka. 14ᵗʰ -16ᵗʰ September.

Kanu, I. A. (2015c). *Igwebuike as an Igbo-African Philosophy of Education.* A paper presented at the International Conference on Law, Education and Humanities. 25ᵗʰ -26ᵗʰ November 2015 University of Paris, France.

Kanu, I. A. (2016a). *Igwebuike* as the consummate foundation of African Bioethical principles. *An African journal of Arts and Humanities* Vol.2 No1 June, pp.23-40.

Kanu, I. A. (2016b) *Igwebuike* as an Expressive Modality of Being in African ontology. *Journal of Environmental and Construction Management. 6. 3.* pp.12-21.

Kanu, I. A. (2017). *Igwebuike* as the Hermeneutic of Individuality and Communality in African Ontology. *NAJOP: Nasara Journal of Philosophy.* Vol. 2. No. 1. pp. 162-179.

Kanu, I. A. (2017a). *Igwebuike* and Question of Superiority in the Scientific Community of Knowledge. *Igwebuike: An African Journal of Arts and Humanities.* Vol.3 No1. pp. 131-138.

Kanu, I. A. (2017b). *Igwebuike* as a Complementary Approach to the Issue of Girl-Child Education. *Nightingale International Journal of Contemporary Education and Research.* Vol. 3. No. 6. pp. 11-17.

Kanu, I. A. (2018). *Igwe Bu Ike* as an Igbo-African Hermeneutics of National Development. *Igbo Studies Review. No. 6.* pp. 59-83.

Kanu, I. A. (2018). Igwebuike as an African Integrative and Progressive Anthropology. *NAJOP: Nasara Journal of Philosophy.* Vol. 2. No. 1. pp. 151-161.

Kanu, I. A. (2018). New Africanism: *Igwebuike* as a philosophical Attribute of Africa in portraying the Image of Life. In Mahmoud Misaeli, Sanni Yaya and Rico Sneller (Eds.).

African Perspectives on Global on Global Development (pp. 92-103). United Kingdom: Cambridge Scholars Publishing.

Kanu, I. A. (2019). *Igwebuike* Research Methodology: A New Trend for Scientific and Wholistic Investigation. *IGWEBUIKE: An African Journal of Arts and Humanities* (IAAJAH). *5. 4.* pp. *95-105.*

Kanu, I. A. (2019). Igwebuikeconomics: The Igbo Apprenticeship for Wealth Creation. *IGWEBUIKE: An African Journal of Arts and Humanities* (IAAJAH). *5. 4.* pp. *56-70.*

Nwodo, C. S. (2004). *Philosophical Perspectives on Chinua Achebe.* Port Harcourt: University of Port Harcourt.

Oguejiofor, O. J. (2009). Negritude as hermeneutics: A reinterpretation of Leopold Sedar Senghor's Philosophy. *American Catholic Philosophical Quaterly. 83. 1.* 79-94.

Ojike, M. (1955). *My Africa.* London: Blandford Press.

Okere, T. (1971). *Can There Be An African Philosophy?* PhD Dissertation, Louvain Belgium.

Okoro, E. (2008). Chi Symbolism in Achebe's *Things Fall Apart*: A Hermeneutical Understanding. https://www.ajd.info.2008.

"CITY BEFORE SELF": A COMPARATIVE STUDY OF PLUTARCH'S ETHICAL-POLITICAL THOUGHT AND IGWEBUIKE COMMUNAL PHILOSOPHY

Kolawole Chabi, O.S.A., PhD
Institutum Patristicum "Augustinianum"
Rome, Italy
kolachabi@gmail.com

EXECUTIVE SUMMARY

This paper studies some aspects of Plutarch's ethical-political thought in comparison with the Igwebuike philosophy. So, it exposes, on the one hand, how Plutarch insists on the need for citizens, especially those involved in politics to seek first the good of the community and give priority to the progress of society above personal achievements. On the other hand, the paper presents the communitarian/communal view that springs from the Igwebuike understanding of life in the community. We present the positions of various African thinkers who reason along the line of this worldview to establish that community does have pride of place in the African conception of life together. The last step in this study is a synthesis of Plutarch's ideas and the Igwebuike philosophy. We discover that mutatis mutandis, *what Plutarch advocates for his Greek compatriots, constitutes the underlining principle of the Igwebuike worldview. Moreover, this confirms the universality of this emerging trend in African philosophy.*

Keywords: Plutarch, Philosophy, Common Good, Igwebuike, Kanu Ikechukwu Anthony, Community, African.

INTRODUCTION

The reading of a new translation of the works of Plutarch[54] recently published in the "Ancient Wisdom for Modern Readers Series" of Princeton University Press prompted me to undertake the present study in order to compare the vision of an ancient Western thinker with the African Igwebuike worldview. The basic principle of Plutarch's political thought, and the

---

[54] Cf. Plutarch, *How to Be a Leader: An Ancient Guide to Wise Leadership. Ancient Wisdom for Modern Readers*, transl. J. Beneker, Princeton University Press, 2019.

common thread to his works in the new translation, can be aptly summarised as 'city before self'. This line of thought seems to rhyme well with the African Igwebuike communal thought.

In this paper, we shall present the underlying presuppositions and orientations of Plutarch's political and moral philosophy, on the one hand, and the Igwebuike worldview, on the other hand, to draw the similarities and differences between a representative of Ancient Western cultural thought and a specific line of African philosophical *pensée*. Both the works of Plutarch and secondary literature on them are abundant, and we shall depend on authoritative studies on the topic to back up our line of argument in the first part of the article. Concerning studies on the *Igwebuike* approach to reality, a lot of studies are going on, and works of I. A. Kanu and other African scholars testify to it. We will precisely depend on most of their scientific research in the field of African philosophical thought in the second part of the paper.

The paper will begin with a brief presentation of Plutarch's biography and an exposition of the significant aspects of his ethical and political thoughts, most notably regarding common life. The second segment of the paper will be devoted to the *Igwebuike* philosophy on communality. In a synthesis of our itinerary, we will draw the similarities in Plutarch's thought and *Igwebuike* understanding of common life before bringing the study to its conclusion.

PLUTARCH AND HIS CONCEPTION OF MORAL VIRTUE AND POLITICAL ENGAGEMENT

Plutarch: A profile

Plutarch was born and educated in Chaeronea, a small village located about sixty-seven miles northwest of Athens. He spoken with warmth of his family: his wife, Timoxena; his father, Autobulus, his grandfather, Lamprias, for whom he expresses special admiration, and his brothers, Timon and Lamprias. Plutarch deeply loved his wife, Timoxena, and their five children, only two of whom survived into adulthood. We have the *Consolation to his wife* (608A–612B) that he wrote after the death of their only daughter at the age of two. It remains a moving testimonial to his love of family. His views on his own marriage can be summed up in one of his memorable quotes: "*Very fortunate is the man who in the entire span of his life knows from the beginning only one woman, the one whom he marries*" (*Cat. Min.* 7.3).[55]

---

[55] Cf. M. Beck, *Introduction. Plutarch in Greece*, in *A Companion to Plutarch*, ed. M. Beck, Wiley Blackwell 2014, 2. It is interesting to note that Plutarch's thought on marriage, women and sexuality has gained interest among scholars of late. Interested readers could see for example S. B. Pomeroy, *Reflections on Plutarch*, "A consolation to his wife", in *Plutarch's "Advice to the bride and groom' and "A consolation to his wife": English translations, commentary, interpretive essays, and bibliography*, ed. S. B. Pomeroy, Oxford University Press 1999, 75-81;

P. A. Stadter, Φιλόσοφος και φίλανδρος: *Plutarch's view of women in the "Moralia" and the "Lives"*, in *Plutarch's "Advice to the bride and groom'*, 173-182. In this paper, Stadter demonstrates that Plutarch's writing addressed to women, especially to Clea ("*Virtues in women*" and "*Isis and Osiris*"), reveals the level of

Although he was born in the "poor, little town" of Chaeronea, Plutarch was hardly the "dull, stupid person" the name has come to connote in modern times. Judging from the respect he got while still living, and the acclaim some of his works handed down through the centuries, he was one bright and witty fellow – so much so that Montaigne would later claim that it was by reading Plutarch's *Lives* that the rest of us "dunces" are *"raised out of the dirt."*[56]

He received much of his early education from the reputed Egyptian philosopher, Ammonius, with whom he lived during an extended stay in Athens as a young man of twenty years.[57] His education was augmented by conversations at the dinner table with his family, relatives, and circle of friends.[58] We can acquire an approximate idea of what these evening sessions may have been like from reading Plutarch's lengthy *Table Talks* (*Quaest. conv.* 612C–748D).[59] By the time he was an older man, he had a reputation of being a very learned and wise man. Much of his adult life was devoted to social, civic and literary activities. He focussed on taking care of his family, serving as a magistrate in Chaeronea, representing his hometown and country on various missions to Rome (where he also briefly gave lectures on philosophy). He also produced a vast body of writings (most notably, the *Parallel Lives*). It is not an exaggeration to say that Plutarch was a prolific writer. His literary legacy testifies to it. The so-called *Lamprias catalogue*, an ancient library catalogue incompletely preserved, supposedly compiled by Plutarch's son Lamprias, lists 227 works, of which several are no longer in existence.[60] Plutarch's works are classified into philosophical and historical-biographical. The latter, the so-called *Lives* of distinguished Greek and Roman men examined in pairs, demonstrate

---

education and philosophical sophistication he expected in them. «*Isis and Osiris*» considers his metaphysical basis for the virtues and limits of female action. Examples of women's virtues in "*Virtues of women*" and the "*Lives*" suggest that he expected women not to act as independent agents.

P. Walcot, *Plutarch on Women*, in Symbolae Osloenses: *Norwegian Journal of Greek and Latin Studies* 74 (1999), 163-183. According to Walcot, the evidence offered by the "*Lives*" and the "*Moralia*" shows that Plutarch had a low opinion of women, regarding them as being deceitful, savage, sexually insatiable, frivolous and gossips. Women are thought to be weak, but at the same time, dangerous. There are, however, notable exceptions, most obviously those women whose stories are related in the "*Mulierum virtues*"; Id., *Plutarch on Sex*, in Greece and Rome: *Journal of the Classical Association* 45/2 (1998), Series 2, 166-187. In this paper Walcot indicates that some of Plutarch's works reveal his heavily prejudiced and grossly inhibited attitude toward sex.

On family and its importance in the development of the person in the thought of Plutarch, see Fr. Albini, *Family and the Formation of Character. Aspects of Plutarch's Thought*, in *Plutarch and his intellectual world. Essays on Plutarch*, ed. J. Mossman, London 1997, 59-70.

J. Beneker, *Sex, eroticism, and politics*, in *A Companion to Plutarch*, 503-515; Id., *The passionate statesman: Eros and politics in Plutarch's « Lives »*, Oxford University Press 2012.

[56] Cf. B. J. Verkamp, *Plutarch*, in *Encyclopaedia of Philosophers on Religion*, ed. B. J. Verkamp, McFarland 2008, 152.

[57] Cf. *Ibid.*

[58] *De tuend. san.* 133E.

[59] Cf. M. Beck, *Introduction. Plutarch in Greece*, 2. An interesting study of the life of Plutarch is that of F. Klotz, *Portraits of the philosopher: Plutarch's self-presentation in the «Quaestiones convivales»*, in *Classical Quarterly* nova series 57/2 (2007), 650-667.

[60] Cf. D. A. Russell, *Plutarch*, London 1973, 18-19.

Plutarch's historical and rhetorical abilities, also showing his interest in character formation and politics.[61] Plutarch's philosophical works, predominantly dialogues (set in Delphi or Chaeronea), cover half of his literary production. In modern times, they have been published under the collective term, *Moralia*. However, as Karamanolis rightly observed, when Plutarch's collection was augmented by many other writings preserved in other manuscripts on various other topics, ranging from metaphysics, psychology, natural philosophy, theology, logic, to philosophy of art, the name was retained with the misleading implication that Plutarch's philosophical works are essentially or primarily ethical.[62]

One can say that, of all the writers of classical antiquity, Plutarch is, without a shadow of a doubt, one of the most popular to contemporary readers. He certainly owes this popularity to the nature of his genius, to the choice of subjects he dealt with, to the eternal interest in the names of the great men whose images he painted. Enough by way of presentation!

PLUTARCH'S ETHICAL AND POLITICAL POSTULATES IN FAVOUR OF COMMON GOOD

In terms of philosophical literary production, Plutarch gives pride of place to ethics in this thought, and this is characteristic of his age. He believes philosophy is a way of life. Such a position was familiar with the Hellenistic philosophers whose worldview he shares from that perspective, even though he criticises Stoics and Epicureans for proposing what he considered misguided ethical ideals.[63] Likewise, concerning the involvement of philosophers in politics, Plutarch criticizes these philosophers. He finds fault with the early Stoics for their abstaining

---

[61] Cf. *Ibid.*, 100-116.

[62] Cf. G. Karamanolis, *Plutarch*, in *Stanford Encyclopaedia of Philosophy* online https://plato.stanford.edu/entries/plutarch/#PluPla accessed on 24/07/2020.

[63] Cf. Plut. *An recte dictum sit latenter esse vivendum* 1129F-1130E. Some scholars have noted elements of exaggeration in Plutarch's attacks on Stoics and Epicureans. That is the position of A. Pierron in the introductory part of his French translation of Plutarch's *Lives*. Pierron wrote: "*Il est certain, d'ailleurs, que son attachement trop exclusif pour le platonisme l'a rendu injuste envers les stoïciens.*" Cf. A. Pierron, *Notice sur Plutarque*, in *Plutarque I. Vies des hommes illustres*, transl. A. Pierronm Paris 1853, iv. Kamaranolis, in his article cited above, justifies Plutarch's reaction to the leading Hellenistic schools of thought thus: "Plutarch engaged in writing so many polemical works against the two main Hellenistic schools of philosophy. One reason for Plutarch's preoccupation must be that the early Stoics and Epicureans both strongly criticized Plato. The Epicurean Colotes, for instance, Plutarch's target in the *Against Colotes*, was critical of Plato's dialogues in his *Against Plato's Lysis* and *Against Plato's Euthydemus* [...] while he also criticized the Republic's myth of Er and the implied view of an immortal human soul [...]. Another reason for Plutarch's engagement was the fact that both Epicureans and Stoics drew freely and extensively for their purposes on Plato without acknowledging it and despite their criticism of Plato." See also M. Montiel – J. Francisco, *Plutarco transmisor de la filosofía epicúrea: el «Contra Colotes» entre polémica y didáctica*, in *Plutarco e l'età ellenistica: atti del convegno internazionale di studi: Firenze, 23-24 settembre 2004*, ed. A. Casanova, Firenze 2005, 337-350; M. Isnardi Parente, *Plutarco contro Colote*, in *Aspetti dello stoicismo e dell'epicureismo in Plutarco. Atti del II Convegno di studi su Plutarco, Ferrara, 2-3 aprile 1987*, ed. I. Gallo, Ferrara, 1988. 65-88.

from taking part in political activities.[64] In the same line of thought, the political quietism of Epicurus and his school, according to him, amounts to abrogating or abolishing laws and political community.[65] Nevertheless, when it comes to some fundamental elements of virtual life in society, for Stoics and Platonists, a man educated in philosophy was expected to mould the character of the people in his community through his example of virtuous conduct, prudent advice and continuous efforts on behalf of the common good.

For Plutarch, as a Platonist, appropriate conduct towards the community meant placing the common welfare ahead of one's private interests, including acts of beneficence towards that community and initiatives to preserve the liberty, harmony and wellbeing of all groups within the State.[66] Plutarch's encouragement to seek common good is a particularly vital element of his thought that calls attention to what we shall see later when examining the communal dimension of *Igwebuike*. The common welfare is supposed to supersede the personal interest to guarantee a better life together.

The concept of "political virtue" (πολιτικὴ ἀρετή) embraces excellence in all these activities— from cultivating moral improvement in others through one's own virtuous character, to taking effective action to improve the conditions of life in the community. As S. Jacobs summarily put it, the distinction between the "virtue" of a statesman (politikos) and that of an ordinary "good man" is based on the sphere in which virtue is exercised (public versus private action) and those on behalf of whom action is taken (the common good of the State as a whole versus the individual caring for his soul). In that light, she argues, both Aristotle and Plutarch agree that the highest expression of practical virtue for human beings is "political virtue". Since public virtue benefits more people than private virtue, public virtue is a "higher degree" of virtue than virtue in private life.[67] Political virtue was deemed the "most complete" or "perfect" virtue (τελεώτατα) because it combined the qualities of a virtuous character (courage, temperance and justice), a willingness to place the good of the community ahead of self-interest (magnanimity) and effective action on behalf of the common good (φρόνησις).[68]

Plutarch's work, *Political Precepts,* treats a wide range of practical functions that require both a moral foundation of temperance, mildness, justice and dedication to the common good, as well as critical judgment about how to administer the city, maintain harmony between groups, foster prosperity and conduct diplomacy to protect its liberty and security. Indeed, in this treatise, moral virtue is not desirable for its own sake, but as a tool of effective leadership: it produces a reputation for incorruptibility that makes a statesman more persuasive, and

---

[64] Cf. Plut., *De Stoic. repugn.* 1033BC.

[65] Cf. Id., *Adv. Col.* 1125C; 1127D.

[66] Cf. Susan Jacobs, *Plutarch's Pragmatic Biographies Lessons for Statesmen and Generals in the Parallel Lives* (Columbia Studies in the Classical Tradition), Leiden-Boston 2018, 18.

[67] Cf. *Ibid.* note 31.

[68] *Ibid.,* 18.

it empowers reason to guide his judgment on behalf of his State.[69] Moreover, sometimes, a politician with the qualities of a philosopher fails as a politician where someone who is less qualified as a philosopher proves to be superior as a politician. In real life, then, the good of a community cannot be reached by philosophy alone, persuasion appears to be a necessary instrument, and popular appeal is a value not to be underestimated.[70]

Giving pride of place to the interests of the community is not only presented as a feature of a philosophical attitude, but also as a morally noble action. Such is the importance that Plutarch places on the good of the community over the individual interest or the satisfaction of a small circle of friends, that we could say that, for him, a specific action, which is *in se* morally reprehensible, may nonetheless be justified if it is beneficial to the State. In his work, *Alcibiades*, Plutarch has one of his characters argue that: "one who had an eye to the general welfare of the community (τὸ συμφέρον) may betray a few dubious persons, if he could thereby save many good men from the anger of the people".[71] Politics is concerned with the highest interests of the community. When it is practised rightly, one does not strive to attain wealth or fame; the purpose is to serve the community.[72]

To bring our study on Plutarch to an end, we deem it fitting to add his opinion on the role older people play in the life of their community. In his work titled "*An seni sit gerenda res publica*" (*Whether an Old Man should engage in public Affairs*), Plutarch argues that older people have much to offer, not only on account of their years of experience, but also because they are less prone than their younger colleagues to give in to their passions. Older people, he maintains, are more reasonable in their judgements and less inclined to impulsiveness than young people. For Plutarch, the primary function of senior politicians was to teach their younger colleagues in both word and deed. He instructs his readers, for example, on how to support young leaders and how to correct them without giving offence or creating hostility. In this way, older politicians could pass on their wisdom and experience to the next generation of leaders. Plutarch beautifully puts his idea thus:

> It is not right to say, or to accept when said by others, that the only time when we do not grow weary is when we are making money. On the contrary, we ought even to emend the saying of Thucydides and believe, not only that "the love of honour never grows old," but that the same is even truer of the spirit of service to the community and the State, which persists to the end even in ants and bees. For no one ever saw a bee that had on account of age become a drone, as some people claim that public men, when they have passed their

[69] *Ibid.*, 24.

[70] Cf. M. van Raalte, More Philosophico: *Political virtue and Philosophy on Plutarch's* Lives, in *The Stateman in Plutarch's Works. Volume II: The Stateman in Plutarch's Greek and Roman Lives*, eds. L. De Blois *et al.*, Leiden-Boston 2005, 111.

[71] Plut., *Alcibiades* 21, 5.

[72] Id., *An seni sit gerenda res publica* 783 E.

prime, should sit down in retirement at home and be fed, allowing their worth in action to be extinguished by idleness as iron is destroyed by rust.[73]

This passage of *Whether an Old Man should engage in public Affairs* summaries the conviction of Plutarch regarding the need for older people to be involved in public affairs, not because they do not wish to hand power over to the younger generation, but because they still have something to contribute to the common good. However, Plutarch does not support those aged men who, for the love of office, involve themselves in a busy restlessness, lying in wait for every opportunity to grab power and relevant positions in the State, seek for themselves discredit and live a toilsome and miserable life. Plutarch opines that,

> to do these things even with the goodwill of others is too burdensome for advanced age, but, in fact, the result is the very opposite: for such old men are hated by the young, who feel that they do not allow them opportunities for public activity and do not permit them to come before the public, and by people, in general, their love of precedence and of office is held in no less disrepute than is other old men's love of wealth and pleasure.[74]

Granted that an old man can be useful in public affairs, there is a code of conduct he ought to observe. Plutarch makes interesting recommendations for elders who still wish to serve the common good, one who still has the honour of setting and making speech in the assembly:

> He should not be constantly jumping up on the platform, nor always, like a cock, crowing in opposition to what is said ; nor should he, by getting involved in controversy, loose the curb of reverence for him in the young men's minds and instil into them the practice and custom of disobedience and unwillingness to listen to him ; but he should sometimes both slacken the reins and allow them to throw up their heads boldly to oppose his opinion and to show their spirit, without even being present or interfering except when the matter at stake is important for the common safety or for honour and decorum.[75]

Plutarch offers a wide range of interesting ideas in favour of communal life and the common good. He calls all citizens to place the city before the self and also exhorts elders to participate in public life with the necessary prudence and wisdom. We shall now expose the *Igwebuike* philosophy.

---

[73] *Ibid.,* 784 A.
[74] *Ibid.,* 793 E.
[75] *Ibid.,* 794 F.

IKECHUKWU ANTHONY KANU

IGWEBUIKE COMMUNALITY/COMPLEMENTARITY WORLDVIEW

A Brief Definition of *Igwebuike* Philosophy

In a recent publication, we have made our first attempt of comparison between the *Igwebuike* philosophy of common life and the Augustinian ideal of community life as expressed in his *Rule* and other essential works.[76] This comparative study helps to establish the universality of the postulates of the new trend in African philosophy being proffered by the emerging *Igwebuike* philosophical worldview.[77]

Igwebuike philosophy was developed by Professor Ikechukwu Anthony Kanu in his attempt to interpret and understand the African reality. "*Igwebuike*" is an Igbo word, which is a combination of three other words. Thus, it can be understood as a word and as a sentence: as a word, it is written thus, Igwebuike, and as a sentence, it is written as, *Igwe bu ike*, with the component words enjoying some independence in terms of space. "*Igwe*" is a noun which means number or population, usually a large number or population. "*Bu*" is a verb, which means is. "*Ike*" is a noun, which means strength or power. Put together, it means 'number is strength', or 'number is power', that is, when human beings come together in solidarity and complementarity, they are powerful or can constitute an insurmountable force".[78] *Igwebuike*

---

[76] Cf. K. Chabi, *Augustine's Ideal of Community vis-à-vis the communal Dimension* of "Igwebuike" *African Philosophy*, in *Perspective on* Igwebuike *Philosophy: Essays in Honour of Professor Kanu, Ikechukwu Anthony, O.S.A.*, 13-33.

[77] For a response to the query whether Igwebuike is exclusive to the Igbo or Africa, see I. A. Kanu, *On the Origin and Principles of Igwebuike Philosophy*, in *Journal of Religion and Human Relations* 11/1 (2019), 159-176. In this paper, Kanu connected Igwebuike philosophy to the oldest philosophical elucubrations of presocratic philosophers such as Thales, Anaximander, and Empedocles to show that it has been in existence for long "beyond the walls of the Igbo traditional society." (Cf. p. 161 of the article).

[78] I. A. Kanu, *Igwebuike as a Trend in African Philosophy*, in *IGWEBUIKE: An African Journal of Arts and Humanities* 2/1 (March 2016), 110. Kanu, Ikechukwu Anthony. *Igwebuike and the Logic (Nka) of African Philosophy*, 14. Kanu, I. A. (2018). *Igwe Bu Ike* as an Igbo-African hermeneutics of national development. *Igbo Studies Review. No. 6. pp. 59-83. Kanu, I. A. (2018). Igwebuike* as an African integrative and progressive anthropology. *NAJOP: Nasara Journal of Philosophy.* Vol. 2. No. 1. pp. 151-161. Kanu, I. A. (2018). New Africanism: *Igwebuike* as a philosophical Attribute of Africa in portraying the Image of Life. In Mahmoud Misaeli, Sanni Yaya and Rico Sneller (Eds.). *African Perspectives on Global on Global Development* (pp. 92-103). United Kingdom: Cambridge Scholars Publishing. Kanu, I. A. (2019). Collaboration within the ecology of mission: An African cultural perspective. *The Catholic Voyage: African Journal of Consecrated Life.* Vol. 15. pp. 125-149. Kanu, I. A. (2019). *Igwebuike* research methodology: A new trend for scientific and wholistic investigation. *IGWEBUIKE: An African Journal of Arts and Humanities* (IAAJAH). 5. 4. pp. 95-105. Kanu, I. A. (2019). *Igwebuikeconomics*: The Igbo apprenticeship for wealth creation. *IGWEBUIKE: An African Journal of Arts and Humanities* (IAAJAH). 5. 4. pp. 56-70. Kanu, I. A. (2019). *Igwebuikecracy*: The Igbo-African participatory cocio-political system of governance. *TOLLE LEGE: An Augustinian Journal of the Philosophy and Theology. 1. 1.* pp. 34-45. Kanu, I. A. (2019). On the origin and principles of *Igwebuike* philosophy. *International Journal of Religion and Human Relations.* Vol. 11. No. 1. pp. 159-176. Kanu, I. A. (2019b). An *Igwebuike* approach to the study of African traditional naming ceremony and baptism. *International Journal of Religion and Human Relations.* Vol. 11. No. 1. pp. 25-50.

is, therefore, along the line of the positions held by such African philosophers as John Mbiti,[79] M. Nkafu Nkembkin,[80] B. I. Ekwulu[81] and many others who pinpoint the importance of the solidarity and complementarity that underline and define the African concept of the person as a relational being. We shall now look concretely at the various expressions of *Igwebuike* philosophy regarding communality and complementarity identifiable in some African philosophers, apart from those already mentioned.

SOME EXPRESSIONS OF IGWEBUIKE WORLDVIEW AMONG AFRICAN PHILOSOPHERS

It may not be a wrong step to take into consideration the thoughts of the major exponents of the first African intellectuals who gave expression to the idea of the primacy of communality in African socio-ethical life. Leopold Sédar Senghor is, without doubt, one of such prominent figures. According to him: "Negro-African society puts more stress on the group than on the individual, more on the communion of persons than on their autonomy. Ours is community society."[82] He further opines that "Negro-African society is collectivist or, more exactly communal, because it is rather a communion of souls than an aggregate of individuals."[83] In these statements, we fine nothing less than the aspect of *Igewbuike* philosophy we are studying in this section of our paper. Where people give primacy to the community, the self continues to exist. But it identifies itself with the organic body (the community) to which it belongs; hence, it does not place itself above the *ensemble*. The same opinion of Senghor holds for other advocates of African socialism, such as Kwame Nkrumah, Jomo Kenyatta and Julius Nyerere, who tenaciously sustained their socialist ideological choice, finding its foundation in the traditional African ideas about society.[84] That is why K. Nkrumah could say that "If one seeks the socio-political ancestor of socialism, one must go to communalism,"[85] which, of course, in their opinion, is the basic principle of reality in the African conception of common life.

---

[79] J. Mbiti, *African religions and philosophy*, Narobi 1970. The study of P. Tempels on the Bantu people of central Africa also affirms some the basic postulates of *Igwebuike* philosophy. He writes: "The living 'muntu' is in a relation of being to being with God, with his clan brethren, with his family and with his descendants. He is in a similar ontological relationship with his patrimony, his land, with all that it contains or produces, with all that grows or lives on it." (P. Tempels, *Bantu Philosophy*, Paris 1959, 66).

[80] Cf. M. Nkafu Nkembkia, *African Vitalogy. A Step forward in African Thinking*, Nairobi 1999.

[81] Cf. B. I. Ekwulu, *Igbo concept of Ibe (the other) as a philosophical solution to the ethnic conflicts in African countries*, in ed. Id., *Philosophical reflections on African issues*, Enugu 2010, 183-192.

[82] L. S. Senghor, *On African Socialism*, transl. Mercer Cook, New York 1964, 93-94.

[83] *Ibid.*, 49.

[84] Cf. K. Gyekye, *Person and Community in African Thought*, in *Person and Community: Ghanaian Philosophical Studies I*, eds. K. Wiredu – K. Gyekye, Washington DC 1992, 103.

[85] K. Nkrumah, *Consciencism – Philosophy and Ideology for Decolonisation and Development in particular Reference to the African Revolution*, London 1964, 73.

Expressing the idea of Man as a communal being in the African culture, specifically from the perspective of his Ghanaian context, N. K. Dzobo opines that:

> The individual's being emerges from a prior social whole which is truly other; it comes into being for the sake of him and exists for his development and growth. Hence, an individual who is cut off from the communal organism is nothing. In Africa, it is true then to say: "As the glow of a coal depends upon its remaining in the fire, so the vitality, the psychic security, the very humanity of man depends on his integration into the family." By living creatively, the individual is also contributing to the life and quality of his community and so can say "we are, therefore I am, and since I am, therefore, we are."[86]

The very last quotation of Dzobo's text, which is another version of Mbiti's famous axiom in expression communitarianism in Africa, has been further examined in a study by I. A. Menkiti which is worth mentioning here. This scholar affirms, based on Mbiti's statement "*I am because we are…*", that from the African perspective, community has an ontological primacy and independence. In his words, "As far as Africans are concerned, the reality of the communal world takes precedence over the reality of the individual life histories, whatever these may be."[87] A few postulates follow in Menkiti's attempt to contrast the African with the Western worldview. He contends that in Africa, "it is the community which defines the person as person, not some isolated static quality of rationality, will or memory".[88] According to him, what we find in the African understanding of the person is the notion of personhood as acquired, "something which has to be achieved, and not given simply because one is born of human seed."[89] For this reason, in African societies, "personhood is something as which individuals could fail."[90]

All these emphatic positions on communal values, collective good and shared goals, could lead to the conclusion that communitarianism conceives the person as entirely constituted by social relationships, that it tends to suppress the moral autonomy of the person, that it makes the being and life of the individual person totally dependent on the activities, values, projects, practices and ends of the community; and as a consequence, that communitarianism would diminish the person's freedom and capacity to choose or question or re-evaluate the shared values of the community.[91] For this reason, some voices rose to critically examine the African communitarian conception of the human person!

---

[86] N. K. Dzobo, The Image of Man in Africa, in *Person and Community: Ghanaian Philosophical Studies I*, eds. K. Wiredu – K. Gyekye, Washington DC 1992, 132.

[87] I. A. Mentiki, *Person and Community in African Traditional Thought*, in *African Philosophy. An Introduction*, ed. R. A. Wright, Lahman, Md, 1984, 171.

[88] *Ibid.*, 172.

[89] *Ibid*, 172.

[90] *Ibid.*, 173.

[91] Cf. K. Gyekye, *Person and Community in African Thought*, 102.

In recent times, some scholars have indicated that the "we existence" ontology of person which characterizes African philosophy, represented by *Igwebuike* and the African philosophers we mentioned above, was more fitting in opposing the Western liberal individualism from a political standpoint, to reclaim human dignity for the colonized African. P. Nnodim is of the view that: "unmeasured emphasis on group-oriented ideas of the person among Africans undermines the broader metaphysical dimensions of personhood existing in the thought systems of many traditional African societies."[92] Such a position is also present in K. Gyekye's article already cited above. According to the Ghanaian philosopher, Menkiti's position that the personhood is defined or conferred by the communal structure of the society cannot be wholly accurate, despite the natural sociality of the human person which places him in a cultural structure.[93] Gyekye posits that the human person is also, by nature, other things besides being a communitarian being. There are various attributes, such as rationality, the capacity for virtue and for evaluating and making moral judgements and choices. The community does not create these attributes but discovers and nurtures them. Moreover, when he fully uses these attributes in her participation in the life of his community, his personhood would be fully defined by the communal structure or social relationships.[94] Instead of an unrestricted communitarianism expressed in the views of Senghor and others, Gyekye advocates a moderate or restricted version of communitarianism which accommodates the communal values as well as values of individuality, social commitments, including duties to self-attention (which is not individualism).

Taking a stand on what we have exposed so far, we contend that community constitutes an essential element in the African understanding of reality. The human person is endowed with a life-force that can only yield and be productive if it is put at the service of common good. We agree with Gyekye that some essential human attributes are natural endowments. However, at the same time, it is vital to emphasise that from the *Igwebuike* point of view, by nature, a human person can only put his worth to bear within a community. V. Mulago's idea on this issue captures the *Igwebuike pensée*:

> The community is the necessary and sufficient condition for the life of the individual person. The individual person is immersed into the natural world and nevertheless emerges from it as an individual and a person within his conscience a freedom given him by the mediation of the community in which he senses a certain presence of the divine.[95]

---

[92] P. Nnodim, The Concept of Person in African Philosophy, in *Life, Body, Person and Self: A Reconsideration of Core Concepts in Bioethics from an Intercultural Perspective*, eds. Graetzel and Guhe, Freiburg 2017, 88.

[93] Cf. K. Gyekye, *Person and Community*, 111.

[94] Cf. *Ibid.*, 111-112.

[95] V. Mulago, *African Heritage and contemporary Christianity*, Nairobi 1989, 115.

This same idea comes in a more straightforward axiom formulated by Kanu: *"To be is to belong and to belong is to be."*[96]

Some anthropological theories, such the Darwinist conflict theory and the Freudian theory, see man as an aggressor and a predator/destroyer by nature, who finds himself obliged to collaborate with other human beings to subjugate his aggressive instincts. From the *Igwebuike* African standpoint, such is not the understanding of the human person. The basic element of life together is the drive to complementarity within the creative synthesis of being which characterizes the African person. Furthermore, in this context, placing the common good ahead of personal interests marks the true spirit of belonging to the body. Thus, the "self", the individual person with all his natural endowments and attributes, works with the common good in mind.

The idea of complementarity that constitutes the underlining principle of *Igwebuike* finds expression also in the vital relationship that exists between the generations in the traditional African environment. Elders are highly regarded in their roles within the traditional African communities. As people who hold the stories and wisdom of the past to enlighten the present, elders have the answers to questions such as "who are we?", "where do we originate from?", "how do we keep alive the heritage handed down to us?" Because of their knowledge and life experience, elders are held in high esteem. As G. J. S. Dei puts it, in traditional African societies, people have "respect for the authority of elderly persons for their wisdom, knowledge of community affairs, and 'closeness' to the ancestors… There is in Africa a general belief that old age comes with wisdom and an understanding of the world."[97] P. O. Onyoyo expresses the

---

[96] I. A. Kanu, *A Hermeneutic Approach to African Traditional Religion, Theology and Philosophy*, Jos Plateau State, 2015, 250. Kanu, I. A. (2017). *Igwebuike* as an Igbo-African philosophy for Christian-Muslim relations in Northern Nigeria. In Mahmoud Misaeli (Ed.). *Spirituality and Global Ethics* (pp. 300-310). United Kingdom: Cambridge Scholars. Kanu, I. A. (2017). *Igwebuike* as an Igbo-African philosophy for the protection of the environment. *Nightingale International Journal of Humanities and Social Sciences*. Vol. 3. No. 4. pp. 28-38. Kanu, I. A. (2017). *Igwebuike* as the hermeneutic of individuality and communality in African ontology. *NAJOP: Nasara Journal of Philosophy*. Vol. 2. No. 1. pp. 162-179. Kanu, I. A. (2017a). *Igwebuike* and question of superiority in the scientific community of knowledge. *Igwebuike: An African Journal of Arts and Humanities*. Vol.3 No1. pp. 131-138. Kanu, I. A. (2017a). *Igwebuike as a philosophical attribute of Africa in portraying the image of life*. A paper presented at the 2017 Oracle of Wisdom International Conference by the Department of Philosophy, Tansian University, Umunya, Anambra State, 27-29 April. Kanu, I. A. (2017b). *Igwebuike* as a complementary approach to the issue of girl-child education. *Nightingale International Journal of Contemporary Education and Research*. Vol. 3. No. 6. pp. 11-17. Kanu, I. A. (2017b). *Igwebuike* as a wholistic response to the problem of evil and human suffering. *Igwebuike: An African Journal of Arts and Humanities*. Vol. 3 No 2, March. Kanu, I. A. (2017e). *Igwebuike* as an Igbo-African modality of peace and conflict resolution. *Journal of African Traditional Religion and Philosophy Scholars*. Vol. 1. No. 1. pp. 31-40. Kanu, I. A. (2017g). *Igwebuike* and the logic (Nka) of African philosophy. *Igwebuike: An African Journal of Arts and Humanities*. 3. 1. pp. 1-13. Kanu, I. A. (2017h). *Igwebuike* philosophy and human rights violation in Africa. *IGWEBUIKE: An African Journal of Arts and Humanities*. Vol. 3. No. 7. pp. 117-136. Kanu, I. A. (2017i). *Igwebuike* as a hermeneutic of personal autonomy in African ontology. *Journal of African Traditional Religion and Philosophy Scholars. Vol. 2. No. 1. pp. 14-22.*

[97] G. J. S. Dei, *Afrocentricity: Cornerstone to Pedagogy*, in *Anthropology and Education Quarterly* 25/1 (1994), 13.

same idea stating that: "… in several African traditional societies in which customary law ruled the lives of people the role of elders was substantial and critical for order and harmony. The elders are construed to be the custodians of customary law, its promulgators and enforcers…"[98] In the Yoruba culture to which I belong, and in several other African ethnic groups, elders preside over religious ceremonies, sit as judges in cases of feud, apply corrective measures to repair the damages caused by offenders, facilitate reconciliation and harmony. As Kanu indicates in one of his studies, elders have such mastery of language that they use folktales in judging in village courts, telling tales in such a way that the people grasp their meanings without requiring further explanation.[99] Those of them with specific roles in priestly lineage pray for the community and offer sacrifice, mediating between God, people, ancestors, and spirits. They have many more vital roles for the good of their community. A very distinctive feature of elders in the Yoruba culture is the desire to hand over their knowledge to the younger generation as the time of their exit from this world draws near. A Yoruba saying states that a divinity whose cult is hidden from the offspring of its priest is doomed to disappear. So, elders are not merely preoccupied with their business in the community without regards to the younger ones. They nurture a sense of complementarity and the desire to transmit the cultural and spiritual patrimony to posterity.

PLUTARCH'S ETHICAL-POLITICAL PHILOSOPHY OF COMMON GOOD AND *IGWEBUIKE*

Having exposed the contents of the two worldviews we set out to compare in this paper, we shall now examine what they have in common and what differentiates them.

Plutarch's ethical-political philosophy which advocates the primacy of "city before self", to express the commitment that a good citizen should have towards the common good, finds *mutatis mutandis*, a corresponding expression in the *Igwebuike* idea of community. Even prior to what we know about his philosophical standpoint, Plutarch's very life as a lover of family, as a man who cherished and remained viscerally attached to the service of his native Chaeronea, indicates that this ancient philosopher had a strong sense of belonging which is characteristic of the traditional African attitude toward life and community.

The same emphasis that Plutarch places on the common good the individual should strive for is present in our African worldview. It confirms the belief that the same seed of wisdom is sown in the spirit of all people of the world, irrespective of the categorisation we make to divide ourselves into groups or factions. The possibility of naturally working for the (common)

---

[98] P. O. Onyoyo, *A Theory of Gerontocracy in the African Customary Law*, a paper published on https://www. academia.edu/9644458/A_Theory_of_Gerontocracy_in_the_African_Customary_Law, accessed on July 27th, 2020.

[99] Cf. I. A. Kanu, *A Hermeneutic Approach to African Traditional Religion*, 77.

good stands in opposition to the anthropological conflict theory sustained by some exponents of Western philosophy in the 19ᵗʰ century.

In the Greek philosopher's thought, the obligation of the good citizen towards the welfare of his social group does not suppress his personality. In his many works, and through the example of his life, Plutarch shows the importance of self-development. He never neglects the importance of the person as an individual with his attributes. Likewise, the African communitarianism affirmed by *Igwebuike* does not obliterate the individual within the society. It only puts to the fore the importance of belonging and working for the good of the body.

Plutarch defends the need for those who, on account of their old age, are considered useless in public affairs to be active and to continue contributing to the life of their community. In the *Igwebuike* framework, elders are never discarded in their old age for retirement as far as the life of the community is considered. No one looks at them as intrusive in matters concerning public life. On the contrary, their opinion is sought and revered. An interesting aspect of Plutarch's recommendation to elders willing to continue their involvement in public life is that of being careful so as not lose the respect and consideration of the youth.

Respect for elders is distinctive of the traditional African code of conduct. But it is worthwhile to mention that, in the real sense, an elder is one who, with the advanced age, also has the wisdom, the goodness and the interest of the community at heart. Among the Yoruba, "*àgbà*" is the word for an elder. When an elderly person is referred to as "*àgbà òshì*" or "*àgbà ìyà*" (that is miserable elder), it is not necessarily because of material indigence. That adjective added to qualify him could portray some aspects of his moral and behavioural stand. A shameless elder who involves himself in baseness belongs to the category of "*àgbà òshì*". Consequently, he cannot be a point of reference to the people of his community. Both in Plutarch's society and our traditional African setting, a person could lose the respect of the community even in his old age.

By and large, we have observed some common points in the Plutarch and *Igwebuike* worldviews concerning life together and the common good. *Igwebuike* is a universal worldview expressed in the language and within the cultural environment of the *Igbo* in Nigeria. That should not come as a surprise, for every trend of thought and every philosophy has a cradle, a point of departure, a culture from which it propagates. This study contributes to the reinforcement of the universal character of this trend as already demonstrated by I. A. Kanu.[100]

---

[100] I. A. Kanu, *On the Origin and Principles of Igwebuike Philosophy*, in *Journal of Religion and Human Relations* 11/1 (2019), 159-176.

CONCLUSION

The Greek philosopher, Plutarch, has consecrated most of his works to revealing the educational power of the past by giving many historical figures as examples for today. In his thought, he laid much emphasis on the need for citizens to seek the common good and to place the well-being of the community before personal or selfish interests. His philosophical *pensée* seems to rhyme with the *Igwebuike* African philosophy in which commonality, complementarity, and seeking the common good have pride of place within the social fabric. For this reason, our study focused on the comparison of the two philosophical worldviews to establish what they have in common and what differentiates them. Apart from the concern for the common good that cut across both philosophies, the aspect of the place and role of elders within the community retained our attention, since it is present in both. Plutarch defends the importance of elders in public life. *Igwebuike* sees elders as the custodians and teachers of culture. However, to be an elder is also earned through the wisdom, kindness and exemplary life an aged person displays within his community.

In the ideal world of traditional Africa, as it was in the ancient Western and Biblical world, ageing was revered and considered a blessing. Living to see one's children's children is blessing beyond measure. In traditional Africa, elderly people were attended to and accompanied in their old age until they rested with the ancestors. It seems, however, that things are much different nowadays. Many elders suffer abuse and neglect. According to Aderemi Suleiman Ajala, among the Yoruba, for example, due to urbanisation and other social factors, the perception of ageing has changed from peaceful retirement to crisis-ridden stage of living. Some of the crises include: neglect of the elderly, poor feeding and poor health status for the aged. Thus, the aged can no longer play their roles as social reformers and custodians of the people's culture.[101] This situation could be a subject for further studies from the *Igwebuike* perspective, to see how we can reconcile structural development and material progress with the core values of our being Africans, with respect to our *Igwebuike* credo.

BIBLIOGRAPHY

B. J. Verkamp, *Plutarch*, in *Encyclopaedia of Philosophers on Religion*, ed. B. J. Verkamp, McFarland 2008.

Fr. Albini, *Family and the Formation of Character. Aspects of Plutarch's Thought*, in *Plutarch and his intellectual world. Essays on Plutarch*, ed. J. Mossman, London 1997.

G. J. S. Dei, *Afrocentricity: Cornerstone to Pedagogy*, in *Anthropology and Education Quarterly* 25/1, 1994.

---

[101] A. S. Ajala, The Changing Perception of Ageing in Yoruba Culture and Its Implications on the Health of the Elderly, in *The Anthropologist* 8/3 (2006), 181-188.

G. Karamanolis, *Plutarch*, in *Stanford Encyclopaedia of Philosophy* online https://plato.stanford. edu/entries/plutarch/#PluPla accessed on 24/07/2020.

I. A. Kanu, *Igwebuike As An Igbo-African Ethic Of Reciprocity*, in Igwebuike: An African Journal of Arts and Humanities Vol. 3 No 2, March 2017.

I. A. Kanu, *Igwebuike as an Igbo-African hermeneutic of globalization* in Igwebuike: An African Journal of Arts and Humanities. 2. 1. 2016.

I. A. Kanu, *Igwebuike as an Igbo-African Philosophy of Education*, A paper presented at the International Conference on Law, Education and Humanities. 25th -26th November 2015 University of Paris, France.

I. A. Kanu, *On the Origin and Principles of the Igwebuike Philosophy*, in Journal of Religion and Human Relations, Volume 11 No. 1, 2019.

I. A. Kanu, *Igwebuike As A Trend In African Philosophy* In Igwebuike: An African Journal of Arts and Humanities Vol. 2, No. 1, 2016.

I. A. Kanu. (2019b). An *Igwebuike* approach to the study of African traditional naming ceremony and baptism. *International Journal of Religion and Human Relations*. Vol. 11. No. 1. pp. 25-50.

I. A. Kanu. *Igwe Bu Ike* as an Igbo-African hermeneutics of national development. *Igbo Studies Review. No. 6.* pp. 59-83. 2018

I. A. Kanu. *Igwebuike* and question of superiority in the scientific community of knowledge. *Igwebuike: An African Journal of Arts and Humanities.* Vol.3 No1. pp. 131-138. 2017

I. A. Kanu. *Igwebuike* and the logic (Nka) of African philosophy. *Igwebuike: An African Journal of Arts and Humanities.* 3. 1. pp. 1-13. 2017

I. A. Kanu. *Igwebuike* as a complementary approach to the issue of girl-child education. *Nightingale International Journal of Contemporary Education and Research.* Vol. 3. No. 6. pp. 11-17. 2017

I. A. Kanu. *Igwebuike* as a wholistic response to the problem of evil and human suffering. *Igwebuike: An African Journal of Arts and Humanities.* Vol. 3 No 2, March. 2017

I. A. Kanu. *Igwebuike* as an African integrative and progressive anthropology. *NAJOP: Nasara Journal of Philosophy.* Vol. 2. No. 1. pp. 151-161. 2018

I. A. Kanu. Igwebuike as an Igbo-African Hermeneutic of Globalization. *Igwebuike: An African Journal of Arts and Humanities*, Vol. 2 no. 1 2016:1-6.

I. A. Kanu. *Igwebuike* as an Igbo-African modality of peace and conflict resolution. *Journal of African Traditional Religion and Philosophy Scholars. Vol. 1. No. 1. pp. 31-40.* 2017

I. A. Kanu. *Igwebuike* as an Igbo-African philosophy for Christian-Muslim relations in Northern Nigeria. In Mahmoud Misaeli (Ed.). *Spirituality and Global Ethics* (pp. 300-310). United Kingdom: Cambridge Scholars. 2017

I. A. Kanu. *Igwebuike* as an Igbo-African philosophy for the protection of the environment. *Nightingale International Journal of Humanities and Social Sciences.* Vol. 3. No. 4. pp. 28-38. 2017

I. A. Kanu. *Igwebuike* as the hermeneutic of individuality and communality in African ontology. *NAJOP: Nasara Journal of Philosophy.* Vol. 2. No. 1. pp. 162-179. 2017

I. A. Kanu. *Igwebuike* philosophy and human rights violation in Africa. *IGWEBUIKE: An African Journal of Arts and Humanities.* Vol. 3. No. 7. pp. 117-136. 2017

I. A. Kanu. *Igwebuike* research methodology: A new trend for scientific and wholistic investigation. *IGWEBUIKE: An African Journal of Arts and Humanities (IAAJAH). 5. 4. pp. 95-105.* 2019

I. A. Kanu. *Igwebuikeconomics*: The Igbo apprenticeship for wealth creation. *IGWEBUIKE: An African Journal of Arts and Humanities (IAAJAH). 5. 4. pp. 56-70.* 2019

I. A. Mentiki, *Person and Community in African Traditional Thought*, in *African Philosophy. An Introduction*, ed. R. A. Wright, Lahman, Md, 1984, 171.

J. Beneker, *Sex, eroticism, and politics*, in *A Companion to Plutarch*, 503-515; Id., *The passionate statesman: Eros and politics in Plutarch's « Lives »*, Oxford University Press 2012.

J. Mbiti, *African religions and philosophy*, Narobi 1970.

K. Chabi, *Augustine's Ideal of Community vis-à-vis the communal Dimension* of "Igwebuike" *African Philosophy*, in *Perspective on* Igwebuike *Philosophy: Essays in Honour of Professor Kanu, Ikechukwu Anthony, O.S.A.*, 13-33. Author House, London.

K. Gyekye, *Person and Community in African Thought*, in *Person and Community: Ghanaian Philosophical Studies I*, eds. K. Wiredu – K. Gyekye, Washington DC 1992.

K. Nkrumah, *Consciencism – Philosophy and Ideology for Decolonisation and Development in particular Reference to the African Revolution*, London 1964.

L. S. Senghor, *On African Socialism*, transl. Mercer Cook, New York 1964.

M. Beck, *Introduction. Plutarch in Greece*, 2. An interesting study of the life of Plutarch is that of F. Klotz, *Portraits of the philosopher: Plutarch's self-presentation in the «Quaestiones convivales»*, in *Classical Quarterly* nova series 57/2 (2007), 650-667.

M. Beck, *Introduction. Plutarch in Greece*, in *A Companion to Plutarch*, ed. M. Beck, Wiley Blackwell 2014

M. Nkafu Nkembkia, *African Vitalogy. A Step forward in African Thinking*, Nairobi 1999.

M. van Raalte, More Philosophico: *Political virtue and Philosophy on Plutarch's* Lives, in *The Stateman in Plutarch's Works. Volume II: The Stateman in Plutarch's Greek and Roman Lives*, eds. L. De Blois *et al.*, Leiden-Boston 2005.

N. K. Dzobo, The Image of Man in Africa, in *Person and Community: Ghanaian Philosophical Studies I*, eds. K. Wiredu – K. Gyekye, Washington DC 1992.

P. Nnodim, The Concept of Person in African Philosophy, in *Life, Body, Person and Self: A Reconsideration of Core Concepts in Bioethics from an Intercultural Perspective*, eds. Graetzel an

P. O. Onyoyo, *A Theory of Gerontocracy in the African Customary Law*, a paper published on https://www.academia.edu/9644458/A_Theory_of_Gerontocracy_in_the_African_Customary_Law, accessed on July 27th, 2020.

P. Tempels, *Bantu Philosophy*, Paris 1959.

Plutarch, *How to Be a Leader: An Ancient Guide to Wise Leadership. Ancient Wisdom for Modern Readers*, transl. J. Beneker, Princeton University Press, 2019.

Susan Jacobs, *Plutarch's Pragmatic Biographies Lessons for Statesmen and Generals in the Parallel Lives* (Columbia Studies in the Classical Tradition), Leiden-Boston 2018.

IGWEBUIKE AND LANGUAGE: IN SEARCH OF AN ONTOLOGICAL TOOLBOX FOR IGBO-AFRICAN PHILOSOPHY

Ikechukwu Anthony KANU
Department of Philosophy and Religious Studies
Tansian University Umunya, Anambra State
ikee_mario@yahoo.com

EXECUTIVE SUMMARY

Human beings are by nature enshrined in an inescapable world-hood web called language. As a symbolic construction and human agenda setting in semantic space, language ensures the application of social meaning, control, culture and social knowledge. As a result of the place that language occupies in the integration, interpretation and internalization of convention for the state of affairs of sociality, it is not surprising that it has always been an attractive area and a fascinating topic for philosophers. The history of philosophical thinking about language is almost impossible to separate from the history of logic and indeed the entire history of philosophy. This piece argued that human beings do not live in the world without the agency of language which becomes the medium of expression within particular societies. It is based on this understanding (that the real world of a people is based on their language habits) that this paper employed Igwebuike as an ontological toolbox that forms the trajectory system of the Igbo-African world. Within the context of Igbo-African philosophy of language, this piece argued for the necessity of the use of the word "Igwebuike" as it captures and communicates the Igbo-African world. Igwebuike is the form (and symbolic) of the Igbo-African mental being, and thus, the gateway to Igbo-African philosophy. Beyond the literal understanding of Igwebuike (Igwe- number; bu-is; ike-strength) as 'there is strength in number', it captures the Igbo philosophy of relationality, complementarity and interconnectedness of reality. The objective of this work is to discover the centrality of language within philosophy and thus give correct bearing to philosophy. For the purpose of this piece, the Igwebuike holistic approach will be employed.

Keywords: Igwebuike, Language, Philosophy, Igbo-African, Ontological, Toolbox

INTRODUCTION

The concept of *Igwebuike* as a toolbox of Igbo-African philosophy is better understood from the background of Wittgenstein's concept of language as a toolbox which contains hammer, plier, saw, screw-driver, ruler, glue pot, nails, screws, etc. From this metaphor, language, therefore, offers functions through words that are as diverse as the objects in the toolbox (1961, p. 18). These functions would include that of communication, identification and instrument of thought. As practical as these objects are, so practical must a language be in its structuring of reality within its original home. It is through language that people are able to practically explore their world and reality. Thus, according to Sefler (1974):

> Language and the world are two sides of one and the same reality. The world I know is known inseparable from the language I use. One cannot split the two and discuss them in isolation without some literal misrepresentation. Such segregation necessitates some metaphysical device, such as local space, to be intelligible, yet its metaphorical character must be preserved and recognized to avoid even in this context misleading conclusions. An investigation of the aspects of language is at the same time an investigation of the formal aspects of the world. To give the essence of propositions is to give the essence of all description, therefore, the essence of the world (p 188).

Arguing along this line, Okonkwo (2002) avers that the language of a people is a reflection of the world of the people:

> The worldhood of man is therefore his language. The language as a 'given' in a worldhood can be called legitimately 'onto-lingustic'. Onto-linguistic defines language as the state of affairs that demarcates and structures the world of man (Dasien) and his being-in-the-world. The world around me is the world made possible through my language. It is my language that concretely arranges, organizes, shapes and delineates my experience and knowledge of my environment, situation and history (p. 180).

Thus, one can argue that human beings do not live in the world without the agency of language, which becomes the medium of expression within the society in question. This implies that one cannot adjust to the realities within a particular people or place without the use of language as an instrument of communication, understanding and reflection. It is from this perspective that *Igwebuike* is employed as a toolbox that forms the trajectory system of the Igbo-African world. Within the context of Igbo-African philosophy of language, this piece argues for the necessity of the use of the word *Igwebuike* as it captures and communicates the Igbo-African world. *Igwebuike* is the form (and it is symbolic) of the Igbo-African mental being and the gateway to Igbo-African philosophy.

Beyond the literal understanding of *Igwebuike* (*Igwe-* number; *bu-*is; *ike-*strength) as "there is strength in number", it captures the Igbo philosophy of relationality, complementarity and interconnectedness of reality (Kanu 2014; 2015; 2016; 2017; 2018; 2019). It concatenates Igbo forms, symbolism, signs, media, meaning, anthropologies, universal cosmic truths, functions, semantic powers, physics, phenomena, faculties, and Igbo environ-mentalities, and symbolizes the propositional powers of Igbo knowledge, perception, identity, phenomenalism, physics, metaphysics, logic, history of analytic character, speculative mindset and positive provisions for definitions of facts.

PHILOSOPHICAL PERSPECTIVES OF LANGUAGE

The human person, not minding place and time, is enshrined in an inescapable world-hood web called language. As a symbolic construction and human agenda setting in semantic space, it ensures the application of social meaning, control, culture and social knowledge. As a result of the place that language occupies in the integration, interpretation and internalization of convention for the state of affairs of sociality, it is not surprising that it has always been an attractive area and a fascinating topic for philosophers. The history of philosophical thinking about language is almost impossible to separate from the history of logic and indeed the entire history of philosophy. Thus, all major philosophers and schools of philosophy have had some doctrine about the relationship between mind and language, and language and the world.

The earliest interaction between philosophy and language dates back to the ancient Greek philosophical era. Heraclitus, understanding *logos* within its semantic and symbolic function, had thought that the word was not merely an anthropological phenomenon but captures what he regarded as a universal cosmic truth. In him, ancient Early Greek thought moved from the study of nature to philosophy of language.

Plato's life-long battle against the Sophists is a typical example of the concerns of the ancients with the phenomenon of language. Plato attacked the Sophists because of their competent but dubious ability to twist language to their own advantage for the sake of making money. He was infuriated by what he saw as the danger and threat that sophistry posed to genuine communication and life in the society (Pierer, 1992).

The Sophists, before Plato, had dealt with linguistic and grammatical problems in a systematic way. Unlike Plato, they were not interested in the problem of language for theoretical purposes. They had a more urgent task to accomplish: to teach how to speak for the sake of political success and to win law suits. Language was the greatest instrument for political struggle in the Athens of the 5th century. Language became an instrument for definite, concrete and practical purposes. The Sophists believed that one had to manipulate language to his or her own advantage, if such a person were to attain their objective. To enhance this purpose, the Sophists began a new branch of knowledge called rhetoric (Cassirer, 1976). As a result of their proficiency in rhetoric, they were able to make the weaker argument the stronger and to sweet-talk something bad into something good and turn black into white (Honderich, 1976).

In the Plato's dialogue, *Cratylus*, he considered another dimension of language: the question of whether the names of things were determined by convention or by nature. In this case, his analysis of language addressed the problem of nomenclature. He criticized conventionalism because it led to the bizarre consequence that anything could be conventionally denominated by any name. Hence, it cannot account for the correct or incorrect application of a name. He claimed that there was a natural correctness to names. To do this, he pointed out that compound words and phrases have a range of correctness. He also argued that primitive names had a natural correctness, because each phoneme represented basic ideas or sentiments. While Plato concerned himself with meaning, Aristotle, in his philosophy of language, steps up his concern to issues of logic and categories. He separated all things into categories of species and genius, and believes that the meaning of a predicate was established through an abstraction of the similarities between various individual things (Kanu, 2010 & 2012).

The Stoics, in their philosophy of language, made important contributions to the analysis of grammar, distinguishing five parts of speech: nouns, verbs, appellatives (names or epithets), conjunctions and articles. They also developed a sophisticated doctrine of the *lektón* associated with each sign of a language, but distinct from both the sign itself and the thing to which it refers. This *lektón* was the meaning (or sense) of every term. The *lektón* of a sentence is what we would now call its propositions. Only propositions were considered "truth bearers" or "truth-vehicles" (i.e. they could be called true or false), while sentences were simply their vehicles of expression (Kanu 2014).

Medieval philosophers were greatly interested in the subtleties of language and its usage. This interest was provoked by the necessity of translating Greek texts into Latin. Furthermore, the scholastics of the high Medieval Period, such as Occam and John Duns Scotus, considered logic as the science of language (*scientia sermocinalis*). More so, the employment of Greek words in the explanation of the Christian faith remains a major contribution of the Patristic and Medieval philosophers and theologians.

In line with the thoughts of the linguists of the Renaissance and Baroque periods, such as Johannes Goropius Becanus, Athanasius Kircher and John Wilkins, Locke (cited in Kanu 2012), in the 17th century, argued that only an adequate or correctly formed language could be a vehicle for communication. He believed that the desire to know reality was the foundation of communication. Even though there is the possibility of lying, Locke argued that lies do not constitute communication, since to lie is to deny reality. To lie is the perpetration of inequality in society, since it denies the other his/her share and portion of reality. To deceive a person is an implicit assumption that he/she she is not worthy to know the truth. This explains why Locke, like Plato, condemned sophistry:

Nor has this mischief stopped in logical Niceties, or curious empty speculations; it hath invaded the great concernment of human life and society; obscured and perplexed the material truths of law and divinity; brought confusion, disorder and uncertainty into the affairs of mankind; and if not destroyed, yet in great measure rendered useless, those two great rules, religion and justice. (p. 486).

In the early 19th century, the Danish philosopher, Soren Kierkegaard, insisted that language ought to play a larger role in Western philosophy. He argued that philosophy had not sufficiently focused on the role language plays in cognition, and that future philosophy ought to proceed with a conscious focus on language. Hence, language began to play a central role in Western philosophy in the late 19th century. The philosophy of language then became so pervasive that for a time, in analytic philosophy circles, philosophy as a whole was understood to be a matter of philosophy of language (Kanu 2014).

During the 20th century, Ayer (1942) averred that our being as human beings was about the inversion of language for the all-encompassing agenda-setting of humanity. As such, humanity has no other choice than the total experimental engagement for the understanding of the workings of language. Wittgenstein (1961), thus, argues that the function of philosophy is not to construct theories but to clarify thought. Therefore, philosophy is an activity of elucidating propositions in order to make them clear, and this can only be done within the boundaries of human knowledge and the use of language.

Keller (1979) and Rorty (1992) speak of modern trends within philosophical inquiry as a method that denotes philosophy as the passage from the philosophy of nature to the philosophy of language. They argue in favour of this linguistic turn on the basis that there is no singular possibility of human sciences outside the data base of human language. Bell (1978) avers that "It is quite an illusion to imagine that one adjusts to reality essentially without the use of language and language is an incidental means of solving specific problems of communication or reflection" (p. 130). Humbolt (1985) further underscores language as the totality of the human spirit which in itself is the central human activity that gives character and structure to human culture and individuality.

LANGUAGE AS THE TRAJECTORY SYSTEM OF AFRICAN PHILOSOPHY

This piece does not argue that African philosophy cannot be done in other languages; rather, it maintains that to engage in African philosophy more profoundly, the African language is indispensable. Mbiti (1970) speaks of language as a very important element in understanding African philosophy:

There is great potential in African scholars studying African Traditional Religion and philosophy, with the aid of scientific tools and methodology and with the advantages of being part of the peoples of Africa, having almost unlimited access to information and speaking the languages which are the key to serious research and understanding of traditional religions and philosophy (p. 14).

Edeh (1985) further writes that: "Our brief consideration of the Igbo language leads us into the culture of the people since it is obvious that a language cannot be divorced from the culture which it expresses" (p. 56). While talking about destiny, Gyekye (1987) brings out the link between language and philosophy as expressed by thinkers:

The first relates to the link that a number of thinkers find between language and thought, or more precisely in the present context, between language and metaphysics. They claim that there is some kind of reality antecedent to language that language is developed to express or depict. Language or linguistic structure, they hold, reflects a deep lying structure of reality or being. (p. 105).

It is within this context that Adeshina (2006) observes that every language system embodies a particular ontology and a system of knowledge about reality. Language, from this perspective, becomes loaded with worldviews and metaphysics, and, more importantly, a person's language determines, at least in part, the way to perceive and conceive the world. Thus, when you lose the language of a people, you also lose a great chunk of their philosophy. It is not surprising that Tempels (1959), Edeh (1985), Gyekye (1987) and Iroegbu (1995) thought it significant to begin from the analysis of language in their philosophical searches.

Wittgenstein (1961), in his *Tractatus,* argues that the structure of language is conditioned by the structure of reality, for language makes us see reality in a structure corresponding to the structure of language. He writes, "What every picture of whatever form must have in common with reality in order to be able to represent it at all… is the logical form, that is, the form of reality" (p. 18). He strongly believes that the structure of the world is pictured by language, which can now be considered a model of reality. Wittgenstein (1974) further writes, "These facts (of which the world is made of) are pictured by language so that by means of language we make to ourselves pictures of facts" (p. 1). In this picture and the pictured, there must be something identical in order that one can be a picture of the other at all. Language is like a mirror of facts, and if it does not correspond to it, it is false. What Wittgenstein is saying is that just as you cannot use human language to talk about divine realities, you also cannot use European languages to talk about African realities, because there are so many things that the European language cannot picture in the African world, and even when it pictures it, it does that inadequately, for the simple reason that there are no such realities in the European world.

Ki-Zerbo (1981) has argued that language is the treasury house of a people's philosophy:

Language is like a bank or museum in which, over the centuries, each ethnic group has deposited all it has built up and accumulated in the way of mental and material tools, memories and resources of the imagination. By means of an in-depth and wide-ranging study of the language (both infra and supra linguistic). (p. 94).

The emphasis on language as an indispensable element for doing profound African philosophy is very evident in the philosophical position of Ethno-philosophers who view African philosophy as the philosophical thought of Africans as could be gotten from their various world views, myths, proverbs, etc. In this sense, it is the philosophy indigenous to Africans, untainted by foreign ideas. It places little or no emphasis on scientificity, logic, criticism and argumentation, and makes more emphases on local relevance or context. In studying ethno-philosophy, we discover the deep relationship between language and philosophy.

In his work, *African religions and philosophy,* Mbiti (1970) begins with an analysis of the African concept of time from the Kikamba and Gikuyu languages, in which he analyses three verbs that speak of the future, covering only a period of six months and not beyond two years at most. Alexis Kagame, in his work, *Philosophie Bantou-Rwandaise de L'Etre,* reveals that from the language of the Rwandans who were called Kinyarwanda they developed their thought through a linguistic ethno-philosophy. Njoku (2010) discovered that *Ntu* is the category of being or the generic meaning of something. This he classified into four: *Umuntu* (human beings), *Ikintu* (non-human beings), *Ahantu* (place and time), and *Ukuntu* (Aristotelian category of quantity). *Ntu* is the unifying notion among all these, even though God does not belong to it. Iroegbu (1995) develops an African concept of being *as Belongingness* from the Igbo principle of *Egbe bere Ugo bere* (let the kite perch, let the eagle perch), which he believes re-enacts the contents and significance of belongingness.

These developments in African philosophy are a pointer to the relevance of African language in doing African philosophy. It is also within the umbrella of this understanding that the *Igwebuike* is adopted as a very significant concept in the understanding and communication of Igbo-African philosophy.

THE TRIPARTITE DIMENSIONAL REASONS FOR *IGWEBUIKE* AS A LANGUAGE-BASED PHILOSOPHY

Okosisi (2012) posits that each language of the world stands out as a configuration and mechanization of the people's book of history and of philosophy, containing and concatenating their implications of real 'worldhood' of facts and metaphysics. Thus, he avers, "The people who use that language are registered and known by the realities of that same language" (p. 9). It is in this regard that *Igwebuike* stands out as a configuration and mechanization of the Igbo-African book of history, and captures the Igbo-African real world of facts and metaphysics.

It is within this context too that it is referred to as the gateway to Igbo-African philosophy or 'worldhood.' To understand better how *Igwebuike* serves as a gateway to the Igbo 'worldhood' of facts and metaphysics, it would be worthwhile to employ the tripartite dimensional functions of language in Okonkwo (1994), which include: the function of communication, the function of interpretation of the real world (thought function) and the function of ontology (Metaphysics or identity), and explain how *Igwebuike* functions in these capacities.

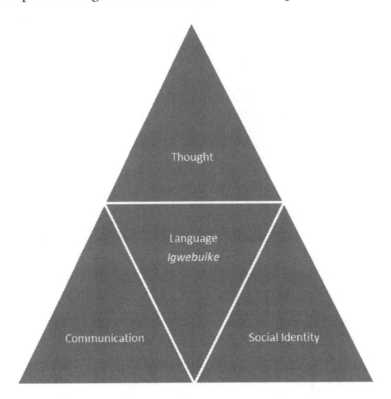

a. ***Igwebuike* as an Instrument of Igbo-African Thought:** *Igwebuike* is an instrument of thought which natures and showcases the Igbo-African human ideas that may be instances and stances of science in a fact of 'worldhood', and this is possible because of the central place of *Igwebuike* in the Igbo-African worldview. Within this context, *Igwebuike* becomes an expression of the Igbo-African world because it captures and expresses Igbo forms, symbolism, signs, media, meaning, anthropologies, universal cosmic truths, functions, semantic powers, physics, phenomena, faculties, and Igbo environ-mentalities, perception, identity, phenomenalism, metaphysics, logic, history of analytic character, speculative mindset and positive provisions for definitions of facts. It is a media for conveying basic facts about our relationship with one another, the environment and super-sensible world.

b. ***Igwebuike* as an Instrument of Igbo-African Social Communication:** Communication speaks of the state of affairs within which human persons share commonly and mutually intelligible and knowledgeable competences. *Igwebuike,* with all it embodies, is an instrument of social communication. This is possible because it is the moving spirit, and therefore captures the entirety, of the African means of communication which involves stories, proverbs, dancing, music, costumes, arts, religious ceremonies, rites and rituals, music, etc., which might be used for the transmission of cultural and religious heritages, skills and knowledge.

c. ***Igwebuike* as an Instrument of Igbo-African Social Identity:** *Igwebuike* captures the social identity of the Igbo-African. As a concept, it gives the Igbo-African the identity of being in an integral framework of relationality. *Igwebuike* is, therefore, not just a word but symbolizes the identity of the Igbo-African. It is based on the worldview of the people which is a background to Igbo behaviour and metaphysics. It explains the Igbo attitude, blueprints, traits, skills, etc., that have registered on their identity, institution, organization, management, etc.

The analysis of *Igwebuike* from the stand point of the functions of language, and the discovery of the fulfilment of these functions by *Igwebuike,* becomes a basis for the insistence on the importance of language in African philosophy and the emphasis on *Igwebuike* as the gateway to Igbo-African philosophy.

CONCLUSION

This study on *Igwebuike* as the ontological toolbox of Igbo-African philosophy, which is a reflection within the parameters of African philosophy of language, has been undertaken on the basis that the Igbo language and Igbo world are merged into the same reality. Any attempt to separate the two points to the impending danger of misrepresentation and misinterpretation. *Igwebuike* is understood within this context as the gateway to Igbo-African philosophy. Thus, an investigation of the structure of *Igwebuike,* which is an Igbo language, is at the same time an investigation of the formal structures and aspects of the Igbo world. It is within this context that Wittgenstein stated that "the limit of my language is the limit of my world".

REFERENCES

Adeshina, A. (2006). The language question in African philosophy. In Olusegun, O. (Ed.). *Core Issues in African philosophy* (pp. 41-58). Ibadan: Hope.

Ayer, A. J. (1942). *Language, truth and logic.* New York: Dover Publications.

Bell, R. (1978). Sociolinguistics: Goals, approaches and problems. London: B. T. Batsford Ltd

Cassirer, E. (1976). *An essay on man: An introduction to a philosophy of human culture.* New haven: Yale university Press.

Edeh, E. (1985). *Towards ab Igbo metaphysics.* Chicago: Loyola University Press.

Gyekye, K. (1987). *An essay on African philosophical thought: The Akan conceptual scheme.* Cambridge: Cambridge University Press.

Honderich, T. (1976). *The Oxford companion to philosophy.* England: Penguin Books.

Iroegbu, P. (1995). *Metaphysics: The kpim of philosophy.* Owerri: International Universities Press.

Kanu, I. A. (2010). Towards an African cultural renaissance. *Professor Andah Journal of Cultural Studies. 3.* 59-70.

Kanu, I. A. (2012). The colonial legacy: The hidden history of Africa's present crisis. *An International Journal of Arts and Humanities 1. 1.* 123-131.

Kanu, I. A. (2014). *Igwebuikology* as an Igbo-African philosophy for Catholic-Pentecostal relations. *Jos Studies. 22. pp.*87-98.

Kanu, I. A. (2015). *African philosophy: An ontologico-existential hermeneutic approach to classical and contemporary issues.* Nigeria: Augustinian Publications.

Kanu, I. A. (2016). *Igwebuike* as an Igbo-African Hermeneutics of Globalisation. *IGWEBUIKE: An African Journal of Arts and Humanities*, Vol. 2 No.1. pp. 61-66.

Kanu, I. A. (2017). *Igwebuike* and Question of Superiority in the Scientific Community of Knowledge. *Igwebuike: An African Journal of Arts and Humanities.* Vol.3 No1. pp. 131-138.

Kanu, I. A. (2018). *Igwebuike* as an African Integrative and Progressive Anthropology. *NAJOP: Nasara Journal of Philosophy.* Vol. 2. No. 1. pp. 151-161.

Kanu, I. A. (2019). *Igwebuike* Research Methodology: A New Trend for Scientific and Wholistic Investigation. *IGWEBUIKE: An African Journal of Arts and Humanities. 5. 4.* pp. *95-105.*

Kanu, I. A. (2012). The Role of Language in the Socio-Political Philosophy of John Locke. *International Journal of Humanities and Social Science.* Vol. 2. No. 14 pp.126-131.

Kanu, I. A. (2014). African Philosophy and the Problem of Language. *Asian Academic Research Journal of Social Science and Humanities.* Vol. 1. No. 21. pp. 248-258.

Kanu, I. A. (2018). *Igwebuike* as an African integrative and progressive anthropology. *NAJOP: Nasara Journal of Philosophy.* Vol. 2. No. 1. pp. 151-161.

Kanu, I. A. (2018). New Africanism: *Igwebuike* as a philosophical Attribute of Africa in portraying the Image of Life. In Mahmoud Misaeli, Sanni Yaya and Rico Sneller (Eds.). *African Perspectives on Global on Global Development* (pp. 92-103). United Kingdom: Cambridge Scholars Publishing.

Kanu, I. A. (2019). Collaboration within the ecology of mission: An African cultural perspective. *The Catholic Voyage: African Journal of Consecrated Life.* Vol. 15. pp. 125-149.

Kanu, I. A. (2019). *Igwebuike* research methodology: A new trend for scientific and wholistic investigation. *IGWEBUIKE: An African Journal of Arts and Humanities* (IAAJAH). *5. 4. pp. 95-105.*

Kanu, I. A. (2019). *Igwebuikeconomics*: The Igbo apprenticeship for wealth creation. *IGWEBUIKE: An African Journal of Arts and Humanities* (IAAJAH). *5. 4. pp. 56-70.*

Kanu, I. A. (2019). *Igwebuikecracy*: The Igbo-African participatory cocio-political system of governance. *TOLLE LEGE: An Augustinian Journal of the Philosophy and Theology. 1. 1.* pp. 34-45.

Kanu, I. A. (2019). On the origin and principles of *Igwebuike* philosophy. *International Journal of Religion and Human Relations.* Vol. 11. No. 1. pp. 159-176.

Kanu, I. A. (2019b). An *Igwebuike* approach to the study of African traditional naming ceremony and baptism. *International Journal of Religion and Human Relations.* Vol. 11. No. 1. pp. 25-50.

Keller, A. (1979). *Sprachphiloosphie.* Muenchen: Verlg Karl Alber.

Ki-Zerbo, J. (1981). *General history of Africa, Methodology and African prehistory.* Berkley: University of California.

Mbiti, J. (1970). *African religions and philosophy.* Nairobi: East African Educational.

Njoku, F. O. C. (2002). *Essays in African philosophy, thought and theology.* Owerri: Claretian Institute of Philosophy.

Njoku, F. O. C. (2010). A search for unifying concepts- destiny and change, freedom and determinism in African Philosophy. In Benjamin Ike Ekwelu (Ed.). *Philosophical reflections on African issues.* Enugu: Delta.

Okonkwo, J. I. (1994). Nationalism and nationism: The sociolinguistic cross-road of the Nigerian National Language Policy. *AAP. 40.* 115-130.

Okonkwo, J. I. (2002). Worldview and life form crisis of the Nigerian Philosophy of culture: An appraisal. *Journal of Nigerian Languages and Culture*. 4. 171-182.

Okosisi, J. I. (2012). *Okwu danahu onu*: The basic principle of Igbo philosophy of language. Inaugural Lecture Series. No. 6. Imo State University, Owerri, Nigeria.

Pierper, F. (1992). *Abuse of language, abuse of power*. San Francisco: Ignatius Press.

Rorty, R. (1992). *The linguistic turn: Essays in philosophical method*. Chicago: Chicago University Press.

Sefler, M. (1974). *Language and the world: A methodological synthesis within the writing of Martin Heidegger and Ludwig Wittgenstein*. New York.

Tempels, P. (1959). *Bantu philosophy*. Paris: Presence Africaine.

Wittgenstein, L. (1961). *Tractatus logico-philosophicus*. London: Reute ledge and Kegan.

THE AFRICAN IDENTITY OF BIBLICAL MOSES: AN IGWEBUIKE DISCOURSE

Hilary Ugwu, MSW
University of Oklahoma
School of Social Work
Norman, USA,
hiugwu@yahoo.com

EXECUTIVE SUMMARY

Why are some Bible-believers and Judeo-Christian and Islamic scholars so reluctant about investigating extra-biblical facts that contradict existing biblical and theological constructs? The answer is simple! It has to do with the problem of theological dogmatism. Webster Dictionary defines dogma as "a system of doctrine proclaimed true by a religious sect," or "principle, belief or idea especially one considered to be absolute truth." Webster equally defines dogmatism as "the expression of an opinion or belief as if it were a fact..." or "a viewpoint or system of ideas based on insufficiently examined premises." Dogmatism of any kind inhibits sound scholarly research. There are dogmatist physicists who refuse to abandon some of the outdated theories of Einsteinian-type classical physics, even in the face of the triumphant new discoveries in Quantum Physics. Such physicists prefer traditionalism over facts. Thus, they have difficulties conceptualizing that solidity and individuation of matter within the realm of perceptible physical world is an illusion. This is because the atomic and the subatomic quantum realm operates with the law of pure potentiality or possibility. It is consciousness that brings density into materialization. This fact has been proven by the new research in "double-slit experiment." In the same way, the dogmatic pharmacological scientist is closed-minded and will not investigate the universal harmonic frequency in order to consider that homeostatic natural foods and herbs are way superior to their big-money-driven allopathic synthetic pills. These pills are not in tune with the human biorhythm and bio-vibratory frequency. The problem with dogmatism of any kind is that they make laws, ordinances, sanctions, rules, and condemn oppositions. Dogmatists often hold the key to certifications, and if you don't agree with them, your certification is frozen. Their arrogance and attitude is much like: 'If you are not with us, you are a heretic and dangerous.' I am certainly one of those who consider theological dogmatism as inhumane, ungodly and absurd. Dogmatism of any kind is counter-research as well as contra-scientific. Dogmatists are nothing but ideological bullies as well as intellectual harassers. This is how dogmatism works: First it displays its version of 'the truth,' like a pre-manufactured industrial consumer goods. It calls this version absolute. Then, it forces the masses into uncritical consumption of that brand or version. Any real or perceived opposition is aggressively and apologetically rejected. Ideological dogmatism is a servant-slave to the status-quo. With theological dogmatism, there is no room for a dialectical scrutiny of the structural components of the belief system in question. Theological dogmatists are closed-minded religious luddites, with rigid authoritarian worldview. They are ecclesio-theological buffers against critical intellectual and historical searchlights. A dogmatist is insecure and will attack every attempt to throw new light on some old information systems. Dogmatism is like a self-preserving narcissistic poltergeist afraid to come out to the sunlight. Religious dogmatists, especially, utilize guilt, shame, condemnation, excommunication, 'sending-to-hell,' character assassination, intimidation, thuggery as well as doctrinal Nazism to create a colonial monopoly of the thought processes of the masses. In theological dogmatism, a point of view is manufactured and imposed as irreducibly infallible wherewith one must swallow or be vilified as a rebel. A typical fanatical dogmatist mindset runs thus: "The Bible is the absolute word of God, end of argument, take it or leave it" or "the church says it and you must follow with no questions." This explains why so many people are not just incapable of looking beyond what is fed to them as 'truth,' but are actually afraid to do so. There are those who can decipher the fallacy of biblical chronology but choose to persist in the error of their fallacy. This might be due to fidelity to statutory ecclesiasticism, cooperate orthodoxy, ritualism, institutional didacticism and mass kerygmatic Pentecostal showmanship. To speak the truth often means compromising a position. This work is meant to push the envelope and invoke a critical examination of the established narrative, particularly relative to the mysterious identity and/ or events surrounding the person of Moses.

Keywords: African, Biblical, Old Testament, Moses, Igwebuike, Philosophy, Kanu Ikechukwu Anthony

INTRODUCTION

Religious and non-religious folks alike study the Bible for moral codes of conduct, spiritual guidance, part-time explorative curiosity, scholarly investigation, etc. Whichever the case may be, the Bible continues to be both a source of simplistic pious inspiration as well as a source of fierce controversial pedagogical debate. My intension is to awaken some critical insights and stretch the mind to a new and higher dimension of reasoning and conceptualization. I do not believe for a moment that the Bible is a book of absolute historical facts. The Bible is more of a compilation of astro-theology, zodiac myths, moral codes, tribal religious rituals, etc. Historical facts in the Bible are very minute and highly corrupted when one considers the book in its entirety. Both the Old and the New Testaments are full of manufactured falsehoods, psydo-epigraphical deceptions, intentionally omitted facts, inaccurate dates and so on.

In the New Testament, for example, ecclesio-patristic regimes created so much intentional forgeries. The brutal repression of the so- called heretics was a form of clampdown of all other facts which the Church feared. Origen Adamantius, also known as Origen of Alexandria or simply Origen, is one of the brightest scholars in the history of Christian theology. But, he fell out of favour with the Church and he was vilified and refused to be according the title of 'sainthood,' despite his undisputed acetic discipline and moral beacon. He was defamed by the claims that he got himself castrated in his quest for purity of the body. This story is probably an ecclesiastical fabrication. What was Origen's error? Part of his vilification was very obvious. He spoke the truth. I am currently looking into the reason why so many Christian scholars and theologians coming out of Africa (Alaxandra in Egypt) as well as Cartage were termed heretics. It has to do with the fact of them being in possession of the original stories from where the New Testament derived. The imperial, expansionist, Euro-Roman church condemned many bright out-of-Africa scholars as heretics. The ecclesiastical regime wanted a monopoly of the religious narratives which was achieved not by the free will and superior intellectual debate but by force and brutality. So many large libraries were destroyed by ecclesiastical regimes, especially those of North Africa church scholars. Many scholars believe that the Church would never have defeated gnostic movements, if it was not through military force, because they possessed superior knowledge. Reading the account of the gnostic movement from the point of view of the Church, one encounters so much propaganda and falsehood. Some of the propaganda are funny and absurd.

Origen linked Jesus and the story of his death and resurrection with the pre-existing religious sect like that of the Dionysian cult. The cult of Dionysus pre-existed in Greece thousands of years before Christianity. Dionysus' birth had an Annunciation from a divine being, his mother was called the virgin, he was born through Immaculate Conception, he taught in the temple at the age of twelve, he had twelve disciples, he was crucified on a tree, and he resurrected and is celebrated in paschal mystery with bread and wine. Dionysus enjoins his followers to drink his blood and eat his flesh to have life— exactly the same doctrinal translations present in the New Testament. We must bear in mind that even the Greek Dionysus was a copycat of the African/Egyptian cult of Horus/Heru. According to the historian, Diodorus, the Africans/ Egyptians mocked the Greeks as infantile because when they copied their astro-theology, they made it real history. The Egyptian god, Set, Shetan (Satan), for example became the Greek god, Typhon. If the ancient Egyptian priests and philosophers were to come back in our own time, they will mock as absurd so many things that the Christians believe today. This is because they would know that the beliefs are mirrors of their ancient astro-theological mythos. The twelve houses of Israel were nothing other than the twelve houses of zodiac astrological constellations. It is difficult to prove the actual existence of the twelve tribes of Israel. Hebrew history scholars are trying to convince us that following the military campaign of the Assyrian kings, Tiglath-pileser III (745–727 B.C.E.), Shalmaneser V (727–722 B.C.E.) and Sargon II (722–705 B.C.E.), the Israelis were permanently deported and from this deportation came the story of the lost tribes. Where is the archeological evidence?

In the New Testament, we see so many fish symbolisms: Mathew 4:18-19; Mathew14:17-21; Mathew 7:9-10; Matthew12:40; Luke 24:42; John 21-13, and there are many more. The New Testament's allusion to fish connotes zodiac astrology. We were told that Jesus fed the people with "two fishes." Anyone who investigates astrological houses will know that PIECES is the 12th sign. It is symbolized by two fish. Two thousand years ago, the sun was in the constellation of pieces. It was called the Age of Pieces or the age of Fish which became esoterically coded in the New Testament. We were told that before the feast of Passover (this is not actual history), the Israelites were asked to slaughter lambs. If Egyptians actually lost every first male child in the last plague, how come they did not record it? How come there were no further records of it by world renounced historians. There is a fragmented piece of archeological document known discovered in Egypt called *The Papyrus Ipuwer or The Admonitions of Ipuwer*. Many biblical scholars are stating that this is an evidence that the Egyptians recorded the famous "Hebrew Plague." But in that papyrus, Ipuwer who might have been a priest, an official scribe or just a private scribe wrote expressing certain tragedy that took place in the land akin to war tragedy or years of national difficulties. It is irresponsible to conclude that this is a sign that the Hebrew sadistic blood thirsty tribal deity, Yahweh, was the cause.

The slaughtering of lambs as Hebrew Passover even was an astrological symbolism as well. Lamb is the symbol of the zodiac sign of Aries. It was a ritual performed in commemoration of the sun leaving the constellation of Aries—that is, passing over to a new zodiac house—that of pieces. It is to mark the ending of an old age and the beginning of a new zodiac era. We also see that Jesus was described feeding the people with fish. This description is purely esoteric because at that time, the sun was in pieces constellation. It takes the sun about 25,000 years to complete its procession through the twelve zodiac houses. When the sun moves into a new zodiac constellation house, it affects earth'smagnetosphere. There have been geomagnetic changes recorded in history due to solar procession through the different consolations. New solar frequencies will trigger the human genetic mutations and DNA updates and people will evolve. There is no doubt that the sun is the major source of genetic evolution of man. If there is a solar flare or solar storm, plasma, solar waves and photons are discharged throughout the space. The earth's ozonosphere will filter radioactive solar materials but will also permit certain passages throughout planet through different electromagnetic frequencies. It is because we are dumb that we condemn the ancient when they venerate the sun. The sun is an active intelligence and it is what activates the code of DNA without this biosphere. The age of pieces is gone. This age was characterized by blind belief systems and rigid religious rituals. With the sun moving into the current Aquarius constellation, we will notice changes in the structure of the human society. Blind religious belief will decline drastically. People will want to know and not just believe. Science, inner reflection, self-awareness, liberation from religious dogmas is going to override simplistic will, override religious mass mind-controls. Institutionalism and traditionalism will decline.

In the gospel of St. Luke 22:10, the pseudo-epigraphical writer(s) made us believe that Jesus said the following: *(He said to them) "Behold, when you have entered the city, a man carrying a jar of water will meet you. Follow him into the house that he enters."* This statement is purely a coded esoteric symbolism, alluding to the sun's procession through the zodiac houses. Remember, from the Age (house) of Aries, the sun moved to the Age (house) of Pieces. Then the next solar age is the Age of Aquarius. So Jesus was referring to the "Aquarius mam." The word Aquarius means "water carrier." If one researches the symbol of Aquarius, it is depicted in all ancient astrological pictographic murals as a man carrying a water pitcher and pouring the water content down. The symbol of the pouring is the "the new spirit' or DNA update or activation. Jesus told them to follow this man into his "House." Each zodiac constellation is called by all ancient scripts as "a house." Jesus was esoterically telling them that the great Age of Pieces in which they were in (symbolized by two fish) will soon end after in about 2000 years. He then pointed them to follow the next age, the Age of Aquarius symbolized in ancient paintings as a man carrying a water jar.

In the grand scheme of things, we are currently in the Age of Aquarius. Any astronomical scientist will tell you that the sun is now entering the constellation of Aquarius and will remain there for the next 2000 years plus before it moves to the next which is the constellation of Sagittarius. This is why the Church does not want people to study astrology and they vilify it as occultic or evil to frighten the people. This is because a sound knowledge of astrology will expose so many information hidden from the ordinary people. The term "Holy Bible" tells it all. It is Greek words for "Helios Byblos" which literarily means "Sun Book" or the book of the Sun. Consequently, the book if full of zodiac symbolism, sun worships and the whole compendium of ancient esoteric astrological events.

Many Bible scholars have never known that there were so many other messianic figures that predate the Christian doctrinal theology. Jesus' story of annunciation, virgin birth, teaching in the temple at the age of twelve, performing miracle, betrayal, crucifixion on a cross and resurrection had the exact repeated pattern of these other historical personages as chronicled in these other sacred texts. Who copied from whom? And why are they hiding it from the people and scaring people from finding out? Christianity is very new and recent compared to others. There is a lot of historicizing of astro-mythology in the New Testament, including the story of Jesus.

My interest in this work is to awaken a critical discussion on a topic which many apologetic Bible scholars shy away from. Many Bible teachers assume the story of the Bible are facts and thus, need no investigation. And, when some actually investigate, they keep to the status quo by subliminally evading the consequences of their research entirely. My sole purpose here is to investigate the African identify of the character identified in the Bible as Moses. I could not have done this without preparing readers to have at the back of their minds, that a lot of things written in the Bible were not facts. There is higher probability that Moses, if indeed he existed, was of African bloodline. Thus, before accusing me of having an Afro-centric view of the Bible, take time to investigate thoroughly any evidence that I will be raising herein. Knowledge of the great ancient African Nile River civilization as one of the major civilizations that shaped humanity's theological conceptions is important. Majority of people who read the Bible do not have access to extra-biblical material facts or sources to compare with the stories they are reading and believing. Thus, a lot of people, including prominent Bible teachers, are prone to digesting the Bible with acute historiographical, historiological and metaphysical blunders. When religious gaffe translates into metaphysical dogmas, the result could be profound mass delusion. Orthodox theological establishment could serve as a fertile ground for mass folie-a-deux as well as anti-fact religious movement. There is need for an authentic epistemo-cognitive praxeology in the examination of the historical claims of all religious documents.

HELLENISM AND THE NAME EGYPT

When reading the Bible, one comes across names like Egypt and Egyptians. Another name which is used in the Old Testament to refer to Egypt is Mizraim (Genesis 10:13). However, the fact remains that the people and the place being referenced to as Egypt or the Egyptians were Africans. These Africans did not identify themselves with such names as Egypt of Egyptians. So, what did the so- called Egyptians call themselves? Before delving into this question, let's look at what led to foreigners' re-naming of Africa land as Egypt. There were historical factors that led to the decline and eventual collapse of the great Nile River civilization of Egypt (Africa). The name 'Egypt' came as a result of Greek invasion. Before the Greeks invaded, there were the Assyrians, the Persians, the Hyksos, etc. Each of these invasions vulturized the black land and its civilization. Alexander the Great, son of Philip of Macedon, arrive in Africa with his army in 332 B.C. By this period, the land had already been weakened militarily, culturally and economically. The Egyptian global influence had waned. The great African pharaohhood had been compromised. This led to the Hellenic foreigners forcing themselves into the pharaohic thrown of the Africans beginning in 334 B.C. The first Hellenic coronation introduced a new era called the Ptolemy Dynasty. Greek invaders even started changing the name of the African god and imposing their own version. For instance, they created the cult of Oserapis. The image of Oserapis would later become the iconic picture of Jesus Christ painted and kept in homes all over the world—continued imperialism of the mind of the Indo-European and Anglo-American psychological warfare. The Ptolomy kings confined the word 'Oserapis' from eclectically combining two names of Egyptian deities, Osiris and Apis (also known as Hapi).

With the Greek take over came the re-naming of Africans, their lands and their culture. The African city of Men-Nefer was misnamed by the Greek as Memphis. This city was where the temple of the god, Ptah, resided. Ptah was the same creator-god that would later emerge in the Hebrew creation myth as the creator-deity of the Garden of Eden myth. This is a replica of Memphite theological construct. The temple of Ptah, situated in Memphis, was called by the African people of the time "HikuPtah," which could translate as 'House of the Soul of Ptah.' Eventually, the Greeks started calling the entire city of Memphis, AigyPtos, which is a mispronounced, Hellenized and misunderstood word for HikuPtah. It is from AigyPtos that we have the name Egypt. From calling the city of Memphis AigyPtos, they proceeded further to apply the name to the entire land. Similarly, the Greek used to call Africans *Aiθίoψ*, Aithiop (Ethiop) which meant "Burnt Face" or black face, a name that now becomes identified specifically with Ethiopia. Due to the re-naming of place and erasing of ancient identities, it is difficult to contextualize history in its purity.

We read books and watch movies. We see how Anglo-America's powerful cinematographic mind-controller—the Hollywood - has produced multiple movies and books in which Egyptians and their people are depicted with Caucasian or Arabic features. I still have to reiterate this fact to many of my non-African friends that Egypt is in Africa. Many Africans who read the Bible are unaware of the level of mind-control they are dealing with. One will be surprised to find out that majority of Bible readers do not know that Mount Sinai, which was significant in the story of Moses and the Exodus, is in Africa as well. The name 'Sinai' has an etymological derivative from the Sumerian word *Sin*. Sin is a moon deity (Natan, 2006). This deity was very popular throughout the Mesopotamian region in ancient times. Sin is the father of the sun god, Shamash. Innana is the mother of Shamash. Inanna took different names in different cultures, such as Anat, Ishtar, Venus, Asherah, and Astarte, Isis and, in the modern time, the Virgin Mary. All named goddesses are referred to as "the queen of heaven." The cult of goddesses was a universal occurrence. These goddesses have Luna crescent as symbols. Many pictures Virgin Mary have her standing with her feet resting on a crescent moon; the same ancient coded esoteric imagery of the ancient mother goddess. Often they are seen carrying a baby or nursing a baby who is the "sun god" or "son of God." This is why Virgin Mary is often drawn standing on a crescent moon. So Mount Sinai is obviously associated with the concept of the mountain of the moon god. Sin, with his female companion Innana, engendered as son, the sun god Shamash.

WHAT DID THE EGYPTIANS CALL THEMSELVES?

But what did the Africans who established one of the greatest civilizations around the Nile River call themselves? They identified themselves with the word KMT or KEMET, which means 'black land,' indicating the colour of the people who lived there. Whether you call it Kemet, Chem or Chemi, they are the same and mean black. The word CHEMISTRY is etymologically derived from the ancient African name, Chem or Kemet. The Arabic word *Kimiya*, probably with a Greek derivation, means black. It is from this Arabic word that the word Alchemy comes. Alchemy initially was an advanced African 'magical' formula of transforming base matter into pure gold. The term 'black magic' is used today in a derogatory way. But the term originally stood for the ancient African (Chem) knowledge of advanced science. It literarily means 'African Science.". The indo-Asiatic/Indo-Aryans called it 'black magic' because it was the science of the ancient (Black, KMT, CHEM) Africans. Black magic, in its original meaning, did not mean evil, as we have been brainwashed to believe. It used to refer to certain knowledge of quantum physics and how to manipulate etheric energy forms to create solutions within the visible spectrum of light. For instance, black magic is not different from the science of manipulating radio waves in the electromagnetic spectrum in order to receive telephone, television and radio signals. Black magic/black science is the ancient African knowledge and application of the law of physics and the quantum realm. It was the ignorance of the Indo-Asiatic and Indo- Euro-Aryanists that termed it "black magic." They called it magic because they did not understand it. Today, many Africans use the term "black magic," not understanding that it is a self-mockery. It is equivalent to calling the use of radio wave frequency to make telephone calls "white magic." Moses as an African was very versed in the Egyptian alchemical black magic—advanced knowledge of the invisible realms and how they interact with the visible light spectrum. These are advanced knowledge.

WHERE DID THE EGYPTIANS ORIGINATE FROM?

The current people in North Africa who are called Egyptians are not the descendants of the original historical Egyptians. These were recent invaders who spread to Africa from Arabia. The original inhabitants of the land of the Pharaohs were blacks. For some racist Europeans who claim that Egyptian civilization is not an African civilization, the great scholar, Dr. Ben-Jochannan (1989), disagrees. According to him, the Egyptians themselves attested to the fact of whom they are and where they came from. He cited an excavated papyrus containing funerary rites belonging to an ancient Egyptian (African) called Hunefer. In this priced archeological document, the Egyptians made it clear that "we came from the beginning of the Nile where God Hapi dwells, at the foothill of the mountain of the moon." This referenced mountain of the moon is not the same as Mount Sinai described above. Rather this is in reference to a mountain range in East Africa, Kenya and Uganda and the democratic Republic of Congo. Mount Kilimanjaro is in Kenya. Mount Ruwenzori is between Uganda and the Democratic Republic of Congo. My curiosity was alerted when the Egyptians identify the god, Hapi, with the Mountain of the Moon in Africa. Hapi is one of the oldest gods on the planet. So, the Egyptians were also attesting to their pre-history as being authentically African. Hapi/Api is the god of the annual flooding. We know for certain that the Nile River in Egypt has its origin in East Africa. The Ugandan word for the Ruwenzori is "Rain Maker." I am just curiously making a connection between the Ugandan word describing the mountain of the moon "Ruwenzori" with "rain' and the Egyptians identity the God who dwell in the same Region with Annual flooding (rain). To any racist who is in denial, Hunefer's papyrus is a strong piece of historical evidence of the African origin of Egyptian civilization. The Egyptologist, Robert Bauval and his colleague Thomas Brophy, published their work under the title of: *Black Genesis: The Prehistoric Origins of Ancient Egypt* in which they made it clear that Egyptian Civilization, with their highly advanced technological prowess, was an authentic black African civilization.

THE NAME MOSES: ETYMOLOGICAL EXPOSITION

The Egyptian word *'ms'* or "msi" (Mose) passed from its Greek linguistic Hellenization to its present construct, Moses. The Hebrew word מֹשֶׁה, transliterates as *Mosheh* (Moses). Hebrew language has the word, מָשָׁה which is different from מֹשֶׁה for those who have at least some elementary understanding of Hebrew. If you have basic knowledge of Hebrew, you will notice diacritical differences in both words. The word, מָשָׁה transliterates as Mashah. Mashah literarily implies "to draw." Therefore, a correlation between Mashah and Mosheh was somehow falsely established (thanks to the nameless Egyptian princess). This correlation was crafted to justify Moses' non-African or rather assumed Hebraic bloodline. Greenberg (2008) is among the researchers who reject this engineered cut-and-join explanation.

Sigmund Freud (1939) of psychoanalytic theory, himself a Jew, rejected the hasty correlation of Mashah and Mosheh as well. Freud exposed a biblical fallacy hiding in plain sight. He stated that it is very "nonsensical" to believe that an Egyptian princess had good knowledge of Hebrew linguistic and cultural etymologies as shown in her naming of baby Moses. Biblical narrator states thus: *"She (Pharaoh's daughter) named him Moses, saying I drew him out of the water"* Exodus 2:8). This is a huge red flag. If the story is true, the Egyptian princess must have been a Hebrew scholar or linguist. She must have lived in Hebraic culture to know their language and naming rituals. This is very unlikely. If the Hebrews were salves in Egypt (it is not very certain), one must also believe that a princess will not copy the inferior culture of the slaves. It is the other way round; the slaves will learn the superior culture of their enslavers and masters.

This is much like assuming that President Trump's daughter, Ivanka, found an abandoned Yoruba (Nigerian tribe) baby from a poor immigrant labourer floating in the Mississippi River in the southern part of USA and gave him an authentic Yoruba name, *Eniolorunopa* and then proceeded further to provide a solid cultural etymology to the name as meaning "the one whose life God will spare." The first mistake is clean. It is very unlikely that Ivanka would understand a single word in Yoruba language. As a highly placed princess of his father, living in super affluence, interacting with the world's most powerful people, it is highly unlikely that she spends time socializing with poor common workers, let alone learning their language and understanding specific linguistic and cultural meanings. Then, compare this to the claim attributed to the Egyptian princess and do the math. The drama of naming of Moses by Pharaoh's daughter was a façade, a historical fabrication, and a lie.

The process of converting Moses from his African root into a Hebrew was gradual. As described above, we saw that the Greeks invaded and controlled the entire Levant region, foisting their colonial culture over the people. Hellenistic elites translated the original Hebrew-stolen African name Mose (Mosheh) to Mosis; then from Greek Mosis to our popularly adopted anglicized (English) translation, Moses. In ancient Egypt, the word "ms" means "is born." The Hebraic corruption of this name is obvious for any scholars who can look deep enough. Hebraic plagiarized version is a mockery to Egyptian child-naming culture.

Egyptians would not just name a child "ms" or Moses. For instance, in Igbo (Nigerian tribe) language, *Chukwubuike* (God is strength) could be corrupted as *"Buike,"* which translates as "is strength." Igbos do not just name a child "Buike." A non-Igbo who decides to plagiarize the name "Buike" and impose such a name on his/her child has committed an epistemological error for those who understand Igbo cultural and linguistic root.

The above analogy provides a picture of the Hebrew corruption of the Egyptian word "ms" (Mose). There is usually a prefix to the name Mose. Egyptians give their children names, such as: Amenmose (Amen-Moses), which means the god Amen is born; Tutmose (Tut/Thot-Moses), the god Tut or Thot is born; Ramses (Ra/Re Moses), the god Ra (sun god) is born; Ptahmose (Ptah-Moses), the god Ptah is born; Ahmose (Ah/Aa/Iah-Moses), the moon (god) is born, etc. In his book, *History of Egypt*, Breasted (1905), the famous Egyptologist, re-echoed similar Hebraic plagiarism of Egyptian baby-naming style. He translated the word "Mose" to mean "a child" is born. Breasted indicated that Amen-Mose could also stand for "Amen-a-Child" (is born). That is, the god, Amen (as a child) has been born. To understand this psychology of child naming, I would like to invoke the New Testament in the gospel of St. Mathew (1:23). The Hebrew לְאָנֻּמָעֵ has the following equivalent English alphabetical transcription: עֵ -Yi/, מ -Ma/ נֻ -nu/ אֵל-El) pronounced Y'Manu-El or Emanuel, El standing for God as in (El'Ohim. The Hebrew word, as translated in the New Testament following Isaiah's prophesy, means "God is with us." So, when the Egyptians name a child Amen-Mose(s), for instance, they are alluding to divine incarnation through the birth of a child. It means God has manifested in the named newborn child. It is worth noting here that it is the same Egyptian god "Amen" deity that Christians and Muslims invoke at the end of prayer when they say "Amen," indicating that all religions came out of the mystery systems, particularly from Egypt. Church fathers have plagiarized an enormous number of documents from ancient Egyptian astro-theologies and deities. The Church destroyed, through years of persecution and death, any documents that would expose origin of their significant theological personalities and doctrinal constructions.

Coming back to our central topic, Sigmund Freud contends that the bearer of Egyptian name, in this case Moses, is Egyptian. Although, to be intellectually fair, bearing of any name from any culture does not necessarily make one part of that culture, as it might just imply cultural adoption, appropriation, or assimilation. However, there are other factors which provide concrete evidence of Moses being an Egyptian and not Hebrew. The problem is that some read the Bible as though it is some scientific historical facts, thus, locking their minds out of any authentic extra-biblical accounts of history. Another possible evidence of Moses being a true Egyptian and not Hebrew could be deciphered in Exodus (4:10):

Moses said to the Lord,
"Pardon your servant, Lord.
I have never been eloquent,
neither in the past nor since you have spoken to your servant.
I am slow of speech and tongue."

Interpretations of this verse often allude to him as being a stammerer, as in verbal impediment. But this could mean that Moses was explaining that he was not familiar with Hebraic language, culture, and the entire social psychology of the population he planned to lead out of Egypt. He could not speak the language. He did not understand them. They were not in the same social, educational, or statutory psychology. Moses belonged to the Egyptian elite. It could mean that as a highly placed scholar, highly learned it would be hard to speak to the understanding of mostly illiterate agrarian community and convey a revolutionary philosophy (in this case, monotheism, which I will come to shortly) to them. He needed an intermediary. Someone who was part of and used to the lower class since Aaron provided a way out. For instance, imagine a Harvard super-elite scholar, who works with the world's superpower president and government all his life, born into wealth, never been close to, nor understands rural village life or the psychology of poor people. Imagine such a person coming back to an impoverished people in rural village, trying to get them to abandon their way of life and to follow him and study quantum physics. That was how it was for Moses, if we follow the trend of the story.

THE APPROPRIATION OF MOSES' AFRICAN IDENTITY

In the book of Exodus Chapter 2, Pharaoh's daughter provided an account of Moses' identity. When subjected to exegetical contextualization, this account is false. Many Bible scholars never questioned why chroniclers of this biblical birth event omitted the specific name of the Egyptian princess who supposedly rescued abandoned baby Moses from the Nile River. This Pharaoic princess (who has no name) went on and testified regarding Moses's identity thus: "This is one of the Hebrew babies" (vs 6). The psychology of this statement has a hideous intent. Those who can read in between the line can detect the lies. Bible writers were carefully emphatic and specifically descriptive in linking the messianic type Moses with Hebraic root. Within this emphasis is a covert implant of fabricated falsehood. The reason was that they were trying to claim the child, so that through him they could manufacture a historical narrative that justifies an existence of a people belonging to a deity who supposedly orders the making of that historical narrative. Prehistoric Israel is non-existent. Extra-biblical, genetic, archaeological and paleontological evidences do not support the existence of prehistoric Israel. The great African scholar, Cheikh Anta Diop (see, *Civilization or Barbarism*), explains that there is a "paleontological vacuum" to the notion of Garden of Eden origin of humanity. He further states that the Levant region was once populated by Negroids.

There was a time when the entire planet was populated by negroid humanity, according to Diop. There was no mongoloid and no Caucasoid. If this, and the science of mitochondrial DNA, is true, it is an assault on human intelligence to credit the creation of man by a group of extra-terrestrial space-invading Elohim beings in the Garden of Eden somewhere in the Middle East. Diop confirms with biological science that all other shades of racial colours results from the synthesis of vitamin D through the sun's ultraviolent frequency. Paleontologists have been able to establish that the oldest anatomically modern human such as Australopithecus

Afarensis came from Africa, that is, assuming that Darwin's evolutionary theory is true. The British Paleontologist, Professor Louis Leaky (1903 – 1972), attested to an African origin of modern humanity. A critical mind would have been asking by now, if humanity existed in Africa millions of years before the Garden of Eden creation, why have theologians continued to promote Garden of Eden fairy tale. Because the Negroid has always existed on the planet before any other race, the goal of many history creators of the past has always been to fabricate a narrative that supports historical emergence of certain people on this planet. In so doing, where facts are lacking, religious myths fill in the gap.

Let us return to Pharaoh's daughter's false testimony that Moses was a Hebrew child. The false testimony was put into the mouth of this nameless Egyptian princess by the religious elites and scholars of the Bible. We see a similar birth story preexisting in Akkadia, Samaria. The story of Sargon of Akkad had exact birth circumstances with Moses and it is questionable if chroniclers of Moses birth did not plagiarize Sagon's messianic symbolism, including his mysterious birth and miraculous survival by being rescued from the rivers by a maiden. Narrator(s) of Moses' birth reported that Pharaoh's daughter named the child, Moses, saying, "I drew him out of the water." Thus, they succeeded in making Pharaoh's daughter to provide a pseudo etymology of the name Moses. The Decipherment of Egyptian hieroglyph has provided an understanding of the historical morphology of the name, Moses. In any case, it is non-Hebraic and has never been. It is rather African, Egyptian.

There is a deceptive reason as to why Bible writers used the general term, Pharaoh, when discussing Egyptian kings. Pharaoh is not a name of a person; it is rather a position, an office, much like the office of the president. If Bible chroniclers had mentioned specific names of individual pharaohs and periods of their reigns, it would have been easy to unearth the complicated inaccuracies of biblical reports when fact-checked against extra-biblical authentic historical records. The fact that they did not shows a hideous intention. For instance, any honest historian would be filled with rage, reading the enter four hundred years of African slavery in America, without specific mention of specific president during specific time. If between 1648 and 1863, a group of scholars were chronicling African slavery in America, and instead of identifying specific names of individuals occupying the office of the president, they resorted to using the world "the President," how would that history be. By using the name pharaoh, this is what scholars who wrote the Bible did—cover their tracks. Granted, they mentioned one or two specific names of pharaoh but that is about it. Therefore, it is difficult to double-check reports of biblical events such as the plagues, with actual factual written histories by the Egyptians themselves. It appears Bible writers knew their tricks ahead of time and that they were trying to hide the non-existence of the ancient history which they had invented.

WHY DID MOSES AND HIS FOLLOWERS LEAVE EGYPT?

It was not any deity commanding Moses to get out of Egypt. A civil war broke out due to religio-ideological factions. Moses was following a new revolutionary teaching—The monotheism. This teaching was invented and promoted by the Pharaoh Akhenaten. Pharaoh Akhenaton (Circa 1353 B.C to 1336 B.C) reigned during Egypt's 18th golden dynasty. He was the Pharaoh Amenophis IV, but took up the name Akhenaton after his spiritual awakening that led him to invent monotheism. Akhenaton stood out prominent in history. Many people, based on the Hebrew Bible, attribute universal monotheism to the Hebrew deity Javhe (Yahweh). This demonstrates lack of knowledge of the Egyptian history. Moses, having been under Pharaoh Akhenaton, was only an ambassador to Pharaoh's universal religious doctrine. Sigmund Freud established an inseparable dependence of the Jewish concept of monotheism on that of the monotheistic emergence out of Egyptian history.

When Akhenaten died, Moses was promoting his monotheistic teaching. It was a radical shift in the human concept of self and the divine—a shift towards the left-brain hemisphere, involving cognitive abstraction. Prior to Akhenaton, gods were represented all over Egypt and, in fact, all over the world in anthropomorphic imageries, concrete symbols, visual pictographs, statues, zoomorphism, etc. This approach uses the famine right-brain hemisphere of conceptualizing reality. Akhenaton destroyed statues of the gods causing so much controversy. He was the first human in history to invent monotheism, not Moses. Moses was just his advanced imitate servant. Monotheism, for the people of that era, was a mathematical abstract concept. It was unnatural to them, unheard of. Akhenaton's new religion condemns representing god in visual images, only abstract universal concept. We can see, historically, that once monotheism got hold of humanity, the art of writing became alphabetical and no longer pictographic. Akhenaton's destroying of the statues of the gods did not go well with the priests and local political establishments. He was hated and they wanted him dead and gone. One could rationally understand why Moses was hesitant in proceeding with his Akhenaton-driven monotheistic mission. After the death of Akhenaton, it was almost suicidal for him to continue to promote monotheism in a society that hated the Pharaoh and all he stood for. Egypt was polytheistic, and the powerful establishment wanted it remain so. For Moses to continue to promote and practices belief in a single universal god, he had to leave the land with all his Akhenaton followers.

Akhenaton died in his seventeenth year of reign as pharaoh. For his role in disturbing and offsetting the established political, religious and social status quo, he was disliked in Egypt. After his death, Egyptian elites sought to erase his memory from history. The city he founded, Amarna, was destroyed and abandoned. His monuments and status were destroyed. His image was defaced on public buildings. Thus, his reputation suffered within the Egyptian society. Sigmund Freud's research work placed Moses as living in the time of Akhenaton. The religion of monotheism which Moses gave to a group of people he led out of Egypt is Akhenaton's religion of Aten.

Akhenaton redirected the motion of history and thinking by initiating an act that was considered treasonable. What he did was unheard of in the annals of Egyptian history and the world of the ancient time. The Old Testament's Psalm 104 was originally Akhenaton's composition known as Hymn to Aten, the one God he promoted.

EXPULSION OF MOSES AND HIS REBELLIOUS GROUP FROM AFRICA (EGYPT)

There are scanty extra-biblical accounts of Exodus. The only evidence for Exodus is the Book of Exodus. Biblical historians and archeologists are still wondering how come there is no archeological evidence of the Israelites' wandering in the desert for forty years through the mountains and deserted places. There is no artifacts, no focalized human bones - nothing. The event did not take forty years as alluded. This paucity of materials makes it somewhat easy to gesticulate that Exodus' of the Hebrews out of Egypt was nothing but dramatic mythic creation. However, the few extra-biblical Egyptian records show series of events which indicate possible mass exodus. Freud placed Exodus out of Egypt around 13th century B.C. He explained the sequence of anarchic events chronicled by Egyptians themselves which might indicate civil unrest and mass movement. Egyptian pharaonic chroniclers did not appear to identify any pharaohs ruling Egypt at this period. This might be due to the fact that Egypt was under what we consider today as military decrees. It was the time of the strong Egyptian military tactician, Haremhab /Horemheb. Haremhab's military strength ended the civil unrests. The great scholar, Greenburg (2008), dated Exodus out of Egypt to be 1315 B.C., following the death of Haremhab. Greenburg concluded that Moses would have been born in 1395 B.C. and may have been about eighty years old during Exodus. Exodus were rebellious sects sent out due to a new religious concept.

The Jewish historian, Josef Ben Matityahu popularly known by his Roman adopted Names Flavius Josephus, commenting on the work of another historian called Manetho, stated that Moses might have been known by the name Osarseph. Monetho, according to Josephus, reported that Moses organized a mass rebellion of the oppressed leprosy-ridden population against the Egyptian authority. This account indicated that Osarseph caused trouble for some years until he was driven out of Egypt into Canaan—the same land the Israelites were said to have settled in after leaving Egypt. As indicated above, many Egyptologists conclude that the exodus occurred in the period following the death of the revolutionary pharaoh Akhenaton. Sigmund Fraud (1939) confirmed this in his brilliant work on monotheism thus: *"all conditions, internal and external, favoring the exodus coincide only in the period immediately after the death of the heretic kind."* A form of civil war erupted in Egypt. The status quo, now emboldened by Akhenaton's death, would no longer put up with monotheism. Moses was having a serious hard time promoting Akhenaton's monotheistic religion. As an ardent believer in Akhenaton's "one God" view of the world, he no longer had a place within the highly polytheistic social, cultural and political system. Thus, this was the beginning of exodus. Many scholars conclude that the people who were expelled from Egypt were native Egyptian rebels in which Moses was the leader—not Hebrews.

EGYPTOLOGY VS BIBLICAL HISTORY

With the advent of Egyptology, we are beginning to have extra-biblical information relative to some events chronicled in the Bible. As I have pointed out above, the Egyptian myth provides insightful back-story into the stories chronicled in both the Old and the New Testaments. One can state, with strong conviction, that the Egyptian astro-theological myth, in addition to so many other astro-mythologies, is what informed the entire Bible. To claim to understand the Bible, without a sound understanding of pre-existing astro-theologies, is tantamount to claiming to be a car engineer without being able to account for the specific inner components of a car engine. Astrological twelve houses of the zodiac were converted, by Hebraic religious scholars, as the symbolic number 12 which continued to reappear throughout the Bible. If biblical stories are factual historical events, then we can conclude that the major players, evidently, learned whatever they knew and wrote from Africa i.e. Egypt. Abraham was from the land of Ur in Chaldea (Genesis 11:28). Chaldea is the modern-day Iraq. My critical mind never ceases to ponder on the absurdity as to how come a full-blooded Babylonian man (Abraham) became the first Hebrew- speaking guy.

If chronology of the Bible is a fact, we were informed that Abraham migrated to the land of Mizraim, i.e. Africa, specifically Egypt. He married an African woman and followed the ancient Egyptian custom of circumcision. Later, biblical myth-makers would claim this ancient African custom of circumcision as Hebraic. But African (Egyptian) records discredit such ridiculous claims. We also see that the Hebrew scribes created a story in which Joseph ended up in Egypt (Genesis, 37:28). Thus, this was how they carefully got the character of Moses carefully interwoven into the history of Egypt and later made him a Hebrew messianic figure (Exodus 2).

The New Testament is not complete without Egyptian association. The pseudo-epigraphic writers of the New Testament created a typology between the old Joseph, who was sold into slavery, and the new Joseph, who became the surrogate father of Jesus. This typology creates an obvious covert psychological game called typology. The two Josephs had a persecutory type connection. The first Joseph was persecuted and sold by his brothers to Egypt. The second Joseph fled from Palestine, out of persecution, with baby Jesus. This is an advanced psychological operation. Anyone who read both stories would make subconscious association and, thus, deep subconscious validation of the latter story, without even being consciously aware of it. Again, they have to like a history to Egypt because Egypt was the light of the work. Jesus was also in Egypt. Thus, Egypt was cardinal in the historical mythologies found in both the New Testament and the Old Testament. What did all these people learn from Egypt when they were there? We know that a latter-day myth took the story of Heru, the Egyptian god, and made it theirs. Heru was the son of god; there was annunciation and Immaculate Conception. He was born on December 25, taught in the temple at the age of twelve, had twelve disciples, engaged in public ministry in his 30s, worked miracle, was betrayed, and killed and rose again. New Testament writers are quite aware of this preexisting story and it surely informed their thought process. Sumerology is another area of studies that has provided much information as to the origin of some of the prominent biblical stories. For instance, the creation of man in Genesis, the deluge and the covenant were all lifted by Hebraic scholars from the original Sumerian stories. The first massive contact of Hebrews with advanced Babylonian philosophies, myths and cosmologies came during the exile of 597 B.C. – 538 B.C.

It is naïve, blindness and uncritical adherence to religious traditions that made the materialist, Karl Marx, voice out his dialectical mockery of religious beliefs as being synonymous with "opium" addiction. Mental health professional will tell you that opiates are neuro-depressant. Opiate absorption causes adverse bio-synaptic impact on the neurotransmitters in such a way that individuals exhibit an altered state of consciousness. Opiate has chemical substances that literally put coherency and cognition to sleep. It creates a sense of false euphoria. Karl Marx, though blatantly anti-religion, presented his historical "opium of the masses" mockery with communist propaganda. His agenda being to replace transcendental beliefs and worship of God(s) with belief in and worship of the almighty state god, The Communist State. Nevertheless, one must not deny the fact that fundamentalism in religion could tranquilize the mind into a state of excitatory delirium to the extent that any facts outside the scriptural canon becomes instantaneously trashed into the mental delete bin. This sort of cognitive ejection of truth and extra-biblical facts, by religious fundamentalists and their fanatical factions, has led materialists, like Richard Dawkins, to write a book titled "The God Delusion."

HOW OOLD IS THE BIBLE?

The Bible is not as old as many would want to believe. Some consider Genesis creation history a factual history. This is such a monumental cognitive error. There is no evidence of the existence of Israel/the Hebrews in terms of nationhood prior to the 13th B.C. The concept "The Land of Israel" is a modern creation through a forceful but systematically induced evolution of religio-national identify by certain rabbinical and Euro-Christian planners. The historical process that went into the formation of the concept "The Land of Israel" is clearly elucidated by Shlomo Sand, in his eye-opening book, *The Invention of The Land of Israel: From Holy Land to Homeland.*

There is no extra-biblical evidence anywhere, no archaeology, no paleontology, nothing pointing to ancient (prehistoric) Israel. There is no existing record of any scriptural texts earlier than the 4th century B.C. We have account of written histories at this period from other nations and cultures, but Israel/Hebrew nation cannot be found. None of these advanced nations with elaborate written culture mentioned Hebrew nation in their official or unofficial chronologies. Some argue the pre-existence of oral history which later was translated into written document (Pentateuch). Let us assume that was the case. This would mean that oral history was transmitted for over a thousand years accurately before being written down in scripts. How possible is this? Even if oral history existed, they were legends, myths, fabricated hero deifications and religio-philosophical speculations. The pre-existing Pentateuchal scripts were not fully developed until late 6th century B.C. Bible writers collected divergent narratives which they used to fashion a comprehensive history. This mishmash of divergent scripts created a big chronological, epistemological, metaphysical and historical discrepancies. This led scholars to study and isolate the multiple sources of biblical composition. One needs to understand that there was a team of religious intellectuals who came together and compiled divergent accounts and myths into a centralized form, the Pentateuch.

Scholars noticed that Pentateuch utilized different names to refer to God, implicating different eras, styles, mindsets, textual contents, compositions, and timelines. During the 19th century A.D., scholars exposed these sources and identified them by letters, such as: the J source which referred to God as Yahweh; the E source which used the name Elohim, the third is the P source named due to its ritualistic priestly nature and, finally the D source (Deuteronomist) which is limited to the Book of Deuteronomy. The J scripts creators appeared to have composed theirs between 922 B.C. to 722 B.C.; E source between 848B.C. to 722 B.C.; P between 722B.C. to 600B.C. and D is sometime around 622 B.C.

Following King Cyrus of Persia's conquest of Babylon in 539 BCE, he (Cyrus) granted freedom to the Jews to return to the land from where they were taken and to rebuild the temple which was previously destroyed by King Nebuchadnezzar. Many years later, the Jews again fell under colonial Hellenism. The Greeks conquered the entire Levant region, including Egypt. At this time, they foisted certain brand of kingship over their subjects, called the Ptolemy Dynasty, as I have described somewhere above. It was the Ptolemy II Philadelphia (282—246 B.C.) who forced Hebrew sacred scripture to be translated into Greek. The Greek translated version of the Hebrew Bible is known as the Septuagint. Septuagint means "the Seventy'. This name came about because the named Greek king selected a group of seventy Hebrew religious scholars, believed to be members of the Essene (group of ascetic, esoteric religious practitioners and intellectuals), and forced them to translate their sacred scriptures from Hebrew to Greek. Reason was that as a colonizing force, Greek was a universal language to the colonizers, much as English is today. So, Greek rulers wanted to liberalize the knowledge contained in the Hebrew scripture and make it available for studies for everyone. Anyone who understands the religious history of the Hebrews and their reverence for their deity Yahweh/Elohim will understand that this request to translate their scripture in into Greek was an abomination. The original document from where the Greek translation was derived was not preserved. Scholars believe that the group of seventy Hebrews who provided the translation gave a deceptive/false interpretation account in Greek. They did not want to provide accurate knowledge of their sacred text and the God to Greek heathens with their ungodly Hellenistic imperialism.

In the year 382 A.D., St. Jerome was assigned by Pope Damasus to translate from the Greek Septuagint into Latin for the Catholic Church. The Romanized imperial church fathers were known for creating a form of rational syncretism between Jesus' teaching and Greek intellectual/rational philosophical worldview. Jerome's translation is known as the Catholic Vulgate. In the late 13th century, John Wycliffe, an English scholar, attempted to translate the Catholic Vulgate version into the English language. This attempted Latin to English translation was later improved by a man known as William Tyndale, another English scholar, during the 15th century A.D. William Tyndale's version was where King James Bible version derived from. King James of England summoned over forty of his scholars and asked them to translate the Bible in his name because he fell out of favour with the authoritarian Catholic Church at the time over some dogmatic altercations regarding polygamous lifestyle. King James Version of the Bible was supervised under the all-seeing eyes of some secret society. We know this because Francis Bacon (1561 – 1626) edited the Bible. Francis Bacon was a high initiate in the Rosicrucian secrete society. That explained why King James Version of the Bible is one of the most corrupt and inaccurate translations—misguided translation. It is specifically sympathetic to Europe and the Church of England, just like the entire New Testament, especially the epistles, was a Roman psychological operation. Many things written there are very sympathetic to the imperial colonizing Roman government—like slaves obey your master; if a man slaps you on one cheek, turn the other one; if someone asks you to carry his luggage for a mile, go two miles; and your pay tax. Any Jewish scholar will tell you that the New Testament was a tool of the imperial Rome for mind-control and to neutralize the possibility of the Jewish messianic uprising and revolution. The Romans had hard times dealing with the Maccabean revolt and they had to find away to destroy the strict Jewish religion. That is why many writers of the New Testament will never be known. They were not meant to be known.

So, there continued to be some questions as to if initial Greek Septuagint Bible translation was even accurate to begin with. And there were many scholars lamenting the monumental corruption in biblical translations down through history. We know this by the publication of Cardinal Ximenes in 1515 A.D titled *the Polyglot of Paris (Paris Polyglot)*. He compared all the historical versions and reported all the biblical translations to be in error. Antonio Fabre d'Olivet (1767 - 1825) also published a work titled *Hebraic Tongue Restored*. He, like Cardinal Ximanes, concluded, through his extensive work, that all the versions were mistranslated based on poor knowledge of Hebraic tongue and culture.

The point we are arriving at is that the Bible is not as old as millions of people presume, coupled with the acts of historical misunderstandings, mistranslations, and blatant inaccuracies. When biblical history is compared to the entire history of the earth, one could metaphorically state that the Bible was written like few minutes ago. The earth is millions of years old. Similarly, when biblical history is compared to the history of human civilization, one wonders how such a book can lay claim to knowledge of the beginning of the world and time.

THE JEWISH MASORETIC ACCOUNT VS THE
CHRISTIAN ACCOUNTS OF CREATION

The Jewish Masoretic chronological account of creation is the most original of all the other biblical versions, like the Sumerian and the Septuagint versions. Masoretic derives from the word *mesorah,* which indicates tradition. So Masoretic text deals with official rabbinic Jewish scholars who were the didactic writers of text in question. According to the Masoretic account, the creation of the world is dated to 3761 B.C. The religious revolutionist/revivalist and an ex-Augustinian monk, Martin Luther critically examined the Genesis chronology and dated the creation of the world to 3960 B.C. During the 17th century, Archbishop James Usher also did a chronological study of creation and he came up with the conclusion that the world was created in 4004 B.C. These scholars were all rock stars in their time, due to the fact that majority of the people did not challenge their religious indoctrination, but accepted myth as facts.

If the Bible is true, Adam died in the year 2831 B.C. At that time in history, Africa (Egypt) had already had thousands of years of established dynasties. This means one thing: people have existed and created advanced civilization before Adam, first human on earth, was even created. And, we are not even talking about the Egyptian Pre-Dynastic period which dates even farther thousands of years back to pre-history. The Egyptian sacred book, called the *Book of the Coming Forth By day and by Night* was written 3400 years before the Hebrew Old Testament and 4200 older than The New Testament (Ben-Jachannan, 1995). Something does not add up and we do not have to accept concocted history simply because the Bible said so. Such is for the illogical, uncritical and infantile minds. The fact of the matter is that the Old Testament is only a few thousand years old. How can a book that is not more than seven thousand years old teach humanity about the history of the planet that is millions of years old?

AGE OF THE EARTH IN PERSPECTIVE: THE GEOLOGIC TIMETABLE

The universe is about 16 million years in formation. Our solar system is about 10 million years old. Paleontologists generally agree that the planet earth, as part of the solar system, came into existence some 4.6 billion years ago. Evidence from the fossil indicates that single-celled organism was on this planet some 3.5 million years ago, which were the only form of life on earth. About 630 millions of years ago, multi-cellular organisms were present on earth. The following is a rough draft of geologic timetable, according modern science:

Era	Period	Years (In Millions)	Prominent Animals
Cenozoic	Holocene	.02	Mammoths and mastodons, saber-toothed tigers present on earth
	Pleistocene	2	Emergency of Australopithecus hominid –homo habilis
	Pliocene	5	Emergence of up-right walking primates
	Miocene	25	First ape in line of humans such as Dryopithecus (Ramapithecus)
	Oligocene	38	First appearance of Ape-like creature on the planet
	Eocene	55	Hoofed mammals present on the planet
	Paleocene	65	Appearance of rodent-like multituberculates
Mesozoic	Cretaceous	144	dinosaurs and lizards
	Jurassic	213	Emergency of gigantic sauropods, like the Diplodocus
	Triassic	248	Age of reptiles populating the planet
	Permian	286	Creatures like finback pelycosaurs
Paleozoic	Carboniferous	360	Amphibians populate the planet
	Devonian	408	Emergency of terrestrial arthropods, including wingless insects
	Silurian	438	Sea creatures were prevalent at this period
	Ordovician	505	diverse marine invertebrates
	Cambrian	590	Emergence of Trilobites –Aquatic arthropods

THE TEN COMMANDMENTS IS COPIED FROM THE EGYPTIAN 42 LAWS OF MA'AT

In ancient Egypt, there was a universal ethical code that was meant to govern all human intentions and behaviours. This code is called the 42 laws of Ma'at, the Negative Confession, or the Declaration of Innocence. Ma'at is the universal principle of righteousness, equity, balance, harmony which ought to govern all humans. Ma'at is anthropomorphized as a goddess with a feather planted on her hair. We see this symbolism copied all over the world today, with people putting feathers on their hats. Ma'at feather represented purity of heart, sincere intention, truth, justice, honesty, righteousness, etc. So next time you see someone with a feather on their hat or cap, you know it is an ancient symbol of godliness from the African universal mother goddess, Ma'at. The Egyptians believe the dead will appear before a panel of 42 judges, each representing one of the moral principles. Everyone will be judged according to if his/her life was in harmony with certain universal laws. For the Egyptians, living according to these set of principles means living in harmony not just with the society, but with the entire universe. Disharmony with these laws implies chaos and disharmony with all of existence. If anyone wants to have a good live on earth, the Egyptians believe he/she must follow these universal codes. Moses, having had an elevated position within the Egyptian elite, was familiar with these universal ethical codes. Many scholars now report that Moses copied his Decalogue (The Ten Commandment) from the 42 laws found in Egyptian mystery system. Below is the Egyptian Negative Confession or 42 Laws of Ma'at. I implore readers to pay keen attention to the following Egyptian Universal moral code:

AFRICAN/EGYPTIAN 42 LAW OF (THE GODDESS) MA'AT:

1. I have not committed iniquity/sin.
2. I have committed robbery with violence.
3. I have not stolen.
4. I have committed murder.
5. I have not defrauded offerings.
6. I have not diminished obligations.
7. I have not plundered the thing that belong to God
8. I have not spoken falsely.
9. I have not snatched away food.
10. I have not caused pain.
11. I have not committed fornication.
12. I have not caused shedding of tears.
13. I have not dealt (with neighbors) deceitfully.
14. I have not transgressed.
15. I have not acted treacherously.
16. I have not laid wasted the ploughed land.
17. I have not eavesdropped.
18. I have not borne false witness against anyone
19. I have not been wrathful for no reason.
20. I have not defiled the wife of any man.
21. I have not defiled the wife of any man.
22. I have not polluted myself.

23. I have not caused terror.
24. I have not transgressed.
25. I have not consumed with rage.
26. I have not turned my ears against truth and righteousness.
27. I have not caused sorrow.
28. I have not acted with insolence.
29. I have not stirred up strife.
30. I have not judged hastily.
31. I have not committed acts of eavesdropping
32. I have not exaggerated my words.
33. I have not done neither harm nor ill.
34. I have never cussed the King.
35. I have polluted the water.
36. I have not been disdainful in my words.
37. I have not cursed the God (s).
38. I have not stolen.
39. I have not swindled the God (s) of their offerings.
40. I have not plundered the offerings of the blessed dead.
41. I have not stolen food from a child.
42. I have not slaughtered with evil intent the cattle of the God(s).

Moses's Ten Commandments switched from Negative Confession to Positive Admonition. Instead of "I have not," Moses used "Thou shall not." Reader can easily fish out the moral codes of the Ten Commandments from the above Egyptian Negative Confession or the 42 Laws of Ma'at. The moral code of the Bible can be authoritatively said to come from ancient Africa - Egypt.

THE BIBLICAL TEN COMMANDMENTS AS COPIED FROM THE 42 LAWS OF MA'AT IN EGYPT

1. Thou shalt have no other gods before me.

In the original Egyptian version, we see respect for God in lines numbers, 37, 39 and 42. Many Christian and non-Christian theologians believe this first biblical code is the origin of monotheism. But as I have discussed above, Moses' idea of monotheism came from his association with Pharaoh Akhenaten, who was the first to make a law abolishing polytheism and uphold the worship of only one God. Moses' association with this radical pharaoh has been established by Egyptologist and historians.

2. Thou shalt not make unto thee any graven image.

The second biblical law is also of Egyptian origin. Refer to earlier discussion on Akhenaton's abolishment of every engagement and physical representation of the gods in any form. Monotheism was not Moses invention. He was only continuing Akhenaton's religious revolution.

3. Thou shalt not take the name of the Lord thy God in vain.

Refer to the Egyptian version above in lines, 7, 37. This moral code deals with, not defiling, abusing or profaning the name of God.

4. Remember the Sabbath day, to keep it holy.

This code could be deciphered from the original Egyptian version in lines 37, 39 and 42.

5. Honor thy father and thy mother.

This code could be decoded from lines 7 and 34 in the above original Egyptian version. Honoring one's parents and elders is intrinsically encoded in the African culture; that it is not even a debate.

6. Thou shalt not kill.

Compare this code with the original Egyptian version in lines 4, 12, 27 and 33.

7. Thou shalt not commit adultery.

Refer to similarity in the original Egyptian lines 20, 21 and 11.

8. Thou shalt not steal.

Compare with the original Egyptian version in lines 2, 3, 5, 38 and 41.

9. Thou shalt not bear false witness.

Compare with the original Egyptian version in lines 8, 15, 17, 18, 30, 31,32 and 36.

10.Thou shalt not covet.

Compare this with the original Egyptian version in lines 11, 21 and 22.

CONCLUSION

So much has been stolen from Africa— philosophical, religious political and cultural ideologies. It becomes difficult to tell Africans that certain things which they assume belong to other races are actually theirs. For instance, the head dress which judges all over the world wear is from Africa. It is a symbol of the god, Anubis or Ampu. Many African scholars have shallow indoctrinated information and have not lived up to the expectation of the term "research scholarship." African scholars are helplessly stuck in pre-colonial, colonial and post-colonial histories/societies when it comes to research. They promote redundant researches of transatlantic slave history, poverty and wars. There is no deep exploration of true history and deep scientific knowledge. Africa should not overly dwell on the European-induced stereotyped information, such repeated slave-inferiority narrative. There have been few outstanding scholars who have done exceptionally brilliant works in the field of pre-historical and historical research relative to Africa. Black African Diasporas, especially in the western hemisphere, have championed the re-investigation of African prehistory and history, and have continued to fight to place Africa in her proper perspective in history. African history and knowable have been stolen, colonized and re-baptized by other races. For instance, the entire idea of the immaculate conception, virgin birth, a virgin /mother carrying a son-God, the concept of the mother of God, the suffering and death of an incarnate God, the ideas of an incarnate God who was tempted, suffered, crucified and rose, the twelve disciple, the twelve (zodiac)houses of Israel etc., were present in Africa hundreds of years before indo-Asiatic civilizations stole such concepts and re-articulated them in their own sacred scriptures and fine-tuned them to their specific cultural psychologies. Ancient historians, such as Herodotus, Erastosthenes, Diodorus and Plutarch, established the superior antiquity of ancient Africa over all others. The Assyrians, the Persians, the Hyksos, the Greeks, the Turks, the Romans, the British, the French and, recently, the Arabs were some of the invaders of Egypt/north Africa. With all these invasions came stealing of African religion, sciences, art forms which are repackaged and given back to Africans as a 'gift of civilization." No doubt, one continues to see 'educated Africans' continue to post pictures of a white man in their homes, believing they are Jesus and God. This is a hypnotically induced mind-control and a form of mental illness. With all these in mind, one would not be distraught to learn that if Moses was an actual historical character, he was an African, and not a Hebrew.

BIBLIOGRAPHY

Cheikh Anta Diop, *Civilization or Barbarism: An Authentic Anthropology,* Lawrence Hill Books, Illinois, 1991

Gary Greenberg, *The Moses Mystery,* Pereset Press Book, NY, 2008

Gerald Massey, *The Egyptian Book of the Dead and the Ancient Mysteries of Amenta,* Cosimo Inc., New York, 2008.

James H. Breasted, *A History of Egypt: from the Earliest time to the Persian Conquest,* The New Era Printing Co., PA, USA, 1905

John G. Jakson, *Christianity Before Christ,* American Atheist Press, NJ, USA, 2002.

John J. Jackson, *Pagan Origins of the Christian Myth,* American Atheist Press, NJ, 2010

Josef Ben-Jochannan, *A Chronology of the Bible: Challenges to the Standard* Version, Black Classic Press, MD 1973

Kanu, I. A. *Igwebuike* as an Igbo-African hermeneutics of globalisation. *IGWEBUIKE: An African Journal of Arts and Humanities,* Vol. 2 No.1. pp. 61-66. 2016

Kanu, I. A. *Igwebuike* as the consummate foundation of African Bioethical principles. *An African journal of Arts and Humanities* Vol.2 No1 June, pp.23-40. 2016

Kanu, I. A. *Igwebuike* as an expressive modality of being in African ontology. *Journal of Environmental and Construction Management.* 6. 3. pp.12-21. 2016

Kanu, I. A. African traditional folktales as an integrated classroom. *Sub-Saharan African Journal of Contemporary Education Research.* Vol.3 No. 6. pp. 107-118. 2016

Kanu, I. A. *Igwebuike* as an Igbo-African philosophy for Christian-Muslim relations in Northern Nigeria. In Mahmoud Misaeli (Ed.). *Spirituality and Global Ethics* (pp. 300-310). United Kingdom: Cambridge Scholars. 2017

Kanu, I. A. *Igwebuike* as an Igbo-African philosophy for the protection of the environment. *Nightingale International Journal of Humanities and Social Sciences.* Vol. 3. No. 4. pp. 28-38. 2017

Kanu, I. A. *Igwebuike* as the hermeneutic of individuality and communality in African ontology. *NAJOP: Nasara Journal of Philosophy.* Vol. 2. No. 1. pp. 162-179. 2017

Kanu, I. A. *Igwebuike* and question of superiority in the scientific community of knowledge. *Igwebuike: An African Journal of Arts and Humanities*. Vol.3 No1. pp. 131-138. 2017

Kanu, I. A. *Igwebuike as a philosophical attribute of Africa in portraying the image of life*. A paper presented at the 2017 Oracle of Wisdom International Conference by the Department of Philosophy, Tansian University, Umunya, Anambra State, 27-29 April. 2017

Kanu, I. A. *Igwebuike* as a complementary approach to the issue of girl-child education. *Nightingale International Journal of Contemporary Education and Research*. Vol. 3. No. 6. pp. 11-17. 2017

Kanu, I. A. *Igwebuike* as a wholistic response to the problem of evil and human suffering. *Igwebuike: An African Journal of Arts and Humanities*. Vol. 3 No 2, March. 2017

Kanu, I. A. *Igwebuike* as an Igbo-African modality of peace and conflict resolution. *Journal of African Traditional Religion and Philosophy Scholars. Vol. 1. No. 1. pp. 31-40.* 2017

Kanu, I. A. *Igwebuike* and the logic (Nka) of African philosophy. *Igwebuike: An African Journal of Arts and Humanities*. 3. 1. pp. 1-13. 2017

Kanu, I. A. *Igwebuike* philosophy and human rights violation in Africa. *IGWEBUIKE: An African Journal of Arts and Humanities*. Vol. 3. No. 7. pp. 117-136. 2017

Kanu, I. A. *Igwebuike* as a hermeneutic of personal autonomy in African ontology. *Journal of African Traditional Religion and Philosophy Scholars. Vol. 2. No. 1. pp. 14-22.* 2017

Kanu, I. A. African philosophy, globalization and the priority of 'otherness'. *Journal of African Studies and Sustainable Development*. Vol. 1. No. 1. pp. 40-57. 2018

Kanu, I. A. *African traditional philosophy of education: Essays in Igwebuike philosophy.* Germany: Lambert Publications. 2018

Kanu, I. A. Igbo-African Gods and Goddesses. *Nnadiebube Journal of Philosophy*. Vol. 2. No. 2. pp. 118-146. 2018

Kanu, I. A. *Igwe Bu Ike* as an Igbo-African hermeneutics of national development. *Igbo Studies Review. No. 6.* pp. 59-83. 2018

Kanu, I. A. *Igwebuike* as an African integrative and progressive anthropology. *NAJOP: Nasara Journal of Philosophy.* Vol. 2. No. 1. pp. 151-161. 2018

Kanu, I. A. New Africanism: *Igwebuike* as a philosophical Attribute of Africa in portraying the Image of Life. In Mahmoud Misaeli, Sanni Yaya and Rico Sneller (Eds.). *African Perspectives on Global on Global Development* (pp. 92-103). United Kingdom: Cambridge Scholars Publishing. 2018

Richard A. Scott John R. Ward Exodus Reality: *Unearthing the Real History of Moses, Identifying the Pharaohs and Examining the Exodus from Egypt,* The Career Press, USA, 2014.

Richard Marlow, *Moses in Ancient Egypt and the Hidden Story of the Bible,* Richard Darlow, 2006.

Robert Bouval and Timothy Brophy: *Black Genesis: The Prehistoric Origins of Ancient Egypt,* Bear & Company, Vermont, USA, 2011.

Shlomo Sand, *The Invention of the Land of Israel: From Holy Land to Home Land,* Verso, NY, 2014.

Sigmund Freud, *Moses and Monotheism,* Vintage Books, NY 1939

Yoel, Natan, *Moon-O-Theism: Religion of a War and Moon God Prophet Vol. I of II,* 2006

IGWEBUIKE: A KEY PRINCIPLE IN AFRICAN LIBERATION THEOLOGY

Nnoruga James
Department of Religion and Human Relations
Nnamdi Azikiwe University, Awka
nnorugajames@gmail.com

EXECUTIVE SUMMARY

The ripples caused by the invasion and partition of African nations by the Europeans many years ago have caused and are still causing havoc to African countries. It has led Africans into bad leadership, migration and human trafficking. The economy of African nations is in constant meltdown. With crisis and political instability, Africa remains undeveloped marginally, when compared to other continents of the world. There have been many advocates of African liberation, each with its own strategy towards the liberation of African nations. We are going to use Igwebuike principles to navigate towards the liberation of African nations. The reflective and theological approach is employed in this research.

Keywords: Igwebuike, African Liberation Theology, Kanu Ikechukwu Anthony, Philosophy, Principle

INTRODUCTION

There are many factors constituting the past and present ugly situation of things found in Africa today. These crises or factors that shaped the situation of African people the way it is today came from internal and external spheres. Hence, we have a lot of challenges that need to be tackled for the development and stability of the African countries. Unfortunately, these crises in Africa touch or spread all through the cultural, religious, political and social aspects of the African people. This accounts for non-development or slow pace of development in almost all the sectors of their lives in different countries of Africa.

It is believed that most of the African countries have gotten their independence, yet they are ruled indirectly by the different strong countries of the world that colonized them initially. This makes Africans to be marginalized in most parts of the world, because they are seen as slaves, undeveloped, and uncultured. Even the colour of their skin (black) segregates them from the white people and makes them third class citizens; hence, today, Africa is regarded as a continent of third world countries.

In the religious sphere, Africans, their God and their worship are regarded as nothing, and they were regarded as incapable of conceiving and worshipping the real Almighty God as the rest of the world. Hence, African traditional religion was called all sorts of names by Europeans and arm-chair researchers. Talbot (1926), Mbiti (1969), Quarcoopome (1987) and Kanu (2015) all affirmed that names like idolatry, fetishism, animism, paganism, primitive were given to African traditional religion, because they fail to understand the culture and language of African people. Achebe (1958) confirms the above:

> Does the white man understand our custom about land, asked Okonkwo, "How can he when he does not even speak our tongue", responded Obierika, and then he continued, but he says our customs are bad, and our own brothers who have taken up his religion also say that our customs are bad. (p. 124)

This confirms the level of degradation Africans were subjected to, even in terms of religion. This level of degradation or subjugation meted out to them is seen through other aspects of their lives. Sequel to the above, many African scholars, including sociologists and theologians, have offered many ways to alleviate the oppressive or ugly state of African situation. Many have advocated many options through which Africa can be developed and sustained, just like other strong continents of the world.

Igwebuike, as a concept or key, will be used as a tool to seek ways to alleviate the condition of the African people. The cry by the advocates of African liberation theology cannot be complete without the Igwebuike principles. This will help in developing African countries when the principles of *Igwebuike* are fully applied. African continent will find real independence, not pseudo independence, as we are having it today. *Igwebuike*, as concept or principle, is advocated for by an African scholar, Professor Ikechukwu Anthony Kanu, just like other advocates of African liberation theology. In this write up, we are going to use the principles of *Igwebuike* to advance further the development, stability and independence of African nations.

AFRICAN SITUATION: AN OVERVIEW

There are fifty four countries in Africa today, according to the United Nations, with other territories which are dependent on stronger countries of the world or being colonized by other countries of the world, territories like Reunion, which is dependent on or being colonized by France; Mayotte, being colonized by France; Saint Helena, which depended on the United Kingdom and Western Sahara, which is still under dispute. But Wikipedia (2020) listed fifty six sovereign states (fifty four of which are member-states of the United Nations), two non-sovereign (dependent) territories of non-African sovereign states, and nine sub-national regions of non-African sovereign states. The African continent is being surrounded by water from all directions, with clearly defined borders. In the north, it is separated from Europe by the Mediterranean Sea; in the north-east, it is separated from Asia by the Suez Canal and farther by the Red Sea. From the east and southeast, it is surrounded by the Indian Ocean, and from the West by the Atlantic Ocean.

The work of liberating African nations, which is a continent of immense diversity, according to Oborji (2005), is not only on the level of geographical areas, but also includes cultural, sociological, political, religious and economic levels. Though Africa is a diversified whole, its unity can be seen in their tenets of African world view, life principles and unity of spirit. According to Kanu (2015), its unity can be seen in their belief in worship of Supreme Being, just like other people, but with a profound sense of sacredness and mystery. Hence, for Africans, it is difficult to separate their day-to-day activities of life from their personal inclination to the divine. No wonder, Mbiti (1969) argued that:

> Wherever the African is, there is his religion. He carries it to the fields where he is sowing seeds or harvesting new crop, he takes it with him to the beer parlour or to attend a funeral ceremony, and if he is educated, he takes religion with him to the examination room at school or in the university, if he is a politician, he takes it to the house of parliament. (p. 2)

Paris (1995) also echoed that "the ubiquity of religious consciousness among African people constitutes their single most important common characteristics" (p. 27).

Comparing African continent in terms of development from all sectors of life with other continents of the world, one will feel a great shock, because it is being ravaged internally and externally by many factors. They stretch from social crisis, political crisis, economic crisis, religious crisis, racism, human trafficking which is new form of slavery, and so on. These crises can be traced to have originated from when the African continent was divided by the strong powers, without the consent of Africans. According to Mbefo (1996):

> It was in Berlin that the master plan and implicit agreement about European intentions in Africa were decided and given active assistance. The result of the conference was that the on-going "scramble for Africa" was organized systematically, according to agreed principles. While it is wrong to claim, as some have done, that Africa was carved out by European powers at this conference, it is right to affirm that it was there the European powers agreed on maintaining colonies in Africa. European powers agreed not to interfere but to respect the "areas of influence" acquired by any given power. It is remarkable that no African was invited to a conference that decided the fate of Africa. (pp. 28-29)

With the invasion by the super powers into Africa, Africa was subjugated, dominated, and the development of Africa was stalled. There are many instances to show that Africans were developed people before even the Europeans came in contact with them. They have their own institutions with their own idea of government. But sadly, Africa has been exploited and dominated over the years by stronger powers. Rodney (2009) showed that using comparative standards, Africa today is underdeveloped in relation to Western Europe and a few other parts of the world, and that the present position has been arrived at, not by separate evolution of Africa, on the one hand, and Europe, on the other, but by exploitation.

In terms of social situation, Africa has continued to deteriorate. This is evidenced by the pressure of urbanization and rural emigration. The decay in educational sector and health infrastructure, growing malnutrition and poverty, the worsening plight of refugees and displaced persons, and wide spread unemployment are signs of decay in African society. Recently the ravage of Acquired Immune Deficiency Syndrome (AIDS) killed many African people. Ebola disease was contained, but many Africans died. As of today, the Corona Virus pandemic (COVID-19) is ravaging the world. Though it is not much in Africa, but it is known that African countries lack the health facilities, quite unlike the other countries of the world, to stop its spread.

Economically, the African situation, according to Drimmelen (cited by Igboamalu, 2003), can be summarized thus:

> Africa as a whole includes 33 of world's 50 poorest countries. The combined Gross National Product (GNP) of the entire continent south of the Sahara is less than that of the Netherlands; the Sub-Saharan Africa is the only region in the world likely to experience an increase in absolute poverty over the next decade. (p. 48)

African counrties are nowhere to be found in the global market economy. The globalization of economy today puts the African countries in the slow lane track. Hence, they remain beggars among the continents of the world. The institutions that are developing economy are not developed, rather they are been looted out, and most African countries keep borrowing for consumption. World economic policies do not favour the African trade. This has contributed enormously to the impoverishment and underdevelopment of Africa. Africa is exploited by their colonizers who take most of their crude oil and agricultural products at a giveaway price only to sell them back to Africa at a high price. Oborji (2005) rightly observed that the present world economy manipulates prices of the raw materials from the African countries and, through the protectionist policies of the industrialized countries, blocks the inflow of manufactured goods from the developing countries. Due to serious crises in African economies, African countries are variously referred to as underdeveloped, developing or less-developed countries. The above reality means that African economy is caged and in bondage, and this is expressed by Adedeji (1984), that the African economy has meaning only to the extent it is allowed to be controlled by the former colonial masters. With this economic system, Africa can never develop fully like other great countries of the world.

Politically, African countries have not found their feet, though they have gotten their independence. Most of the African countries are still being ruled indirectly by strong powers that colonized them. According to Igboamalu (2003), one of the major problems or crises of the African countries and other developing countries, with regard to the issue of global governance, is the tendency of the West and America or the colonizers to impose their socio-cultural and political standards and values, which they want, on the rest of the world. Hence, Africa is always suppressed politically, without these super powers remembering that we have our own ideas of government before their advent. This led to the enthronement of puppet leaders and presidents who would always obey the strong powers that put them put them in office. m. Hence, Achebe (1983) rightly observed that leadership remains the problem of African countries. This continues to make African countries to be political slaves to most nations in the world. This affirms Oborji(2005) claim that "the newly independent African states were modeled politically and economically on the nations which had colonized them" (p. 34). Again, Dudley (1984) pointed out that the constitution handed over to the new nations was not founded on African cultural environment or atmosphere. By implication, the independence lacked the ingredients of its new nations; this accounts for political instability in most of the African nations. This political instability led to several military coups d' etat in Africa. This well-known military rule in Africa helped in reducing Africa to abject poverty.

Slavery and colonization were great blows to the African continent, judging from all aspects of African lives. This in particular perpetuated poverty in Africa today. African countries gradually became poor with the conquest of African nations. African states were divided at the Berlin conference, for self interest and exploitation. Offiong (2001) asserted that:

> The conference produced the Berlin act, an instrument to which the major European powers were signatories. It had as its aims those of fostering the development of trade and civilization… the moral and material wellbeing of the native populations. This was non-sensical because in all their undertakings, their interests came first and all was designed to enhance the exploitation of the people. (p. 9)

It is well known that the conquest and occupation of the continent of Africa by Europeans spanned four centuries. During these centuries, Africans were dominated, exploited. This led to the formulation of colonial policies and disorganization of the traditional pattern of societal organization in Africa. This makes African countries to be stooges to the stronger countries of the world. These situations above, in a nut shell, show the image of bondage in Africa which has held the African people hostage for centuries. The African continent has been promised liberation (even by our colonizers), through many ways, out of their poverty, political instability and underdevelopment, yet things keep on becoming worse and backward when compared to this age of globalization.

IGWEBUIKE AS A PRINCIPLE OF LIBERATION

With the critical situation of the African continent, which is being ravaged by constant wars because of forceful divisions or partition of African borders by the world powers, poverty now takes place in a continent known to be full of agricultural raw materials and crude oil. World powers rose to a greater height of industrial growth by impoverishing Africa through slave trade and other exploitations. Mbefo (1996) lamented that as of today, African nations are still undergoing new forms of slavery through our youths going back freely, and on their own, to Europe, because of bad state of the economy and the political instability in Africa. Mbefo called it slavery in reverse gear. With the above situation, many scholars have advocated for many solutions to the African state of crisis. We apply the principles of *Igwebuike* in seeking to control and redirect or restructure the African continent.

According to Kanu (2015), *Igwebuike* is the modality of being, and *being* in Igbo ontology is '*idi*', that is 'to be'. *Igwebuike* is an Igbo word which is a combination of three words. According to him:

> It can be understood as a word and as a sentence: as a word, it is written thus *Igwebuike*, and as a sentence, it is written thus, *Igwe bu ike*, with the component words enjoying some independence in terms of space [and meaning]. (p. 67)

He went further to explain the three words that make up the word *Igwebuike. Igwe* is a noun, which means number or population, usually a large number or population; *Bu* is a verb which means 'is'; *Ike* is a noun, which means strength or power. When these words are put together, it means 'number is strength' or 'number is power.' This, in effect, means when a good number, group or society of human beings come together in solidarity, they are powerful. Again, solidarity combines with complementarity, because everybody needs each other to make a complete whole; it constitutes a powerful group and an insurmountable force. At this level, Kanu asserted that no task is beyond their collective capability. Again, this analysis provides or proves an African ontology that presents being as that which possesses a relational character of mutual relations. Mbiti (1960) also asserted that "man is at the very centre of existence, and African people see everything else in its relation to this central position of man… it is as if God exists for the sake of man" (p. 92). Metuh (1991) affirmed that "everything else in African worldview seems to get its bearing and significance from the position, meaning and end of man" (p. 109).

The above analysis shows that for man to achieve his aims or objectives in this world, he has to be in relational character with the other people around him. This will ensure a formidable force. The human person, following the African worldview, is understood in his relation with God and his fellow human beings. Ideologically, Kanu (2015) argued that 'to be' is to live in solidarity and complementarity, and to live outside the parameters of solidarity and complementarity is to suffer alienation. 'To be' is to be with the other in a community of being. Onwubiko (1991) expressed this sense of community rightly with Lozi proverb which says: "Go the way that many people go; if you go alone you will have reason to lament" (p. 13).

Anchoring or explaining *Igwebuike* on the basis of the African world view, Iroegbu (1994) described it as being characterized by a common origin, common worldview, common language, common historical experiences and common destiny. Determining the role of community to the individual or human beings, Mbiti (1969) asserted that "I am because we are and since we are, therefore I am" (p. 108). The sense of community here portrays family-hood or brotherhood, which means collaboration in existence. Achebe (cited by Kanu, 2015) in order to bring out the essential nature of the Igbo African communal relationship, related that:

> We do not ask for wealth because he that has health and children will also have wealth. We do not pray to have more money but to have more kinsmen. We are better than animals because we have kinsmen. An animal rubs its itching flank against a tree, a man asks his kinsmen to scratch him. (p. 68)

The quotation above shows that life is shared in the African worldview which makes life meaningful. So it is in relationship or coming together that each completes a whole. Thus, according to Kanu (2015), every being has a missing part and is at the same time a missing part. Ekwulu (cited by Kanu, 2015) confirmed the above view by saying that "if the other is my part or a piece of me, it means that I need him for me to be complete, for me to be what I really am. The other completes rather than diminishes me" (p. 68).

This rightly explains why Igbo-African worldview would refer to the other as '*ibe*', which means a piece of or a part of, as in '*ibe ji*' (a piece of yam), or '*ibe ede*' (a piece of cocoyam). Kanu (2015) asserted that the Igbo-African refers to the other person as '*ibe*,' which means 'my piece', or '*mmadu ibe m*' (my fellow human being). This concept is also employed in relation to relationships and reciprocity: love one another *(hunu ibe unu n'anya)*, help one another *(nyere nu ibe unu aka)*, respect one another *(sopuru nu ibe unu)* etc. From the above, we see that *Igwebuike* portrays the African sense of commonality, solidarity, brotherhood, familyhood and complementality as the root of the African world view, thought and the ontological quality of real African, which is needed to liberate the African people from the state of anarchy seen in all aspects of their lives.

IGWEBUIKE AS A TOOL IN AFRICAN LIBERATION THEOLOGY

The theology of liberation or liberation of Africa has gone through many phases. And it arises out of the concern of African scholars or African theologians to address the people's experience of exploitation, oppression and injustice that are going on through different means. In June 2020, there was a protest in all the states of America because of a black man killed by an officer of the law who is meant to protect life. Though not African, the blacks protested against such oppression and injustice.

African scholars continued to seek solutions to the current situation of exploitation, poverty, oppression and injustice in a continent which for a long time has suffered from subjugation, according to Oborji (2005), in the forms of imperialism: slave trade, colonialism, multinational corporations, the activities of the national bourgeoisie, despotic regimes and racism. Okolo (1994) asserted that the theology of liberation emerged as a response to experiences of negation, grinding poverty caused by greed, exploitation and oppression from world leaders and African leaders. Though this critical reflection by Okolo was in the light of the gospel, it was with the aim of inspiring in African people and their leaders the confidence to stop the horrors of oppression in Africa and to build a more just and human African society.

Liberation has been a major theme or emergent theological thought in Africa, in a bid to liberate Africa from its current state of anarchy. Oborji (2005) linked or related theology of liberation in Africa with inculturation. According to him:

> The aim of inculturation is to facilitate an in-depth evangelization of a particular socio-cultural context or milieu. On the other hand, liberation theology seek, through the gospel, to address the oppressive elements in a traditional culture, and focus on political and economic situation of the particular cultural context so as to liberate people from the forces of sin and death, reinforce their identity, and give a new orientation to their advancement. (p. 154)

This implies that for any liberation to be real or authentic, it must be inculturated, in the sense that the social and cultural milieu of the particular people must be involved. This will make it easy and meaningful. It must not be transported or forced into people, so that their initial world view would be abandoned, rather it would start with their world view. This is exactly the aim of *Igwebuike* as a tool of liberation in Africa. *Igwebuike* liberation constitutes majorly of using African world view, which is based on solidarity and complementarity, to seek freedom for African people in their state of anarchy that is still ongoing in this age of globalization.

There have been many advocates of African liberation through their philosophical and theological critical reflections. Many of the African scholars or advocates of African liberation hammered so much on the poverty of the African nations. Many remarked that it is as if Africans got political independence in order to enjoy poverty. Ezeanya (1992) remarked that today in Africa wherever anyone goes, he sees or notices poverty and suffering starring in the face of African people. Surely, Christ is suffering terribly among the African people. Many African countries have gotten their independence yet under colonial yoke. Going further, Morrow (cited by Oborji, 2005) described African poverty situation thus:

> Africa-Sub Saharan Africa, at least has begun to look like an immense illustration of chaos theory, although some hope is forming at the margins. Much of the continent has turned into a battleground of contending dooms: AIDS and overpopulation, poverty, starvation, illiteracy, corruption, social breakdown, vanishing resources, overcrowded cities, drought, war, and the homelessness of war refugees. Africa has become the basket case of the planet, the "third world of the third world", a vast continent in free fall, a sort of pre-colonial breakdown. (p. 158)

This is the reason why most advocates of African liberation (or African writers) conducted their critical reflection for a better socio-political cultural-cum-religious, and economic order in the nations of Africa. At this time of the Corona Virus pandemic, world leaders in other continents of the world are projecting that it will later spread more in Africa because health facilities are not in place, or are not found in most health centers in African countries. With their prediction, the world powers are evacuating their citizens from African countries back to their countries. One of the advocates, Uzukwu (1996) traced the poverty of African nations to dependency status of African nations, seeing it as the major cause of poverty in the continent. This is because dependency is a system problem which is destroying the African nations from inside and makes the African countries to be beggar countries, and a beggar has no respect. Hence, Uzukwu advocated for an end to foreign aid to Africa. In its stead, Africa needs committed leadership at all levels of government who are not influenced by the world powers.

Igwebuike, as a tool for African liberation, hinges on the solidarity and complementarity of African people based on African world view, which is quite different from other principles of African liberation theology or black liberation theology. Cone and Wilmore (1979) described Black theology or Black liberation theology thus:

> Black theology is that theology which arises out of the need to articulate the religious significance of black presence in a hostile white world. It is black people reflecting on Black experience under the guidance of the Holy Spirit, attempting to redefine the relevance of the Christian gospel for their lives…- Black subjugation under white oppression. (p. 468)

Here, liberation from white oppression is based on the Christian world view as a basis which is different from *Igwebuike* as a tool for liberation, which is based on purely African world view. Theology of black liberation was seen again, as we have noted before, with the protest of all Blacks in America recently in June 2020, when a police man killed a black man for no reason. Again Cone and Wilmore (1979) described African liberation theology as a theology which is based on the biblical faith and speaks to the African soul:

> To speak of African theology involves formulating clearly a Christian attitude to other religions. It must be pointed out that the emphasis is on Christian theology, which could be expressed through African thinking and culture. (p. 473)

Mbiti (1979) also echoed the same when he described Black theology as emerging from the pains of oppression of the Negro's experience in America in the social, economic, political, cultural and educational spheres of their lives, while African liberation theology grew out of joy in the experience of the Christian faith preached to Africans.

All we are trying to establish above is that it is *Igwebuike* as a tool that would touch fundamentally the African world view which needed liberation, than implanting another world view on the African soil, and then using it for liberation. The complementary role of *Igwebuike* from its point of ideology will be used in solving the problems of African continent and advancing the quality of life in Africa (Kanu 2018). From the analysis done before, the ideology of complementarity in the African world view reaches to individual basis, ontological basis and social basis. The embracing of these entire bases will give a whole solution in which all the units when put together will give a formidable and dynamic force to achieve freedom and development. In Africa today, what is needed is a formidable and dynamic force in pursuing a goal, like wiping away hunger or poverty in Africa. When the efforts of our governments or leaders are combined as a unit whole with that of the masses, great achievements will be made in the economic and political lives of the Africans. This automatically will ensure security and the employment of our youths. The communal life which is already in the African world view will help in great advancement of the African continent for which *Igwebuike*, as a tool for liberation, is seriously advocating. This is also echoed by Asiegbu (2010), in expressing the African world view as a fundamental constituent for an authentic dimension of thoroughgoing complementarism.

The collective efforts seen in the *Igwebuike* ideology relates again to the social dimension of action in any African society. Here, the role of sharing life in a community makes life meaningful (Kanu 2016). When conceived in terms of complementarity, a community life is full of relation and relationships. This brings in vividly teamwork which is against the choice of isolation. Teamwork or team spirit is going on in the African continent to see how the Corona Virus pandemic can be contained, which is against the choice of the world powers, each are trying to work out something to be the first country to contain the pandemic.

Igwebuike again advocates complementary attitudinal change of all Africans. Africans from unit to the whole should liberate their psyche and undergo a total transformation that starts from the African world view than from other world views. This type of re-education ensures an authentic new understanding towards life as an independent being, not as a dependent being (Kanu 2017). This again is in line with Asouzu's (2004) line of thought that the liberation of African nations constitutes a complementary attitudinal change of psyche which comprises their whole being, attitude and vision.

The *Igwebuike* ideology consists also of solidarity that, in the words of Nnoruka (2009), means people coming together. In Igbo expression: *Ayili n'igwe n'aga egwu a naghi atu* (when people are marching together, there is no fear). People coming together stand for a reasonable number of people who have come together to achieve a common purpose, a common objective. No one loses his identity in a group. The solidarity of the African Union (AU) needs to be revamped. African solidarity is needed continually to fight insecurity and wars prevalent in African nations. With this solidarity, African countries will engage in more introverted economies which have some built-in protectionism and some trade barriers argued (Offiong, 2001).

Religiously, Africa has, to some extent, achieved religion indigenous to Africa, seen in the emergence of African Independence Churches (A. I. C.). According to Ndiokwere (2019):

> As African saw it, it was not only the Europeans who had the divine mandate to go and make disciples of all nations (Mt. 28:19). Discipleship was the universal vocation of every Christian, but Africans are not stopping at founding churches and religious movements... African prophets and self-acclaimed religious leaders found and run "churches" of their grass root tastes. (pp. 9-10)

The above originated after the partition of Africa by the colonial Masters of Europe, in which Christian missionary organizations followed the flags of their respective nations to the shores of African nations. This supports the view that *Igwebuike* as an ideology has a common origin, common shared culture, common historical experience and common destiny. Today many African people are introducing new religious movements which bear features of the African traditional religion. This is possible because the common historical experience and cultures shared by Africans necessitate this. This necessitates also the common trend today about the need for dialogue between the African traditional religion and Christianity. From the dialogue so far, the question of how to merge the two religions (African traditional religion and Christianity) become a problem. Many theologians and African scholars have proposed inculturation, adaptation, hybridization, indigenization, translation and contextualization. Muonwe (2014) argued that before the emergence of inculturation, a plethora of terms, as we see above, had been employed over the years in an attempt to fashion out the best model or approach to be adopted in relating the Christian faith with the African traditional religion or culture. As a tool for liberation in Africa, *Igwebuike* is firmly grounded in the African sense of solidarity and complementarity and on the ontological quality of the African.

CONCLUSION

The principle of *Igwebuike*, when understood and properly applied towards the critical situation of Africa, will go a long way in helping African nations to salvage themselves from all crises. Its ideology is all embracing; hence, it is oriented towards the coming together of all people of Africa. This will start from African leaders looking inwards than outside for the solution to the critical situation of the African continent. Though there are internal and external factors constituting the deplorable state of African nations, it is true that many scholars have advocated for solutions *Igwebuike*, as a key, ushers in a new ideology and combines with all other possible solutions for the liberation of African people. The *Igwebuike* ideology comes from African world views; hence, it can trace and deal properly with the problems of Africans themselves.

REFERENCES

Achebe, C. (1958). *Things fall apart.* London: Heinemann.

Achebe, C. (1983). *The trouble with Nigeria.* Enugu: Fourth Dimension Publishers.

Adedeji A. (1948). The economic evolution of developing Africa. In M. Crowder

(Ed.). *The cambridge history of Africa.* (pp.192-250) University Press.

Asiegbu M. F. (2010). African renaissance, globalization and philosophy. In A. B. C. Chiegboka and T. C Udoh-Ezeajughi G. I. Udechukwu (Eds*.). The Humanities and Globalization in the third Millenium.*(Pp 77-92). Nimo: Rex

Charles & Patrick.

Asouzu, I. I. (2004). *The method and principles of complementary reflection in and beyond African philosophy.* Calabar. University of Calabar Press.

Cone J. H. and Wilmore G. S. (1979). Black Theology and African Theology: Considerations for Dialogue, Critique and Integration. *In G.S. Wilmore & J. H. Cone (Eds.). Black Theology.* A documentary history. 1966-1979. (pp.463-476). New York Orbis book.

Dudley, B. J. (1984). Decolonization and the problem of independence. In M. Crowther (Ed.). The Cambridge of Africa. (pp. 52-94). Cambridge: University Press.

Ezeanya, S. N. (1992). *The poor in our midst.* Onitsha: Tabansi Press.

Igboamalu, U. B. (2003). *Globalization and the future of Africa.* Enugu: San Press. Iroegbu, P. (1995). *Metaphysics: The kpim of philosophy.* Owerri: International University Press.

Kanu, I. A. (2019). *Igwebuike* research methodology: A new trend for scientific and wholistic investigation. *IGWEBUIKE: An African Journal of Arts and Humanities* (IAAJAH). *5. 4.* pp. *95-105.*

Kanu, I. A. (2019). *Igwebuikeconomics:* The Igbo apprenticeship for wealth creation. *IGWEBUIKE: An African Journal of Arts and Humanities* (IAAJAH). *5. 4.* pp. *56-70.*

Kanu, I. A. (2019). *Igwebuikecracy:* The Igbo-African participatory cocio-political system of governance. *TOLLE LEGE: An Augustinian Journal of the Philosophy and Theology. 1. 1.* pp. 34-45.

Kanu, I. A. (2016a). *Igwebuike* as an Igbo-African hermeneutics of globalisation. *IGWEBUIKE: An African Journal of Arts and Humanities*, Vol. 2 No.1. pp. 61-66.

Kanu, I. A. (2016a). *Igwebuike* as the consummate foundation of African Bioethical principles. *An African journal of Arts and Humanities* Vol.2 No1 June, pp.23-40.

Kanu, I. A. (2016b) *Igwebuike* as an expressive modality of being in African ontology. *Journal of Environmental and Construction Management. 6. 3.* pp.12-21.

Kanu, I. A. (2017). *Igwebuike* as an Igbo-African philosophy for Christian-Muslim relations in Northern Nigeria. In Mahmoud Misaeli (Ed.). *Spirituality and Global Ethics* (pp. 300-310). United Kingdom: Cambridge Scholars.

Kanu, I. A. (2017). *Igwebuike* as an Igbo-African philosophy for the protection of the environment. *Nightingale International Journal of Humanities and Social Sciences.* Vol. 3. No. 4. pp. 28-38.

Kanu, I. A. (2017). *Igwebuike* as the hermeneutic of individuality and communality in African ontology. *NAJOP: Nasara Journal of Philosophy.* Vol. 2. No. 1. pp. 162-179.

Kanu, I. A. (2017a). *Igwebuike* and question of superiority in the scientific community of knowledge. *Igwebuike: An African Journal of Arts and Humanities.* Vol.3 No1. pp. 131-138.

Kanu, I. A. (2017a). *Igwebuike as a philosophical attribute of Africa in portraying the image of life.* A paper presented at the 2017 Oracle of Wisdom International Conference by the Department of Philosophy, Tansian University, Umunya, Anambra State, 27-29 April.

Kanu, I. A. (2017b). *Igwebuike* as a complementary approach to the issue of girl-child education. *Nightingale International Journal of Contemporary Education and Research.* Vol. 3. No. 6. pp. 11-17.

Kanu, I. A. (2017b). *Igwebuike* as a wholistic response to the problem of evil and human suffering. *Igwebuike: An African Journal of Arts and Humanities.* Vol. 3 No 2, March.

Kanu, I. A. (2017e). *Igwebuike* as an Igbo-African modality of peace and conflict resolution. *Journal of African Traditional Religion and Philosophy Scholars. Vol. 1. No. 1. pp. 31-40.*

Kanu, I. A. (2017g). *Igwebuike* and the logic (Nka) of African philosophy. *Igwebuike: An African Journal of Arts and Humanities.* 3. 1. pp. 1-13.

Kanu, I. A. (2017h). *Igwebuike* philosophy and human rights violation in Africa. *IGWEBUIKE: An African Journal of Arts and Humanities.* Vol. 3. No. 7. pp. 117-136.

Kanu, I. A. (2017i). *Igwebuike* as a hermeneutic of personal autonomy in African ontology. *Journal of African Traditional Religion and Philosophy Scholars. Vol. 2. No. 1. pp. 14-22.*

Kanu, I. A. (2018). *Igwe Bu Ike* as an Igbo-African hermeneutics of national development. *Igbo Studies Review. No. 6. pp. 59-83.*

Kanu, I. A. (2018). *Igwebuike* as an African integrative and progressive anthropology. *NAJOP: Nasara Journal of Philosophy.* Vol. 2. No. 1. pp. 151-161.

Kanu, I. A. (2018). New Africanism: *Igwebuike* as a philosophical Attribute of Africa in portraying the Image of Life. In Mahmoud Misaeli, Sanni Yaya and Rico Sneller (Eds.). *African Perspectives on Global on Global Development* (pp. 92-103). United Kingdom: Cambridge Scholars Publishing.

Mbefo, L. N. (1996). *Coping with Nigeria's two-fold heritage.* Enugu: Snap Press

Mbiti (1969). *African Religions and Philosophy.* London: Heinemann.

Mbiti, J. S. (1979). An African views American black theology. *In G. S. Wilmore &*

J. S. Cone (Eds.). Black Theology: A documentary history, 1966-1979 (pp.477-482). New York Orbis books.

Metuh, I. E. (1991). *African religions in western /conceptual schemes.* Jos: Imico.

Muonwe, M. (2014). *Dialetics of faith-culture integration- inculturation or syncretism.* Bloomington: Liberty drive.

Ndiokwere, N. I. (2019). *Christianity in turmoil: The African scenario.* Owerri: Lui House of Excellence Ventures.

Nnoruka, S. I. (2009). *Solidarity: a principle of sociality. A phenomenological-hermeneutic approach in the context of the philosophy of Alfred Schutz and an African culture.* Owerri: Living Flame Resources.

Oborji, A. O. (2005) *Trend in Africa theology since Vatican II; A missiological orientation.* Italy: Leberit Press.

Offiong, D. A. (2001). *Globalization: Post-neodependency and poverty in Africa.* Enugu: Fourth Dimension.

Okolo, B. C. (1994). *African liberation theology: Concept and necessity.* In SEDOS Bulletin. Pp. 102-103

Onwubiko, O. A. (1991). *The christian mission and culture in Africa.* African Thought, religion and culture. Enugu: Snapp Press.

Paris, P. J. (1995). *The spirituality of African peoples, the search for a common Moral Discourse.* Minneapolis.

Quarcoopome, T. N. O. (1987). *West African traditional religion.* Ibadan: African University Press.

Rodney, W. (2009). *How europe underdeveloped Africa.* Abuja: Panaf Publishing. Talbot, P. A. (1926). *The peoples of southern Nigeria*: O. U. P.

Uzukwu, E. E. (1991). *A listening church: Autonomy and communion in African churches. New York:* Orbis Books.

Wikipedia (2008). *Sovereign states and dependent territories in Africa.* Retrieved July, 27, 2020. http://en.wikipedia.

IGWEBUIKE, INDIVIDUAL FREEDOM AND RESPONSIBILITY IN AFRICAN ETHICS

Jude I. Onebunne, PhD
Department of Philosophy
Nnamdi Azikiwe University, Awka
juno.anyi@gmail.com
&
Mirian N. Alike, PhD
Department of Philosophy
Nnamdi Azikiwe University, Awka
mirianngozialike@gmail.com

EXECUTIVE SUMMARY

The concept of Igwebuike as a philosophy of inclusive action in unity still respects the individual person in the African world view. Igwebuike is possible when the individuals congregate, defined by a common interest as a goal. The individuals, therefore, make up the Igwe (populace, unison, people) that exercises or has the enormous Ike (Strength). Hence, Igwe is Ike. By and large, the morality or the ethical demand of the individual is not lost amidst the population or in the Igwe, with regard to the exercise of Ike; rather, the individual is responsible for every action within the Igwe, and the Igwe, via individual actions, has a cooperate responsibility to bear and as such there is an individual responsibility in Igwebuike as regards African ethics. The act of belonging within the African community entails a duty within the limits of the communal ethics. Applying the method of critical analysis, this paper explores and finds out that the communalistic relationship between Igwebuike and the individual person is within the bounds of African Ethics.

Keywords: Igwebuike, individual person, Kanu Ikechukwu Anthony, freedom, responsibility, African ethics

INTRODUCTION

This work proposes *Igwebuike* as the key in understanding African philosophy and, by implication, African Ethics as its main branch. *Igwebuike* is a relational concept that defines a communal action in the African world view. Man, the individual human person, is always, to a great extent, the product of his environment, that is, the community known for communion

111

and other forms of human interactions. The community must be understood as being one and the same with the society, environment or group of people, though with differential nuances. However, Maritain (1951:2) maintains that "a community is more of a work of nature and more nearly related to the biological; a society is more of a work of reason, and more nearly related to the intellectual and spiritual properties of a man". In both senses, however, community is synonymously interchanged with the state. The human person interplays out his life within the community as an individual within a group. In this sense, it is applicable to say that, *no individual, no community;* that is, if there is no individual person, there is no group formation as a result of the aggregate of individual persons. This is the hallmark of *Igwebuike.*

Igwebuike, as an African relational concept, is the modality of being in African metaphysics. It is an Igbo concept, which is a combination of three words. Therefore, as Kanu (2017:23) explains, it can be employed as a word or used as a sentence: as a word, it is written as *Igwebuike,* and as a sentence, it is written as, *Igwe bu ike,* with the component words enjoying some form of spatial independence. According to Kanu, *Igwebuike* is anchored on the African world view. Kanu (2017:23), the apostle of *Igwebuike,* defines it as "the expressive modality of being in Igbo Ontology". For him, *Igwebuike,* which, according to Asouzu (2007:11) is literally *strength in togetherness,* is the locus of meeting of beings in Igbo communalist metaphysics, with special reference to existentialism and leadership. Onebunne (2020), in a paper titled *Belongingness as Igwebuike and African Philosophy: A Critical Relationship* (Unpublished), sees a crucial but necessary relationship between *Igwebuike* and belongingness. In developing the fundamental character of *Being as Belongingness,* however, Iroegbu (1996:45) initially defines belongingness as *a definitive principle in African communalism.* He used belongingness as a principle of membership applied to a given community. This membership is not a mere identification, but a kind of belonging that is security-assured. In this understanding, belongingness implies the basic commonness that makes a community a community, and in our context, it is what makes a given African community as such. This feeling of belonging is a basic need and a unique term in the dynamics of living and existence. Hence, Iroegbu (1995:19) asserts that "belongingness makes sure that all belong and none is marginalized, both contributively (duties and responsibilities) and distributively (sharing of communal cake)". This is the locus of *Igwebuike* at play. One does not necessarily belong. One is ever conscious of where one is putting up or belonging. Continuing, one can therefore appreciate *Belongingness as Igwebuike;* hence, they are being characterized by a common origin, common worldview, common language, shared culture, shared race, colour and habits, common historical experience and a common destiny. The communal-individuality of the African life is expressed in the Igbo-African proverb: *Ngwere ghara ukwu osisi, aka akparaya* (If a lizard stays off from the foot of a tree, it would be caught); *Otu osisi anaghi emebe ohia* (A tree does not make a forest); *Gidigidi bu ugwueze* (The dignity of a king is the number of his supportive followers); *Mmetuko ahu bu utondu* (The beauty of life is in mixing up with others). Mbiti (1970:108) has classically proverbialized the community by determining role of the individual when he wrote, *I am because we are and since we are, therefore I am.* This would mean that the confidence of being is because others are in being. The existence of others assures me of their solidarity and complementarity without which I cannot be. Achebe (1958:133) brings the essential nature of the Igbo-African communal relationship to a higher and more fundamental focus when he wrote:

> A man who calls his kinsmen to a feast does not do so to save them from starving. They all have food in their own homes. When we gather together in the moonlight village ground it is not because of the moon. Everyman can see it in his own compound. We come together because it is good for kinsmen to do so.

The community in question is ever guided by principles which, of course, are the hallmark of personal actions of the individual persons. Hence, the individual person in *Igwebuike* has a defined responsibility within a defined group that opts for it. Such is the thrust of African ethics, guiding the operations of *Igwebuike* in a *communal state*. The full understanding of this kind of relationship is properly expressed in the meaning of community and or a state, as already referred to above as *communal state*. Maritain (1951:2), however, maintains that "both community and society are ethico-social and truly human, not mere biological realities". As a consequence, therefore, if they are truly human and more real Africans, they need a moral principle and should be under moral obligation as well as have a practice of African value system as the cardinal points of African ethics.

These cardinal practices are regarded as African way of life, at least, in pristine and still in modern African societies and groups. Such cardinal acts are more of communalistic in nature. This understanding underlines the key characteristics of a human *communal state*, namely: mutual participation, social relationship, fellowship and equal sharing of certain fundamental rights, origin (root), good or orientation in the community. It entails sharing a defined locality and communality, which are often expressed in the concept of a nation as people from the same root, *natus*. Many will refer to this form of communal nature as mere communalism as such. According to Ekennia (1998: 348), the idea of communalism expressed in a *communal state* "refers to social relationship, fellowship, socialites, organized society. It invokes obligingness". In our popular parlance and understanding, it invokes belongingness. Belongingness has been identified as an ontological abstract term that specifies that a human person is because he belongs within the *communal state*. A human person, as the primary subject of African ethics, displays and defines himself more in belongingness. Belongingness, in this understanding, is the propulsive move of a human person to perfect himself so as to operate within an environment, a kind of *communal state*. Onebunne (2019a:2) expatiates on this idea of belongingness, thus:

> Belongingness is a fundamental quality in understanding being. No being can be understood in terms of its completeness but in its relation to other beings, defining itself through other beings. Every being is defined by a relation, that is, a being is in relation to something, or with an attribute of engaging in something. And this fact of *beingness*, which is a form of relation, is a form of

belonging to, belonging with, and belonging in. Relation, therefore, becomes a kind of state by which being realizes itself among others and others within it.

Belongingness, to this extent, concretizes one in existence in relation to others within the spatial temporality like the *communal state*. The *communal state* in question is understood as a nexus of inter-relational relationship for human actions and interactions, that is, existence in the broadest perception. *Igwebuike*, nevertheless, becomes a practical expression of communal interaction and responsibility in this *communal state*, since it is the basis for a communal life that demands a just ordered and well-organized society as African ethics demands and opines.

CONCEPT OF *IGWEBUIKE*

Igwebuike is the action of human beings as an entity. It is the modality of human beings. In our context, and as a concept, *Igwebuike* is the African mode of human beings' style of belonging in African communalistic metaphysics and socio-political philosophy. Therefore, it is the *actus humanus* of a being to belong within a communal setting. It is the mode of any and every reality as such in African philosophy. Kanu (2017:1) was clear in placing *Igwebuike* at the hub of African philosophical enterprise on which many African institutions and societal interactions are built. It is, therefore, the background to meaningful communal interaction and significant existence. Hence, there are values of *Igwebuike*, for Kanu, A. They are in its complementary character, solidarity form, unitary nature and concordance style. *Igwebuike* is an Igbo word, which is a combination of three words. Therefore, it can be employed as a word or used as a sentence: as a word, it is written as *Igwebuike*, and as a sentence, it is written as, *Igwe bu ike*, with the component words enjoying some independence in terms of space. The three words involved: *Igwe* is a noun, which means number or population, usually a huge number or population. *Bu* is a verb, which means *is*. *Ike* is another verb, which means strength or power. Thus, put together, it means 'Number is strength' or 'Number is power'. It was employed by Igbo traditional philosophers as a theory based on an illustrative statement to teach that when human beings come together in solidarity and complementary relationship, they are powerful or can constitute an insurmountable force to express their world of relationship, harmony, continuality and balance. At this level, no task is beyond their collective capability. This provides an ontological horizon that presents human beings as that which possess relational character of mutual interest. As an ideology, *Igwebuike* argues that t*o be* is to live in solidarity and harmony, and to live outside the parameters of complementary solidarity is to suffer alienation. *To be* is to be with the other, in a community of human beings. This is based on the African sense of community, which is the underlying principle and unity of African philosophy. *Igwebuike* philosophy is, therefore, sourced from the proper and professional but critical interpretation of the African world view and praxis, with regard to their thoughts and culture mostly embedded in the African orature. This, to a large extent, has to do with the African myths, folklore, symbols, proverb and songs.

PERSON

The concept of person, with its root in Latin as *persona* and in Greek as *prosopon* meaning *mask* or *disguising,* explains concretely the human being, often the man. Sacred Scripture was apt to acknowledge that *Man*, a living thing, is a creature of God with body and soul, made in the image and likeness of God (cf. Gen. 1²⁶ff). Man was created by the immediate hand of God, and is generically different from all other creatures. His complex nature is composed of two elements, two distinct substances, viz: body and soul. The Scriptures, nevertheless, appreciate man based on the Hebrew word *'Adam,* used as the proper name of the first man. Hence, the first man was called Adam because he was formed from the red earth (cf. Gen.1-8). The name is derived from a word meaning *to be red.* It is also the generic name of the human race. Its equivalents are the Latin *homo* and the Greek *anthropos.* The Hebrew *'ish'* denotes also man in opposition to *woman, h'isha.* Equally, human evolution has it that human beings have common *ancestorship* with the apes, the chimpanzees, as characterized by a number of morphological, developmental, physiological constituents and behavioural changes unto the moment of *homo erectus,* irrespective of the discovery of the much-lauded missing link of man's ancestry. It was Charles Darwin's 1958 publication on *The Origin of Species* which, according to Bowden (1991: x), "provided evidence to show how the very diverse animals now existing had evolved from earlier primitive life over a long period of time". This is the beginning of the great controversial theory of human evolution, which is the evolutionary process that led to the emergence of anatomically modern humans, beginning with the evolutionary history of primates—in particular, *genus Homo*—and leading to the emergence of *Homo sapiens* as a distinct species of the hominid family, the great apes. Amidst these theories of human evolution, Pierre Teihard *de* Chardin's *Hominization,* in line with *the becoming of man,* along with *the crossing the threshold of reflection,* culminating in his *omega point, is* against the mere physical science that man is not uniquely man but *ape-man.* According to Lewis (1969:3), "scientists generally accept the fact that human beings evolved from ape-like ancestors". Scientific human evolution based on evidence from comparative anatomy, paleontology and embryology and as a result of mutation, adaptation and natural selection acknowledges man as human person, that is *homo sapiens, homo faber, homo loquens,* and a *homo cogitans.* All these definitional concepts differentially define the human person as a rational animal than an animal with instinctual nature.

In the words of Mondin (1985:243), "historically the word *person* marks the line of demarcation between pagan and Christian culture…until the advent of Christianity, there did not exist, either in Greek or in Latin, a word to express the concept of a person, because in pagan culture such a concept did not exist, these cultures did not recognize the absolute value of the individual as such, and made their absolute value depend essentially on class rank, wealth and race." Mondin (1985: 256) continuing, gave an authoritative definition of a person, thus, "the person can be defined as a subsistent gifted with self-consciousness, communication and self transcendence." Isaka Seme was one of the first western-educated Africans to challenge the European colonialism and malevolent explorations then sweeping across the continental

Africa. In 1906, however, he addressed the Royal African Society in London. Below is the excerpt from his speech titled *Regeneration of Africa*:

> Man, the crowning achievement of nature, defies analysis. He is a mystery through all ages and for all time. The races of mankind are composed of free and unique individuals. An attempt to compare them on the basis of equality can never be finally satisfactory. Each is self.

The speech was an epoch-making event that woke up the Europeans to the fact that Africans are human beings as a result of their human personhood. Their personality gives them the title of a human person with defined rights and responsibility. He reminded them that the years of slavery, yokes of dehumanization of Africans as mere object and plundering of Africa are over. Africa, therefore, must be *regenerated* as they have *degenerated* it. The starting of course is the recognition that *the races of mankind are composed of free and unique individuals* as African persons as such.

AFRICAN PERSON

African persons are people who are native to Africa, descendants of natives of Africa, or individuals who trace their ancestry to indigenous inhabitants of Africa. This person in question enjoys the quality of a human person and, added to that, the singular privilege of being culture-bound. Africanity, therefore, becomes another defining character and peculiar value amidst other continents and comity of nations in the new world order. An African person is a human person with African *weltanschauung* as a basic background.

Continental Africa has lot of possibilities, in spite of the rare privilege of Africa being the cradle of ancient civilization and mother of civilization of all civilizations. As Oguejiofor (2001:24) puts it: "the African continent was also host to ancient civilizations such as Egypt, Kush, Napata and Meroe, Nubia and Axum. When these had had their days, the continent kept pace with the rest of the world". The contemporary and renewed continuation of the scramble for Africa, after the much-lauded *independence* and *end to open slavery*, leaves every good-thinking man with a lot of questions, with regard to Africa's coming of age *to be* (amidst the inherent racism and resurgence of white supremacy). The beauty of Africa, as PLO Mulumba would alert, makes Africa still attractive to the *West* and the rest of the world. This attractiveness is very much seen and exceptionally dependent both on the human and natural resources within the African continent. Explaining further, PLO Mulumba said:

> When I look at Africa and see how attractive she is, one word comes to mind globalization. When they talk about globalization, they talk about it as if it were new. Africans were once globalized as a commodity in the slave market, we were sold everywhere in the world, that was globalization. Then we were

globalized again through colonization. Then, again, through neo-colonization. Now we are being globalised again in the context of opening our markets: It was Julius Nyerere who in many of his enlightened moments said, "We should open our markets in the name of globalization and they say that the rules are the same." "I laugh," he said. Then he went on to say, "it's like a boxing match, the rules are the same but you don't put a heavyweight boxer with a lightweight boxer in the same ring and say the rules are the same, it's murder.

The African person, therefore, is appreciated more from the context that human beings are the centre of all reality, based on the fact that human life, from the ethical point of view, is of primary value. Mondin (1985:25) puts it thus: "of all the forms of human action, the most elementary and fundamental one, and the one which at the same time emerges as the most complex and rich with content, is life." Human life, not animal life, nor plant life, therefore, places the human person as the locus of creation and created things. This is why human life is a primary value. It is the value of all values, and without it, no other value is valuable. Human life, therefore, vivifies the human person and as a consequence the African person. As Iroegbu (1994:136) rightly puts it, "there is in African anthropology an anthropocentricism that is nonetheless a humanism and an integralism." An African person, therefore, has a holistic personality that is very dynamic and exceedingly unique, in line with the Shakespearean (Hamlet, Act II, Scene II) descriptive exaltation of man, thus:

> What a piece of work is man! How noble in reason! How infinite in faculty! In form and moving how express and admirable! In action how like an Angel! In apprehension how like a god! The beauty of the world! The paragon of animals!

The African person, therefore, is fundamentally culture-bound and communally understood and appreciated. This is the background knowledge of a person through the sense of extended family system and super hunger for human interaction. The African person of the 21st century unfortunately must once again be liberated from the shackles of structural imperialism, racial discrimination and white supremacy. Back then in 1906, Isaka Seme daringly spoke boldly fearless, thus:

> By this term regeneration I wish to be understood to mean the entrance into a new life, embracing the diverse phases of a higher, complex existence. The basic factor which assures their regeneration resides in the awakened race consciousness. This gives them a clear perception of their elemental needs and of their underdeveloped powers. It therefore must lead them to the attainment of that higher and advanced standard of life.

Concluding, Isaka Seme was vehement in addressing the issue of reviving Africa from all forms of mis-educated and misguided ideas imported into Africa. He was blunt against the carting away of what they branded *blackishly evil* and *despicably demonized*. A civilization

117

they *wickedly denounced*, yet they cherished to covertly import and appropriate them. Seme, however, concluded thus:

> The regeneration of Africa means that a new and unique civilization is soon to be added to the world. The African is not a proletarian in the world of science and art: he has precious creations of his own—of ivory; of copper and of gold; of fine, plaited willow-ware; and weapons of superior workmanship. Civilization resembles an organic being in its development—it is born, it perishes, and it can propagate itself. More particularly, it resembles a plant; it takes root in the teeming earth, and when the seeds fall in other soils, new varieties sprout up. The most essential departure of this new civilization is that it shall be thoroughly spiritual and humanistic-indeed, a regeneration moral and eternal.

FREEDOM AND RESPONSIBILITY

Rousseau's renowned phrase, in his *Social Contract,* is that *man is born free, but he is everywhere in chains.* With this form of *chained freedom,* he asserts his exalted idea of the contemporary nature of humanity. This chained freedom, nevertheless, suppresses the basic expression of freedom that is our birthright and is absolute against every natural instinct that is mere animalistic, and for this reason, man enters into civil society with every duty and responsibility. It is, therefore, freedom in *responsibility*. It is freedom that is accounted for and such is a responsible freedom. It has to do with the ability to respond as need be in the cause of exercising free actions. You are free to the extent you can account for it. This is responsibility. It is freedom in responsibility. Freedom to this extent is duty-bound. In this is basic understanding that *man is free but everywhere in chains,* according to J. P. Sartre. Man is free as long as his freedom respects others' free acts. Man is free within boundaries. This is a limited freedom. This is the fundamental idea behind *freedom to* and *freedom from.*

The concept of freedom is from the Latin word, *libertas,* and the Greek word, *eleutheria,* both of which indicate a condition of independence, a kind of autonomy, a form of self-determination. Freedom is the liberty, license or ability to do something. It is a rational concept reflecting an inalienable human right to realize one's human will in form of freedom to and freedom from. Freedom, according to online Webster's Dictionary, is the quality or state of being free: such as (a): the absence of necessity, coercion, or constraint in choice or action, (b): liberation from slavery or restraint or from the power of another: independence, (c): the quality or state of being exempt or released usually from something onerous.

The word, *freedom,* therefore, stands for something greater than just the right to act in whichever way one wishes to act. It also stands for securing to everyone an equal opportunity to life, emancipation, and the pursuit of happiness. Freedom is a term which is synonymous with liberty. It has been a point of deliberation among various epochs of philosophy in both ethical and political circles. A man is said to be free to the extent that he can choose his goals or the course of his conduct, without being compelled to act as he would not himself choose to act. It is the absence of the imposition of one's will by any other authority or power. Karl Jasper is reputed for his philosophy of freedom which he considers not free but gained. According to Jasper (1959: 32), "freedom is not absolute; it is always bound at the same time. I do not have it, I gain it." The exercise of freedom in real practice, at the long, necessitates a kind of limit to what an individual does in a community. The whole idea is about the place of African ethics in a community.

AFRICAN ETHICS

Ethics, western ethics to be precise, deals with the moral value of human actions and decency of human behaviour against all forms of animality. The human actions and behaviour, by this understanding, must be accounted for as long as one confronts confusing but decisive moments in living out his daily experience on what is right or bad and what ought to be done or not. From this ethical appreciation, one moves unto traditional African ethics. Traditional ethics has to do with norms, precepts, doctrines, principles and moral codes, which regulate the conduct and actions of individuals in African societies. Kanu (2015:166) confirms that "traditional African Societies had had their traditional ethics". Traditional, however, informs African ethics as it tries to maintain and ensure social order and stability in conventional African societies. African ethics is a realistic and pragmatic philosophy that involves and engages the African person with regard to limits of freedom and, as a result, his responsibility in a communal engagement. African ethics is a main branch of African philosophy. It is a practical philosophy which, according to Maritain (2005:177), "is for the good man". Iroegbu (1994: 136), defines African ethics, thus:

> This is a horizontal aspect of metaphysics and the consequence of epistemology. Ethics in African Philosophy has been argued to be independent of religion. To this we say *Yes and No*. While God does not directly determine all moral norms, the fear of God makes the realization of those norms effective.

Ethics, as a branch of practical philosophy, deals directly with human actions in relation to others. However, philosophers today usually divide ethical theories into three general subject areas: meta-ethics, normative ethics and applied ethics. Stanford Online dictionary, however, gave a general descriptive definition of Ethics thus:

> The ethics of a society is embedded in the ideas and beliefs about what is right or wrong, what is a good or bad character; it is also embedded in the conceptions of satisfactory social relations and attitudes held by the members of the society; it is embedded, furthermore, in the forms or patterns of behavior that are considered by the members of the society to bring about social harmony and cooperative

living, justice, and fairness. The ideas and beliefs about moral conduct are articulated, analyzed, and interpreted by the moral thinkers of the society.

Here, we see the difference between morality (that is value) and religious innuendoes (nuances of belief), as regards the fear of God. It is all about the question of the defining differential nuances between moral instruction and religious education. Onebunne and Alike (2017) reiterate that "religion and morality are not synonymous. Religion and morality are concepts whose conceptual relationships are expressed between religious views and informed conduct of morals…Morality does not necessarily depend upon religion". However, African ethics is all about value, rather than religious belief. Over the years, Stanford Online Dictionary offers that "African societies, as organized and functioning human communities, have undoubtedly evolved ethical systems—ethical values, principles, rules—intended to guide social and moral behaviour". Hence, there are outstanding African values which are the thrust of African ethics; they include: respect for the sacredness of human life, extended family system, large family system, industry, hard work, respect for senior members of the society, religion, value for private property, language, to mention but a few. African ethics, therefore, has to do with the conduct and action of the human person within a specified community. Maritain (2005:173) maintains that, "Ethics is as practical to any true science in the strict sense can be, for it teaches not only the most general rules of remote applications but also the particular rules applicable to the particular action to be performed." It has the good of man in every explicit term by defining what is right and determining what is wrong.

In spite of the progress already made in science and technology amidst *transvaluation* of values and disparagement of the fundamentals of African culture and the threat of monoculture via globalization, an African man is still very conscious of his root and identity as an African. An African man by nature is morally conscious of his attitude, especially within the community. Hence, he lives on the pretext of what community identity offers, approves or disapproves. The communal life often determines the African man with the spirit of extended family system already in practice.

African ethics is African morality. It is the African value. It has to do with African value system, with regard to the norms and morality of the African human person's right or bad conduct within the community of persons. It is the *modus operandi* as well as the *modus vivendum* of an African man as an African. African ethics is operational within the African world view which is holistic and encompassing. Hence, African ethics starts with the individual in the community and extends beyond that. Kanu (2015:170), explains it, thus, "the community in Africa survives on the contributions of individual endowments. " According to Bujo (2003:20), African ethics is "realized primarily by means of a relational network that is equally anthropocentric, cosmic and theocentric". From this, one discovers that African ethics is a kind of relationship with man at the centre in relation to *uwa* as a generic term that englobes all that is. *Uwa*, however, is the locus of operation for human living and necessary interaction. However, against other philosophers who have delved into philosophical excursus, Iroegbu was very rigorous in adopting from

Okere the uses of the concept of *uwa,* which is an Igbo word meaning *world.* For Iroegbu, *uwa* is the totality and fullness of being in its self expression. It is the theatre of activity for *being as belongingness.* To this view, Asouzu (2007:204) appreciates thus, that. "this ethnocentric flavour notwithstanding, what I find very positive in Iroegbu's use of the concept *Uwa,* is that this concept gives us some feelings concerning the comprehensiveness, totality and wholeness of reality itself; an understanding of reality quite in consonance with the teaching of traditional philosophers of the complementary system of thought". Through different mutual dynamics of relationship, the term, *uwa,* remains a universalising concept, respecting the boundaries of African ethics in any community living and interaction. Bujo (2003:20) further reiterates that "the main goal of African Ethics is fundamentally life itself. The community must guarantee the promotion and protection of life by specifying or ordaining ethics and morality."

IGWEBUIKE EXPRESSING AFRICAN ETHICS OF LIVING

Igwebuike is a *lived out* principle of participation. The concept of *Igwebuike* expresses concretely the African ethics of living. Something, of course, is holding and binding them so as to form and be referred to as *Igwebuike.* There is an underlying fact or rightly put, a guiding principle of operation. *Igwebuike* is a practical expression of communal attitude with underlying guidance, based on the value system of the people, and in our context, African value system. *Igwebuike* specifically spells out the communal strength that is exerted in moments of communal need in order to execute or achieve a feat. Such communal enterprise, nevertheless, is within specified principles as African ethics.

It is the individuals that actually make up the population that is identified and empowered as such as Igwebuike. These individual persons are very conscious of their individuality and responsibility towards the other and the community in general as a result of their free will to associate and relate as such. Bujo (:114) explains that "it must be recalled that African Ethics does not define the person as self-realization or as ontological act; rather, it describes the person as a process of coming into existence in the reciprocal relatedness of individual and community...." There is a collective responsibility that is rightly translated as *Igwebuike* in this context.

Personal responsibility succinctly defines a response-able person. That is, an individual who is capable of giving a response, albeit in every situation that demands so. Such idea of responsibility defines a permissible person, with regard to age and the expected accountability. This has to do with the idea that a human being is ever the architect of his ideas, with a status within the bounds of moral obligation. This is the border line of an African person as an individual in the *Igwebuike* crusade. Hence, the attended personal responsibility attunes one into the level of individual commitment which all congregating individuals are willing to make or sacrifice in setting clear goals needed for full responsibility in their achievement of the *Igwebuike* mandate. Bujo (2003:112) affirms accordingly that "the position of the individual and the community in ethical behaviour is very important". There must be a morally bottom line of action. The individual responsibility in question is as a result of the aggregates of acceptable single individual behaviour that is of course bordered on choice. However, Bujo (2003:115) explains further that:

> The individual becomes a person only through active participation in the life of the community. It is not membership in a community as such that constitutes the identity: only common action makes the human person a human person and keeps him from becoming an unfettered ego.

The community becomes a veritable ground for the true meaning and expression of the individual participation in and for the community based on *Igwebuike*. This is solidarity in the form of concrete expression of *Igwebuike*. Therefore, every form of interaction of the individual in the community is based on the needed solidarity. Bujo (2003:117) continues to buttress that "life in a community demands alertness and the maintenance of one's own individuality". Igwebuike, therefore, respects and recognizes the individual amidst other persons. Though *Igwebuike* thrives on the strength of the *Igwe* (number, population), yet it appreciates the *minor* individual, as well, the concrete contributions of each in strengthening the other are recognized.

A good understanding of the individual persons' response-ability, as well as the responsible freedom in a community, while expressing their appreciable solidarity in their best interest too, is what *Igwebuike* is all about. Part of the African value system is a well-defined relationship that is well spelt out on mutual interest and common good of all. *Igwebuike* is for the common good. *Igwebuike* is a unification of communal talents and possibilities harnessed for the general interest. Bye and large, such interest and communal expression must be under some guiding principles. This is what African ethics is all about.

CONCLUSION

Life is of primary value. According to Iroegbu (2000:179), "life is the highest, foundation and end-point of all values". The life in question, especially human life, is the locus of operation for the concepts like *Igwebuike* and African ethics in the exercise of freedom and practice of responsibility. However, Iroegbu (2000:182) buttresses this enduring fact, thus "every life has meaning. The highest meaning of life is to live for somebody, for something, for others, for society…making others alive". *Igwebuike* is possible as a result of the individual persons acting as a group within the bounds of peculiar moral guidance for the good of all in a communal setting. African ethics, however, is that value parameter that vivifies *Igwebuike* as the modality of human beings in the African community. Contemporary African philosophers have tried to give sustained reflective attention to the implementation of African ethics as it contributes to the understanding of the African human person. Through the African human person and

African language of morality expressed as such in the practise of *Igwebuike*, African ethics is given a prominent place through the individual's responsible freedom and responsibility. In the exercise of the communal effort, informed most probably by the spirit of *Igwebuike*, African ethics becomes the yardstick for the involved individuals.

REFERENCES

Achebe, C. *Things Fall Apart*. England: Heinemann. 1958

Asouzu, I.I (2007) *Ibuanyidanda: New Complementary Ontology*. Zurich: lit, Verlag GmbH & Co; Wien

Boweden, M. *Science vs Evolution*. Kent: Sovereign Publications. 1991.

Bujo, B. *Foundation of an African Ethic: Beyond the Universal Claims of Western Morality*. Nairobi: Paulines Publications Africa. 2003.

Ekennia, J. *African Communalism and Political Rationality: A Critique in African philosophy and public Affairs*. Enugu: Delta Publications, 1998.

Iroegbu, P. *Enwisdomization & African Philosophy*. Owerri: International Universities Press Ltd, 1994

Iroegbu, P., *Metaphysics: Kpim of Philosophy* (Owerri: International University Press), 1995.

Iroegbu, P. *Kpim of Politics: Communalism,* Owerri: International University Press. 1996

Iroegbu, P. *Kpim of Personality: Treatise on the Human Person*. Owerri: Eustel Pubs. 2000

Jaspers, K. *Philosophy Vol. 2 Trans*. New York: Chicago Press. 1959.

Kanu, A. *African Philosophy: An Ontologico-Existential Hermeneutic Approach to Classical and Contemporary Issues*. Awka: Fab-Anieh Ltd. 2015.

Kanu, I. A. *Igwebuike and Being in Igbo Ontology* in Igwebuike: An African Journal of Arts and Humanities. Vol. 4 No 5. [12-21]. 2017

Kanu, I. A "Sources of Igwebuike Philosophy: Towards A Socio-Cultural Foundation" Traditional African personality, Identity and Philosophy: Challenges and Ways Forward. 5thInternational Annual Conference of the Association of African Traditional Religion and Philosophy Scholars, 28th-30th June 2017, School of Postgraduate Studies Conference Hall, Nnamdi Azikiwe University, Awka Anambra State, Nigeria.

Kanu, I. A. (2014). *Igwebuikology* as an Igbo-African philosophy for Catholic-Pentecostal relations. *Jos Studies. 22. pp.*87-98.

Kanu, I. A. (2015b). *Igwebuike as an ontological precondition for African ethics.* International Conference of the Society for Research and Academic Excellence. University of Nigeria, Nsukka. 14th -16th September.

Kanu, I. A. (2015c). *Igwebuike as an Igbo-African philosophy of education.* A paper presented at the International Conference on Law, Education and Humanities. 25th -26th November 2015 University of Paris, France.

Kanu, I. A. (2016a). *Igwebuike* as an Igbo-African hermeneutics of globalisation. *IGWEBUIKE: An African Journal of Arts and Humanities,* Vol. 2 No.1. pp. 61-66.

Kanu, I. A. (2016a). *Igwebuike* as the consummate foundation of African Bioethical principles. *An African journal of Arts and Humanities* Vol.2 No1 June, pp.23-40.

Kanu, I. A. (2016b) *Igwebuike* as an expressive modality of being in African ontology. *Journal of Environmental and Construction Management. 6. 3.* pp.12-21.

Kanu, I. A. (2017). *Igwebuike* as an Igbo-African philosophy for Christian-Muslim relations in Northern Nigeria. In Mahmoud Misaeli (Ed.). *Spirituality and Global Ethics* (pp. 300-310). United Kingdom: Cambridge Scholars.

Kanu, I. A. (2017). *Igwebuike* as an Igbo-African philosophy for the protection of the environment. *Nightingale International Journal of Humanities and Social Sciences.* Vol. 3. No. 4. pp. 28-38.

Kanu, I. A. (2017). *Igwebuike* as the hermeneutic of individuality and communality in African ontology. *NAJOP: Nasara Journal of Philosophy.* Vol. 2. No. 1. pp. 162-179.

Kanu, I. A. (2017a). *Igwebuike* and question of superiority in the scientific community of knowledge. *Igwebuike: An African Journal of Arts and Humanities.* Vol.3 No1. pp. 131-138.

Kanu, I. A. (2017a). *Igwebuike as a philosophical attribute of Africa in portraying the image of life.* A paper presented at the 2017 Oracle of Wisdom International Conference by the Department of Philosophy, Tansian University, Umunya, Anambra State, 27-29 April.

Kanu, I. A. (2017b). *Igwebuike* as a complementary approach to the issue of girl-child education. *Nightingale International Journal of Contemporary Education and Research.* Vol. 3. No. 6. pp. 11-17.

Kanu, I. A. (2017b). *Igwebuike* as a wholistic response to the problem of evil and human suffering. *Igwebuike: An African Journal of Arts and Humanities.* Vol. 3 No 2, March.

Kanu, I. A. (2017e). *Igwebuike* as an Igbo-African modality of peace and conflict resolution. *Journal of African Traditional Religion and Philosophy Scholars. Vol. 1. No. 1. pp. 31-40.*

Kanu, I. A. (2017g). *Igwebuike* and the logic (Nka) of African philosophy. *Igwebuike: An African Journal of Arts and Humanities.* 3. 1. pp. 1-13.

Kanu, I. A. (2017h). *Igwebuike* philosophy and human rights violation in Africa. *IGWEBUIKE: An African Journal of Arts and Humanities.* Vol. 3. No. 7. pp. 117-136.

Kanu, I. A. (2017i). *Igwebuike* as a hermeneutic of personal autonomy in African ontology. *Journal of African Traditional Religion and Philosophy Scholars. Vol. 2. No. 1. pp. 14-22.*

Lewis, J. *Anthropology Made Simple.* Great Britain: Richard Clay (the Chancer Press) Ltd. 1969.

Maritain, J. *Man and the State.* Chicago: University of Chicago Press, 1951

Maritain, J., *An Introduction to Philosophy,* London: Continuum, 2005

Mbiti, J. S. African *Religion and Philosophy.* London: Heinemann. 1969.

Mondin, B. *A history of Medieval Philosophy.* India: Theological Pub.1991

Onebunne, J.I., *Being as Belongingness: Expanding the Hermeneutics of African Metaphysics of To Be,* Awka: Fab Anieh Nig Ltd,. 2019a

Onebunne, J. & Alike, M. *Religious and or Moral Education: In Search for a Critically Defining Difference* in Ejikemeuwa J.O. & Ejikeme, P.O. (eds). Society and Human Development: Essays in Honour of J.B. Akam. NG: Bobpecco Pub. 2017. p. 335-353.

Online Webster's Dictionary, https://www.merriam-webster.com/dictionary/freedom. Retrieved 04/07/2020

Shakespeare, W. *Hamlet,* Act II, Scene II

Stanford Online Dictionary, https://plato.stanford.edu/entries/african-ethics/. Retrieved 10/07/2020

Seme, I. https://www.blackpast.org/global-african-history/1906-isaka-seme-regeneration-africa/. Retrieved on 04/07/2020

IGWEBUIKE IDEOLOGY AND MARTIN BUBER'S I-THOU THEORY: TOWARDS A MODEL FOR AUTHENTIC EXISTENCE

Ejikemeuwa J. O. NDUBISI, PhD
Department of Philosophy and Religious Studies,
Tansian University, Umunya, Anambra State, Nigeria
ejikon4u@yahoo.com

EXECUTIVE SUMMARY

Our contemporary society is such that emphasizes individualism. There is less emphasis on interpersonal relationship. Many people tend to live and behave as though they do not need the other. Today, there is high rate of frustration, hopelessness, suicide actions and rejections among the young and the old. In this regard, this paper burdens itself with a phenomenological inquiry into the existential problem of human interaction. It states that both Igwebuike ideology and the I – Thou theory are geared towards an authentic human existence. This study argues that the human person can only authenticate his/her existence as a social being when he/she collaborates with the other in a relationship that is hinged on openness, reciprocity, trust, sincerity, truth, mutuality, respect for the other, justice, among others. It, therefore, submits that the overemphasis on the 'I' cannot bring about an authentic human existence and, as such, our contemporary society needs to understand and appreciate this model for an authentic human existence as derived from the Igwebuike *ideology and Buber's I – Thou theory.*

Keywords: Igwebuike Ideology, Kanu, I-Thou, Buber, Human relation

INTRODUCTION

Experience has shown that the issue of interpersonal relationship has been the concern of many philosophers and thinkers. Philosophers, such as Aristotle, Aquinas, Kierkegaard, Gabriel Marcel, Heidegger, Levinas, Nietzsche, Ozumba, Nyerere, among others, have written volumes on human relationship. One thing that is clear in the submissions of most philosophers and thinkers mentioned above is that the human person is a being that cannot but interact with others; the human person is a relational being.

Emphasizing the importance of human relationship, Aristotle (1953) argued that it is not possible for a human person to live without friends (p. 258). This explains the existential fact that the human person is a social being. Existentialists affirm that the human person is a being-with-others. The nature of the human person is that of relationship with the other. One cannot actually see one's face without the aid of a mirror; and as such, it can be said that one cannot actually know oneself or discover oneself fully without the other. In the view of Kaitholil (2001), a human being is said to be more human when he interacts with others (p. 13). The implication here is that without interaction, a particular human person becomes less human.

In our contemporary society, experience has shown that there is much emphasis on individualism. Some people tend to believe that they are comfortable without relating with others. This, among others, has constituted a serious threat to the essential aspect of the human person as a being-with-others. Today, suicide is on the increase; family relation is being crushed; frustration and hopelessness have become the order of the day. The pertinent question now is: How can a human person live a meaningful life without interacting or relating with others? In an attempt to address this and other related questions, this study is set to phenomenologically analyze the *Igwebuike* Ideology from Igbo-African perspective, especially as championed by Professor Kanu, and also Buber's theory of I-Thou relationship. The paper begins with a basic understanding of the *Igwebuike* ideology and a brief exposition of Buber's I–Thou theory. It further presents the *Igwebuike* ideolog and the I–Thou theory as a model for an authentic human existence in our contemporary society, and thereafter ends with a conclusion.

THE UNDERSTANDING OF THE *IGWEBUIKE* IDEOLOGY

The power of effectively pulling forces together to achieve a common goal cannot be undermined or overemphasized. There is always stronger and unquenchable strength in unity. The Igbo adage has it that a single broom can easily be broken, but when they are united as a bundle of broom, it then becomes very difficult, if not impossible, to break. This understanding is the brain behind the Igbo-African ideology of *Igwebuike*. The notion of *Igwebuike* hinges on the existential fact that 'united we stand, but divided we fall'. Ndubisi (2019) opines that *Igwebuike* is an all-embracing ideology and as such, it "captures the philosophical, religious, political, economic and social life of the African people" (p.142). As a concept, *Igwebuike* is derived from three Igbo words: *Igwe bu ike*. This Igbo expression can be understood as 'strength in number', strength in many' or 'power in multitude'. In this regard, one can say that *Igwebuike* has to do with synergy in human relationship.

It is important to note at this point that the contemporary understanding and usage of *Igwebuike* in African discourse was popularized by Professor Ikechukwu Anthony Kanu, a renowned contemporary African scholar. Kanu (2016a) explains that "when human beings come together in solidarity and complementarity, they are powerful or can constitute an insurmountable force. At this level, no task is beyond their collaborative capacity" (p.3). The point here is that *Igwebuike*, as an ideology, underscores the existential reality that a part can never be bigger than a whole. It hinges on the need for a cordial interrelationship and interaction among human beings. Kanu (2016a) further explains:

> As an ideology, Igwebuike rests on the African principles of solidarity and complementarity. It argues that 'to be' is to live in solidarity and complementarity and to live outside that parameters of solidarity and complementarity is to suffer alienation. 'To be' is 'to be with the other' in a community of beings. This is based on the African philosophy of harmony and complementarity, which is the underlying principle and unity of African Traditional Religious and Philosophical experience (p. 3).

The above citation amplifies the understanding of *Igwebuike* as an ideology. One thing to note here is that *Igwebuike* is an ideology of togetherness; it is an ideology that tends to unite the views and ingenuity of people to achieve a common goal. *Igwebuike* is a philosophy of complementarity and solidarity. Experience has shown that every human person needs the other in order to survive or to make meaning in life. Kanu, as cited in Ogbaki (2019), avers that *Igwebuike* has to do with sharing. He relates:

> Igwebuike as a complementary philosophy understands life as a shared reality. And it is only within the context of complementarity that life makes meaning. Life is a life of sharedness. One in which another is part thereof. A relationship, though of separate and separated entities or individuals but with a joining of the same whole. It is a relationship in which case the two or more coming together make each a complete whole; it is a diversity of being one with the other … if the other is my part or a piece of me, it means that I need him for me to be complete, for me to be what I really am. The other completes rather than diminishes me. His language and culture make my own stand out and at the same time, they enrich and complement my own (Kanu as cited in Ogbaki, 2019, p. 170).

The above reflection pictures the existential and complementary nature of *Igwebuike*. The ideology presupposes that no one is actually complete without the other. In a musical parlance, it is said that a particular music is melodious when all the musical instruments and voices are harmonized together. Without the harmonization of the instruments and voices, it will be very difficult to perceive the melody of the particular music. One thing we must note is that "Kanu's perception of Igwebuike is such that is all-embracing: it is a philosophy of inclusiveness" (Ndubisi, 2019, p 143). In this regard, Kanu affirms that *Igwebuike*, as an ideology, is the Igbo-African search for meaning in all spheres of life (Kanu 2016b, p.5; Kanu 2017, p. 9). The Igbo-African, in particular, and the human person, in general, can only find meaning in life through the proper understanding and application of the *Igwebuike* ideology. For sure, no man is an island. The *Igwebuike* ideology, as understood and championed by Kanu, sees complementarity as the fundamental requirement for human existence. For one "to live outside the parameters of solidarity and complementarity is to suffer alienation" (Kanu 2016a, p.3). It, therefore, follows that the authentic human existence can be understood and achieved in the other. Aliba (2019) corroborates: "In Igwebuike, co-relating with each other is an essential part of survival because it aids mutual understanding and co-existence. This gives the idea that whatever happens to an individual person affects the community" (p. 163). Onebunne (2019) relates the *Igwebuike* ideology to belongingness. He argues that *Igwebuike* ideology is expressed in the philosophy of belongingness. Every human person belongs to each other; every human person depends on the other in order to survive. He strongly argues that it is the "experience of life that gave recourse to the idea of complementarity as a measure to survive the challenges posed by other vicissitudes of life. Inter-dependence, inter-relationship, collectivism and mutual co-existence form the basis for Igbo life pattern as expressed in Igwebuike and Belongingness: the metaphysics of effective communal relationship" (p. 71).

One thing that is clear is that the *Igwebuike* ideology is at the heart of Igbo-African understanding of reality; it explains how the Igbo-African relates to reality within and around him. It can be seen as the totality of African pPhilosophy, religion and socio-political experiences.

Following the nature of this study and also having given the basic understanding of the *Igwebuike* ideology, the next subtopic shall focus on Martin Buber's theory of I-Thou relationship.

I – THOU THEORY IN MARTIN BUBER: A BRIEF EXPOSÉ

It was in 1923 that Martin Buber wrote his famous essay, *Ich und Du* (I and Thou). It is in this work that he expressed his doctrine of I–Thou relation as the mode of human existence. Buber explained that there are two modes of encountering the world, namely, I–Thou and I–It. He used these two modes to explain interpersonal relationship in the world. One can relate to things in the world as either persons (Thou) or as objects (It) (Buber, 1958; Buber, 1968; Buber, 1970). The understanding of the I–Thou relationship, according to Buber as cited in Okonkwo (2014), is that of "a relationship of mutuality, openness, recognition, directness, reciprocity and above all presence. It is a relationship in which the whole being of an individual is engaged in an unassuming relationship with the other" (p.21). One important thing to note about Buber's notion of I–Thou is that it is essentially a relationship of mutuality. It is such a relationship where mutual relationship among human beings is enthroned. In this type of relationship, the particular human person only discovers himself/herself f not in relation to himself/herself, but in relation to others. This, for Buber, is possible when individualism is removed and mutuality is emphasized.

More so, Buber maintained that the I–Thou relation is possible in an atmosphere of openness. Both the 'I' and the 'Thou' must be open to each other. The fact is that the other can only exist for me, and I exist for the other when there is openness. This type of openness is devoid of deception. Buber remarked that the I–Thou relation is devoid of any prejudice or pre-conceived ideas. Any form of prejudice, according to Buber, constitutes a barrier to I–Thou relation (Buber, 1958, p. 11).

Another important element in I–Thou relation, as conceived by Buber, is reciprocity. This understanding entails a mutual response of individuals to the actions of the other. There is no intention whatsoever of individual in I–Thou relationship to gain from the other. As soon as a person sets goals or objectives to be achieved prior to the relationship, there can be no mutuality because one's intention in the relationship would be to realize an objective which is very often at the expense of the other. In this regard, I–Thou is seen as mutual relationship and not a parasitic or exploitative type of relationship (Buber, 1970, p.115).

It is important to note that Buber's strong position is that no one can be fully human without experiencing the other, the world around him/her and also God. It follows that these tripartite expressions constitute, for Buber, the essential elements for one to be fully human and to experience an authentic existence. Furthermore, another important thing to note in Buber's position is that the doctrine of I–Thou is not only related to other human beings alone; it also relates to things (I- It) and the Eternal Thou (God). This means that the particular human person can find meaning in life as he/she relates with other human beings, the environment and God. Buber argues that I–It relationship is very essential as it helps the human person to develop and accumulate knowledge. He explains: "The primary relation of man to the world of *It* is comprised in experiencing, which continually reconstitutes the world, and using, which leads the world to its manifold aim, the sustaining, relieving and equipping of human life" (Buber, 1958, p. 38). As the individual relates with the *Thou* and the *It,* there remains the *third* party, which Buber called the *Eternal Thou (God).* It is the relationship with the *Eternal Thou* that helps to authenticate one's existence. In sum, Buber's relational mode for authentic existence is manifested in a triad relation: I–Thou, I–It and I–Eternal Thou. This is a kind of existential relationship that is required for a harmonious interpersonal relationship (Koyeli and Roy, 2002, p. 192).

IGWEBUIKE IDEOLOGY AND BUBER'S I–THOU THEORY: A MODEL FOR AUTHENTIC EXISTENCE

So far, we have been able to discuss the *Igwebuike* ideology as propounded by Kanu and also presented a highlight of Buber's I–Thou theory. One thing that is clear is that both the *Igwebuike* ideology and the I–Thou theory are geared towards an authentic human existence. The human person can only authenticate his/her existence as a social being when he/she collaborates with the other. The overemphasis on the 'I' cannot bring about an authentic existence. The human person, in the light of this study, is required to move beyond the 'I' in order to have meaningful relationship with the other. It is in a relationship with the other that life can be said to be meaningful to an individual person. This explains the reason this present study argues that both the *Igwebuike* ideology and Buber's I–Thou theory can be seen as a model for an authentic human existence, especially in our contemporary society that is carried away by individualism and scientism.

It is an existential truism that no human person or anything at all can be said to be absolutely useless. And so, a particular individual can gain from another individual when they engage in a relationship. As a model for an authentic human existence, it means that the Igwebuike ideology and the I–Thou theory emphasize the essential character of complementarity. In a society such as Nigeria, it should be noted that all of us need the other in order to experience an authentic human existence as Nigerians. There is something in an Igbo person that the Hausa person needs; there is also something in the Yoruba person that the Tiv person or the Fulani person needs. This is an existential fact! No person, tribe or nation can exist in isolation; there is always the need for complementarity.

One important thing to note is that the emphasis on *Igwebuike* and/or Buber's I–Thou theory does not in any way negate individual differences, choices and interests. It means that individuals in a relationship have to work together to achieve a common goal. Without working to achieve a common goal, it will be difficult, if not impossible, to achieve anything or derive meaning in life. Uzukwu (2019) discusses the importance of the Igwebuike ideology, thus: "The social, economic, political, religious, physical and gender differences of the members [of a particular society] are important for the varieties of contributions and as well as the proportionate strength of the group" (p. 145). The implication of Uzukwu's position is that the strength of economic growth, peaceful coexistence, political stability, etc., that is observed in a particular society is highly dependent on the level of synergy or collaboration experienced in that particular society.

CONCLUSION

The *Igwebuike* ideology and Buber's I–Thou theory constitute, in the view of this study, a model for an authentic existence. No one can claim to live for oneself alone. There is no way an individual's history can be written without reference to the 'thou'. Authentic existence implies living in solidarity, collaboration, synergy and complementarity with other human beings. There is always the essential need to foster a common ground for human relationship. As Aliba (2019) avers: "Human association remains an inalienable aspect of our human nature. The human person as a being, is not independent, but rather needs the other to foster his own existence" (p.163).

The fact is that human relationship is inevitable and very essential for an authentic human existence. This relationship, to achieve its goal, in the light of the *Igwebuike* ideology and Buber's I–Thou theory, should be hinged on openness, reciprocity, trust, sincerity, truth, mutuality, respect for the other, justice, among others. It should be devoid of deceit, bias, inferiority or superiority complex, objectifying the other, using the other simply as a means to an end and not as an end in itself, etc. Our contemporary society needs to understand and appreciate this model for authentic human existence as derived from the *Igwebuike* ideology and Buber's I–Thou theory.

REFERENCES

Aliba, S. I. (2019). "A Comparative Study of Igwebuike Philosophy and Ujamaa: Towards a Common Brotherhood". *Journal of African Studies and Sustainable Development, Vol. 2, No. 4.* Pp. 156- 165.

Aristotle (1953). *The Nichomachean Ethics.* J. A. K. Thomson, trans. London: George Allen and Unwin.

Buber, M. (1958). *I – Thou.* G. R. Smith, trans. New York: Charles Scribers

Buber, M. (1968). *Between Man and Man.* London: Collins

Buber, M. (1970). *A Believing Humanism: My Testament.* New York: Simon and Schuster

Kaitholil, G. (2010). *Communion in Community: A Renewal Programme for Religious, 6ᵗʰ ed.* Mumbai: St. Pauls

Kanu, I. A. (2017). Igwebuike and the Question of Superiority in the Scientific Community of Knowledge. *Igwebuike: An African Journal of Arts and Humanities, Vol. 3, No. 1. Pp. 9 – 18.*

Kanu, I. A. (2016a). Igwebuike as an Igbo-African hermeneutic of globalization. *Igwebuike: An African Journal of Arts and Humanities. Vol. 2, No. 1. Pp. 1-6.*

Kanu, I. A. (2016b). Igwebuike as an Igbo-African Philosophy for Christian-Muslim Relations in Northern Nigeria. *Igwebuike: An African Journal of Arts and Humanities. Vol. 2. No. 2. Pp. 1 – 9*

Kanu, I. A. (2017). *Igwebuike* as an Igbo-African philosophy for Christian-Muslim relations in Northern Nigeria. In Mahmoud Misaeli (Ed.). *Spirituality and Global Ethics* (pp. 300-310). United Kingdom: Cambridge Scholars.

Kanu, I. A. (2017). *Igwebuike* as an Igbo-African philosophy for the protection of the environment. *Nightingale International Journal of Humanities and Social Sciences.* Vol. 3. No. 4. pp. 28-38.

Kanu, I. A. (2017). *Igwebuike* as the hermeneutic of individuality and communality in African ontology. *NAJOP: Nasara Journal of Philosophy.* Vol. 2. No. 1. pp. 162-179.

Kanu, I. A. (2017a). *Igwebuike* and question of superiority in the scientific community of knowledge. *Igwebuike: An African Journal of Arts and Humanities.* Vol.3 No1. pp. 131-138.

Kanu, I. A. (2017a). *Igwebuike as a philosophical attribute of Africa in portraying the image of life.* A paper presented at the 2017 Oracle of Wisdom International Conference by the Department of Philosophy, Tansian University, Umunya, Anambra State, 27-29 April.

Kanu, I. A. (2017b). *Igwebuike* as a complementary approach to the issue of girl-child education. *Nightingale International Journal of Contemporary Education and Research.* Vol. 3. No. 6. pp. 11-17.

Kanu, I. A. (2017b). *Igwebuike* as a wholistic response to the problem of evil and human suffering. *Igwebuike: An African Journal of Arts and Humanities.* Vol. 3 No 2, March.

Kanu, I. A. (2017e). *Igwebuike* as an Igbo-African modality of peace and conflict resolution. *Journal of African Traditional Religion and Philosophy Scholars. Vol. 1. No. 1. pp. 31-40.*

Kanu, I. A. (2017g). *Igwebuike* and the logic (Nka) of African philosophy. *Igwebuike: An African Journal of Arts and Humanities.* 3. 1. pp. 1-13.

Kanu, I. A. (2017h). *Igwebuike* philosophy and human rights violation in Africa. *IGWEBUIKE: An African Journal of Arts and Humanities.* Vol. 3. No. 7. pp. 117-136.

Kanu, I. A. (2017i). *Igwebuike* as a hermeneutic of personal autonomy in African ontology. *Journal of African Traditional Religion and Philosophy Scholars. Vol. 2. No. 1. pp. 14-22.*

Koyeli, C. and Roy, A. (2002). *Interpersonal Relationship and Human Dignity. Indian Philosophical Quarterly, 29.* Pp. 2 – 13.

Ndubisi, E. J. O. (2019). "Igwebuike Philosophy in I. A. Kanu vis-à-vis the Validity of Truth-claim in African Epistemology". *Journal of African Studies and Sustainable Development, Vol. 2, No. 3.* Pp. 141- 147.

Ogbaki, P. E. (2019). Nigeria and the Debate of Leadership and good governance: Perspectives from Igwebuike Philosophy". In E. J. O. Ndubisi, A. A. Ichaba and J. Nnoruga (Eds.).

Igwebuike Philosophy: An African Philosophy of Integrative Humanism: A Book of Readings in Honour of Professor Kanu, Ikechukwu Anthony. Bloomington, USA: Author House. Pp. 154 – 208.

Okonkwo, I. E. (2014). "I -Thou Relationship in Martin Buber's Existentialism: A Critical Analysis". (Unpublished Project, Department of Philosophy and Religious Studies, Tansian University, Umunya).

Onebunne, J. I. (2019). "Igwebuike: An African Metaphysics of Communal Strength" in J. I. Onebunne, P. T. Haaga and E. J. O. Ndubisi (Eds.). *Igwebuike Ontology: An African Philosophy of Humanity Towards the Other: Papers in Honour of Professor Kanu, Ikechukwu Anthony, OSA.* Bloomington, USA: Author House. Pp. 63 – 81.

Uzukwu, G. N. (2019). "Igwebuike as an African Expression of the Pauline Theology of Collaboration in Mission". *Journal of African Studies and Sustainable Development, Vol. 2, No. 4.* Pp. 141- 155.

THE TEACHINGS OF THE CHURCH ON THE DIALOGUE BETWEEN CHRISTIANS AND MUSLIMS IN THE CURRENT WORLD A MODEL FOR IGWEBUIKE PHILOSPHY

Naanmiap Baamlong, OSA
Estudio Teologico de Valladolid
Spain
fadabaamlong@yahoo.com

EXECUTIVE SUMMARY

Going through the history of the human beings, it is clear that, the human person is a religious and social being. Religious because he believes and professes belief in the existence of a deity (a Supreme Being, God, a creator of the universe) and realities that are supreme to the realities surrounding man. He is social because he lives not alone but with other humans in the society. With the diversity of nature of the human person, it has become very necessary to always cultivate dialogue and interraction for peaceful coexitence. Interreligious dialogue is one aspect of the different forms of dialogues existent amongst humans. In this brief reflection, we are going to present the teachings of the Catholic Church about dialogue between Christians and Muslims. In a document of the Second Vatican Council Nostra aetate, these guidelines and teachings about dialogue are discussed. In view of this, from the theological point of view, this paper aims at demonstrating how the message about interreligious dialogue can contribute more lessons and values to the principle of complementarity of the Igwebuike philosphy, illustrating, therefore, how theological values can help to improve, as well, the values already existent in the Igwebiuke philosophy.

Keywords: God, *Nostra aetate,* dialogue, Kanu Ikechukwu Anthony, interreligious dialogue, Igwebuike philosophy, Christians, muslims, unity.

INTRODUCTION

Interreligious dialogue, also referred to as interfaith dialogue, is about people of different faiths coming to a mutual understanding and respect that allow them to live and cooperate with one another, in spite of their differences. The term refers to cooperative and positive interaction

137

among people of different religious traditions, at both the individual and institutional levels. Each party remains true to their own beliefs, while respecting the right of the other to practise their faith freely. Although interreligious dialogue is a recent term in the vocabulary of the Church, its reality is not new, but has always been existent in the Church[102]. The document *Nostra aetate* of the Second Vatican Council is a document that presents the Church's relations with non-Christian religions. It gives us some key guidelines for establishing a fraternal dialogue, of relations, of mutual trust and respect between Christians and Muslims. Certainly, when they promulgated the document, the council fathers took into account the pluralism of both religions and cultures and ideologies. Although basically, the texts deal with questions concerning what practical relationships between Christians and Muslims should look like; however, they also offer suggestions on aspects of a new Catholic Theology on dealings with Muslims.

The following reflection will be based on this document and other texts of the Popes (encyclicals and messages), in order to present some of the teachings of the Magisterium on the dialogues of the Catholic Church in reference to Islam, with special emphasis on the practical demonstrations of these teachings of the Popes from Vatican II. This paper will point out very important aspects about inter-faith dialogue beneficial to the *Igwebuike* philosophy. This philosophy is based on the Igbo-African worldview of complementarity, that is, the manner of being in African ontology. It is a worldview in which individuating differences must work towards a corporate existence, where the 'I' does not stand as the 'I' but as a 'We', where life and living makes meaning. In a scenario of this kind, difference does not divide nor does it constitute a threat, but rather unites and gives hope that future existence would have meaning. In a cosmogony of this kind, while the ontology of the person is founded on the particularity of the individual, implying that it is the metaphysics of the particular that founds identity, it is the community that gives meaning to such an existence and grounds such an identity[103]. The Church always calls for dialogue between all people. It calls all to a dialogue and solidarity as human persons, to work for the common good of all[104].

---

[102] Cf. Dupuis, R, "Cristología fundamental", en *Diccionario de Teología Fundamental*, Latourelle, R., Fisichella, R. y Pié-Ninot, S. (directores), Madrid, Ediciones Paulinas 1992,

[103] Cf. Kanu, I. A. (2017a). *Igwebuike as a philosophical attribute of Africa in portraying the image of life*. A paper presented at the 2017 Oracle of Wisdom International Conference by the Department of Philosophy, Tansian University, Umunya, Anambra State, 27-29 April. Kanu, I. A. (2017b). *Igwebuike* as a complementary approach to the issue of girl-child education. *Nightingale International Journal of Contemporary Education and Research*. Vol. 3. No. 6. pp. 11-17. Kanu, I. A. (2017b). *Igwebuike* as a wholistic response to the problem of evil and human suffering. *Igwebuike: An African Journal of Arts and Humanities*. Vol. 3 No 2, March. Kanu, I. A. (2017e). *Igwebuike* as an Igbo-African modality of peace and conflict resolution. *Journal of African Traditional Religion and Philosophy Scholars*. Vol. 1. No. 1. pp. 31-40. Kanu, I. A. (2017g). *Igwebuike* and the logic (Nka) of African philosophy. *Igwebuike: An African Journal of Arts and Humanities*. 3. 1. pp. 1-13. Kanu, I. A. (2017h). *Igwebuike* philosophy and human rights violation in Africa. *IGWEBUIKE: An African Journal of Arts and Humanities*. Vol. 3. No. 7. pp. 117-136. Kanu, I. A. (2017i). *Igwebuike* as a hermeneutic of personal autonomy in African ontology. *Journal of African Traditional Religion and Philosophy Scholars*. Vol. 2. No. 1. pp. 14-22.

[104] Cf. http://w2.vatican.va/content/francesco/en/apost_exhortations/documents/papa-francesco_esortazione-ap_20131124_evangelii-gaudium.html. accessed 10/07/2020. *Evanglii gaudium*, nn. 217-237.

THE TEACHINGS OF THE CHURCH ON DIALOGUE

The beginning of this document indicates that all peoples form one community and have the same origin, because God made all humanity dwell on the whole face of the earth[105]. The text continues with an affirmation of Islam's link to biblical tradition, as can be read in number 3; *"The Church also looks with appreciation at the Muslims, who worship one living and subsisting God, merciful and omnipotent, creator of heaven and earth, who spoke to men, to whose cult designs seek to submit entirely, as was submitted to God Abraham, to whom the Islamic faith refers willingly"*.

Although the reference to Muslims' professing to Abraham's faith seems to be on a subjective level, its position as one of the non-Christian monotheistic religions can be clearly seen. This is inferred from the phrases that speak of Muslims who worship the one God, merciful, omnipotent, and creator of everything, and also wait for the Day of Dudgment, when God will reward all men once they are resurrected. Therefore, they appreciate moral life and venerate God above all, with prayer, alms and fasting[106].

The document states that the Church sees Muslims with great appreciation. They worship one God of mercy and almighty creator of everything. Two things attract attention to the document reader. The first thing is that it emphasizes what Muslims and Christians have in common and at the same time emphasizes the essential point of difference, with reference to Christ, whom Islam venerates as a prophet, and does not recognize him as God. In addition, they also honour Mary the mother of Jesus Christ and sometimes even invoke her devoutly. The document states that the Church sees Muslims with great appreciation[107].

Undoubtedly, a mention of Jesus and Mary is a sign of the special place they occupy within the Quran. It describes Jesus not only as a prophet and messenger of God, but also as the Word of God (cf., Quran 3:45; 4.171) strengthened by the Holy Spirit (cf. Quran 2:87, 235; 5.110). These notes mentioned above also open up the possibility of cooperation between the two religions, in situations of religious conflict, especially in today's world. The phrases at the beginning of this document appear only as an ordinary preamble, but it is a fact that makes the statement exceptional.

This official declaration on Islam made by a Church council should be seen as a point of reference and an absolutely new beginning. The Creed and the worship of one God are the center of the Muslim religion, as it is also for Christians whose faith solemnly professes, *"Credo in unum Deum"*. The document briefly mentions some aspects of Islamic eschatology, referring to the final judgment. This aspect is essential for both the Christian religion and Islam. As you study these aspects in more details in both religions, you will no doubt see that there are

---

[105] Cf. *Nostra aetate*, n.1.

[106] *Ibíd.*, n.3

[107] *Ibíd.*

notable differences. However, in both the New Testament and the Quran, it is mentioned that in the final judgment, each will receive his/her reward, according to the actions performed during his/her pilgrimage in the world. In addition, if you look closely at the document, three basic elements of the Muslim religion are also mentioned in it: prayer (salat), alms (zakat) and fasting (sawm)[108]. As regards to its profession of faith, (shahada; there is no God but Allaah), it has been mentioned in the beginning of the document.

The second part of the document deals with the prospects for understanding and collaboration between Christianity and Islam in the present and in the future. The hatred and war of the past must be forgotten, not ignored but overcome, in order to achieve a mutual understanding, which is the goal that the two religions must secure. It says; *"Since in the course of centuries not a few quarrels and hostilities have arisen between Christians and Muslims, this sacred synod urges all to forget the past and to work sincerely for mutual understanding and to preserve as well as to promote together for the benefit of all mankind social justice and moral welfare, as well as peace and freedom[109].*

To succeed, therefore, in addition to seeking sincere understanding, believers have the responsibility and need to go beyond a simple dialogue between Christians and Muslims. Our greatest responsibility as believers is to actively cooperate in preaching and in the experience of the message of peace and dialogue that our faith in God demands. In this message, we are all called to reproach as alien to the Spirit of Christ, any discrimination against men or harassment of them because of their race, colour, condition of life, or religion. On the contrary, following in the footsteps of the holy Apostles Peter and Paul, this sacred synod ardently implores the Christian faithful to maintain good fellowship among the nations (1 Peter 2,12), and, if possible, to live for their part in peace with all men, so that they may truly be sons of the Father who is in heaven, thereby building a better world[110].

PRACTICAL ACTIONS OF THE POPES IN RELATION TO THE DECLARATION *NOSTRA AETATE*

The progress of interreligious dialogue since the Second Vatican Council has certainly been positive and deserves praise. The first protagonists of this are the Popes themselves. It is worth emphasizing the role of the Popes in this mission as a service to the unity exercised by them on behalf of the whole Church, so that the prayer of Jesus, *"that all may be one"* (Jn 17,21) may continue to strengthen his Church.

Pope John XXIII himself, when he convened the Ecumenical Council, had in his mind the idea of dialogue, which we know or we heard of his famous saying; "let the wind of change blows

---

[108] *Ibíd.*

[109] *Ibíd.*

[110] *Ibíd.*, n.5.

into the Church." This is a clear sign of his desire for dialogue. It can be said that this idea underlies the whole Council. If we take a look at his encyclical *Pacem in terris* of 11 April 1963, it speaks on peace among all peoples that will be founded on truth, justice, love and freedom; an encyclical intended not only for Christians, but also for all men of good will.

Paul VI, in whose hands was the task of presiding over and concluding the Second Vatican Council, was thinking of the prevailing need for dialogue among all humanity. This is evident in his encyclical *Ecclesiam suam* of 6 October 1964, which deals with the Church's mandate in the contemporary world. Number 27 of the document deals specifically with this idea of dialogue. For its part, the practicality of its actions is a very significant element, of its willingness to promote a Church in dialogue with the world. In January 1964, he paid a visit to the holy land, where he embraced the patriarch of Constantinople Atengoras. That same year, he went to Bombay in India, preaching once again the gospel of dialogue. He then paid a visit in 1969 to Africa in Kampala Uganda, during which he had some meetings with Muslims. And in Manila, the Philipines in 1970, he made great praise of the religious wealth of the Asian continent.

It is almost impossible to cover all the teachings of John Paul II, on Christian-Muslim dialogue. But he certainly kept in line with his predecessors by emphasizing the need for dialogue. In most of his papal trips, he had meetings and conversations with different Muslim leaders, for example, his speech to young Muslims in Casablanca in Morocco in 1985 and his visit to Egypt in 2000. On one of his visits to Turkey, he addressed the people with words of dialogue. On the other hand, it shows much of the dialogue and relational character that the Church must play, with his gesture when he entered a mosque in Damascus on 6 May, 2001, an action that many people today remember as a great display of love and dialogue.

Benedict XVI also made works to strengthen dialogue between Christians and Muslims, like the meeting with representatives of Muslim communities in Germany in August, 2005. Also, the current Pope, whose pontificate is still young, has already made many visits to the Middle East, Central Africa, preaching a message of peace and mercy. It is worth mentioning the importance of his commentary on the current situation of terrorism in the world as the beginning of the third world war.

These practical examples presented show the evident actions and efforts of the Popes in the implementation of the Council's teachings not only in their words, but above all in their actions. If we look at the efforts and the results that have come out of all of them, we can confidently say that, although it has not been easy, and despite the apparent setbacks, progress has been made on the path of reconciliation.

As Christians and Catholics, at this time full of challenges and difficult situations to manage, let us not forget the words of Jesus: "I am with you always, to the close of the age" (Mt 28:20). We must encourage one another to preach peace and dialogue. Our Christian conduct towards dialogue must be a translation of the values of the Gospel, which we are called to live with hope, even if the other does not want it. That is not why we must be discouraged, because, "though the fig tree do not blossom, no fruit be on the vines, the produce of the olive fail and the fields yield no food, the flock be cut off the fold and there be no herd in the stalls, yet I will rejoice in the Lord, I will joy in the God of my salvation" (Habakkuk 3, 17-19).

BENEFITS CHURCH'S TEACHING ON INTERRELIGIOUS DIALOGUE TO IGWEBUIKE PHILOSOPHY

From the above discourse on the Church and interligious dailogue, it is clear that the central message is about peaceful coexistence amongst people of distinct religious beliefs and practices; this will rightly contribute good ideas to this African philosophy of complementarity. One of the principles of the *Igwebuike* philospohy is unity. In fact, it is the inner or underlying principle of this African philosophy[111]. This unity stems from the coming together and putting into one place the various and different exiting realities. The principle points to the fact that in spite of the contrariety of reality, in spite of the singular identity of each reality, there is something common to everything. *Igwebuike* understands every individual reality as part and completion of the whole, and thus there is a unity in the midst of diversity. *Igwebuike* presents being as that which possesses a relational character of mutual relations. Thus, 'to be' is to live in solidarity and complementarity, and to live outside the parameters of solidarity and complementarity is to suffer alienation. 'To be' is 'to be with the other', in a community of beings. "I am because we are and since we are, therefore I am"[112].

The document *Nostra aetate* emphasizes aspects that Muslims and Christians have in common. And like we have seen, at the heart of this similarity is the act of belief in only one God. God is the binding force and the belief in this one supreme God is at the heart of the interaction and dialogue. It is, therefore, obvious that what is involved here is very important and serves as the basis on which all other dialogues can be established. Consequently, this of course,

---

[111] Cf. Kanu, I. A. (2017). *Igwebuike* as an Igbo-African philosophy for Christian-Muslim relations in Northern Nigeria. In Mahmoud Misaeli (Ed.). *Spirituality and Global Ethics* (pp. 300-310). United Kingdom: Cambridge Scholars. Kanu, I. A. (2017). *Igwebuike* as an Igbo-African philosophy for the protection of the environment. *Nightingale International Journal of Humanities and Social Sciences*. Vol. 3. No. 4. pp. 28-38. Kanu, I. A. (2017). *Igwebuike* as the hermeneutic of individuality and communality in African ontology. *NAJOP: Nasara Journal of Philosophy*. Vol. 2. No. 1. pp. 162-179. Kanu, I. A. (2017a). *Igwebuike* and question of superiority in the scientific community of knowledge. *Igwebuike: An African Journal of Arts and Humanities*. Vol.3 No1. pp. 131-138.

[112] Cf. Kanu, I. A. *Igwebuike and the Logic (Nka) of African Philosophy,* 14. Kanu, I. A. (2018). *Igwe Bu Ike* as an Igbo-African hermeneutics of national development. *Igbo Studies Review. No. 6*. pp. 59-83. Kanu, I. A. (2018). *Igwebuike* as an African integrative and progressive anthropology. *NAJOP: Nasara Journal of Philosophy*. Vol. 2. No. 1. pp. 151-161. Kanu, I. A. (2018). New Africanism: *Igwebuike* as a philosophical Attribute of Africa in portraying the Image of Life. In Mahmoud Misaeli, Sanni Yaya and Rico Sneller (Eds.). *African Perspectives on Global on Global Development* (pp. 92-103). United Kingdom: Cambridge Scholars Publishing.

without any doubt, fits well for the *Igwebuike* philosophy which preaches complementarity and unity. *"I am because we are and since we are, therefore I am"*. And because of this strong sense of togetherness and unity, everyone in a given community considers the next person as a brother. As such dialogue can easily be made, and by the very nature of this belongingness and togethernes, there is intimately in existence dialogue because no one is considered different or outside of the circle that binds the community. To be identified as an individual one is first considered as part of the whole group. It is the whole that gives meaning and importance to the individual or a particular reality and aspect. That is dialogue in play.

Interreligious dialogue increases the understanding Christians and non-Christians have of the beliefs and practices of the other. This enhanced understanding can lead to a more peaceable coexistence in the pluralistic culture of the 21st century Africa. As people of different religious communities encounter another in mutual service in schools, in government, and in civic activities, the foundations established through dialogue will enable these people to know the areas in which mutual activity can enhance society (as well as to know in advance the areas in which religious differences can make mutual undertakings difficult).

As stated above, dialogue enhances the efficacy of peaceful coexistence. The clarified understanding of other religions will be published in books and articles about the religions, many of which will be read by all, as well as transmitted to everybody person. This, therefore, effectively addresses and shapes the thinking of one group of people about the beliefs and cultures of the other group. It helps each group to better understand their own faith. Because the focus of interreligious dialogue is on the differences between religions, people are forced to examine their own beliefs in order to support these positions. This examination will increase the self-understanding of Christians and Muslims, helping them to see the great values they both possess. This enables both groups to identify and contextualize the teachings of other religions, and to present a reason as to why each believes differently.

Finally, interreligious dialogue increases and breeds love and unity. This is another aspect that the *Igwebuike* philosophy stresses, the advantage that stems from this union of various parts. According to the study of Kanu, *Igwebuike* strongly holds that the whole is greater than the corresponding parts. It is also a view that maintains that by the coming together of the individuals or parts, a viable and sustainable whole will emerge, and by this, the parts will get to the brim purpose of their existence[113]. The coming together of the parts to form one single unit makes the various parts strong and powerful. In line with this, it will be relevant the teaching of Nostra aetate.

---

[113] *Cf.* Kanu, I. A. (2019). *Igwebuikecracy*: The Igbo-African participatory cocio-political system of governance. *TOLLE LEGE: An Augustinian Journal of the Philosophy and Theology. 1. 1.* pp. 34-45. Kanu, I. A. (2019). On the origin and principles of *Igwebuike* philosophy. *International Journal of Religion and Human Relations.* Vol. 11. No. 1. pp. 159-176. Kanu, I. A. (2019b). An *Igwebuike* approach to the study of African traditional naming ceremony and baptism. *International Journal of Religion and Human Relations.* Vol. 11. No. 1. pp. 25-50.

It emphasizes this concept of dialogue, because to produce fruit, there has to be strongly in place understanding and integration - a community that is together in harmony and dialogue. *Igwebuike* philosophy preaches harmony and relationship. According to the study done by Kanu, *Igwebuike* is an ordered relationship, even though the idea of Igwe (large number of people or group) may give the impression of a mob or disordered relationship. *Igwebuike* is a relationship guided by the Igbo-African principle: egbe bere ugo bere (Let the kite perch, let the eagle perch).

The idea of egbe (kite) and ugo (eagle) speaks of a variety of positions, personality, creed, culture, etc., and in fact, differences in life, which is found in the world, and yet must coexist together. When the egbe settles in the uwa (the world) and imagines that the ugo has no right of existence and then begins to castigate ugo and to push it out of being, at that point, the egbe alienates the being of the ugo. When egbe castigates and condemns the ugo, it thinks that it is making progress; it is rather alienating itself, because the being of the ugo has an existential and fundamental contribution to make to the being of the egbe. It is such that when egbe kills the uUgo, the egbe also kills itself. To be in the world, Kanu assert that the egbe and the ugo must dialogue. The world is such that differences would always exist and to try to destroy the other as a result of difference is to waste one's time; to end the variation of reality is to end reality itself, for reality is by its nature variegated. Egbe beru, ugo beru (Let the kite perch, let the eagle perch).

This implies they must dialogue and, therefore, must have a relationship. They have the options of either relating and being happy or being in perpetual discord which alienates their being in the uUwa. When the egbe and ugo harness their energies towards a common project, need and desire, they can constitute an insurmountable force in pursuing their collective vision. Only then can they overcome their collective difficulties. In the same way, only when Muslims and Christians come together in existential solidarity, which is a correlative and complementary solidarity, a 'we' relationship, can they fulfill their divine mandates. Both religions have something to learn from each other, and to avoid or alienate the other is to deny oneself of knowledge and growth, and, thus, expanding the capacity of ignorance. When both religions slight each other, look down on each other, segregate each other and reject the contribution of each other, they are committing the ontological evil of alienation[114]. Nostra aetate, in the concluding part, warns against all these negative aspects amongst the different religions calling for dialogue and understanding.[115]

---

[114] Cf. Kanu, I. A. (2019). Collaboration within the ecology of mission: An African cultural perspective. *The Catholic Voyage: African Journal of Consecrated Life.* Vol. 15. pp. 125-149. Kanu, I. A. (2019). *Igwebuike* research methodology: A new trend for scientific and wholistic investigation. *IGWEBUIKE: An African Journal of Arts and Humanities* (IAAJAH). *5. 4.* pp. 95-105. Kanu, I. A. (2019). *Igwebuikeconomics*: The Igbo apprenticeship for wealth creation. *IGWEBUIKE: An African Journal of Arts and Humanities* (IAAJAH). *5. 4.* pp. 56-70.

[115] Cf. *Nostra aetate*, n.5.

CONCLUSION

Interreligious dialogue involves meeting people themselves and getting to know their religious traditions. Inter-faith dialogue is not just words or talk. It includes human interaction and relationships. It can take place between individuals and communities and on many levels. For example, between neighbours, in schools and in places of work - it can take place in both formal and informal settings. In Nigeria, for example, Muslims and Christians live on the same streets, use the same shops, buses, and attend the same schools. Normal life means that we come into daily contact with each other. Dialogue, therefore, is not just something that takes place on an official or academic level only – it is part of daily life during which different cultural and religious groups interact with another directly, and where tensions between them are the most tangible. Christian-Muslim dialogue should always aim at providing a positive alternative to destructive violence, especially in situations of tension and strife. The situation in Nigeria calls for dialogue, if people must live in peace with one another. Wherever Christians and Muslims live in peace, dialogue between them should aim at addressing common problems for the good and peaceful coexistence of the society. This is important because today Muslims and Christians are now neighbours, colleagues at work, members of the same political parties and football clubs. Their children attend the same nurseries, schools and universities. Having seen the relationship between the teaching of the Church on dialogue and philosophy, one can see how theological values can help to improve as well the values already existent in the *Igwebiuke* philosophy.

IGWEBUIKE PHILOSOPHY, STRATEGIC RELIGIOUS ACTION AND THE THEORY OF CHANGE

Mike Boni Bazza, PhD
Veritas University Abuja
(The Catholic University of Nigeria)
Department of History and International Relations
danbazza68@gmail.com

EXECUTIVE SUMMARY

*This paper examines the root causes of the problems of religious tensions, violent conflicts and killings, using the North Central Region of Nigeria as a case study. Consequently, the paper develops a Strategic Religious Action to tackle the menace. The research uses the tools of an indigenous African philosophy called Igwebuike, which is a substratum of African traditional values, philosophy and religion. It embodies an integral principle of African philosophical experience which enhances the unity of all Africans. Igwebuike philosophy is an accepted tactics of soft power, i.e. the ability to attract and co-opt people, expose problems about Human Rights on Freedom of Religion or Belief (FoRB), and then proffer a strategic religious action. The submission quickly addresses all the contentious issues that facilitate agitations from different sections and players in the region under focus, and submits that traditional African values, in relation to the Igwebuike philosophy, strategic religious action and the theory of change (collectively speaking), are **sine qua non** for prosecuting the problems in question. To achieve the goal of this study, historical and phenomenological methods of enquiry are deployed in the collection and analysis of data, while the 'indigenous holistic theory' and the 'theory of change' were adopted for the interpretation and understanding of the problems at hand. Furthermore, it concludes by stating the ultimate aim of the study, which is basically to examine the root causes of the aforementioned problems in the middle belt of Nigeria, namely: religious tensions, violent conflicts and killings and proffer a strategic religious action within the context and framework of the Theory of Change (ToC).*

Keywords: Igwebuike, Philosophy, Kanu Ikechukwu Anthony, Human Rights, Freedom of Religion, African traditional values, Theory of Change

INTRODUCTION

Professor Ikechukwu Anthony Kanu developed the concept of 'Igwebuike' to describe the unity of the African philosophical experience, which profoundly relates to a perspective-driven ideology and epitomizes the manner of being in African ontology. This, according to him, includes African cherished traditional values such as complementarity, harmony, communality, etc. Thus, *Igwebuike,* being the inner or underlying principle of African philosophy, has successfully been used as a holistic response to the problem of evil, and sometimes it has been applied to define the logic of African philosophy, inclusive leadership and even the issue of national development. For the purpose of this discourse, *Igwebuike* philosophy is adopted as a solution to the problems about Human Rights on Freedom of Religion or Belief (FoRB) which, on the long run, encompasses a strategic religious action.

Strategic religious action promotes and builds on its extensive experience and best practices, which specifically focus on women and youth as contained in Article 18 of the Universal Declaration of Human Rights on Freedom of Religion or Belief (FoRB).[1] While admitting that FoRB is a fundamental human right enshrined in international treaties and constitutional provisions in most countries, the actual practice of FoRB encounters many challenges, particularly in the sphere of religious tensions, violent conflicts and killings.[2] Our ultimate aim in this paper is to examine the root causes of the aforementioned problems in the north central region, i.e., the middle belt of Nigeria and proffer a strategic religious action within the context and framework of the theory of change (ToC).[3]

THE PRESENTATION

In presenting the *Igwebuike* philosophy as an accepted tactics of soft power about Human Rights on Freedom of Religion or Belief (FoRB), we will like to explore the Kanu school of thought as a remedy for almost every human problem. Doing so will enable us to appreciate immensely the apt and scholarly interpretation of *Igwebuike* from this perspective. According to this school of thought, *Igwebuike* is from an Igbo composite word and metaphor: Igwebuike, a combination of three words. Therefore, it can be employed as a word or used as a sentence: as a word, it is written as Igwebuike, and as a sentence, it is written as, Igwe bu ike, with the component words enjoying some independence in terms of space.[4] The three words involved are explained thus: Igwe is a noun, which means 'number' or 'population', usually a huge number or population. Bu is a verb, which means 'is'. Ike is another verb, which means 'strength' or 'power.' Thus, put together, it means 'number is strength' or 'number is power'; that is, when human beings come together in solidarity and complementarity, they are powerful or can constitute an insurmountable force or strength, and at this level, no task is beyond their collective capability.[5] *Igwebuike* is, therefore, a philosophy of harmonization and complementation. It understands the world immanent realities to be related to one another in the most natural, mutual, harmonious and compatible ways possible.[6]

TACKLING THE ROOT CAUSES OF RELIGIOUS TENSIONS, VIOLENT CONFLICTS AND KILLINGS BY APPLYING THE PPRINCIPLE OF IGWEBUIKE PHILOSOPHY

The root causes of the above-listed problems in the north central region (Middle Belt) of Nigeria can be understood by using a 'causal factor' approach. Using this approach, the root causes of the problems can be classified into factors which include: economic, political and socio-cultural factors.

Economically, the root causes of the identified problems in the north central region of Nigeria include the scramble for economic opportunities and resources. The economic opportunities in the north central region are scarce. These opportunities include employment and trade. As a result of the scarcity, the ethno-religious backgrounds are resorted to, in order to get access to these opportunities, on the one hand. On the other hand, the inability of some people to have access to these opportunities is interpreted along ethno-religious lines. With this situation, a "**we** versus **them**" construct is created among the people of various backgrounds in the region, thereby deepening the differences among the people and raising conflictive tendencies, which eventually manifest in the problems within the region.[7]

The dominant and most important economic resource in the region is land. Acquiring portions of land in the region is tantamount to wealth acquisition, as the land can be used for farming or grazing livestock. Accordingly, farmers-herders dimension of the identified problems in the region is basically as a result of clashes over land.

Politically, the identified problems in the north central region of Nigeria are as a result of the weak government institutions, lack of political will by the government agencies and political leaders, the quest for territorial expansion by migrating stock of people into the region, the struggle for the control and domination of the region among the diverse ethnic groups found therein,[8] et cetera.

Government institutions which are supposed to control human behaviours in the society and ensure social order have not been performing their duties. The police, courts, military, have even been accused of partiality, partisanship, and even connivance as perpetrators of the problems within the region.

Weakness of the institutions has eventually ossified into a lack of political will by the institutions and political leaders to finding lasting solutions to the problems. Hence, the problems have become a daily reoccurrence in the region.[9] As a matter of fact, many political leaders have been associated with all the identified conflicts in the states within the region, but of course, because "this is Nigeria," nothing has been done to bring them to book.

Constitutional weakness has also been one of the root causes of the identified problems in the region. The Nigerian constitution makes provisions for citizenship and indigenity.

Constitutional provisions, by virtue of their ambiguity over the terms "indigene" and "residency" for accessing citizenship rights, have not been satisfactorily clarified. It appears that the indigene principle promoted in Section 147 (3)[10] is not in line with the citizenship provisions of Section 15 (3) (b),[11] which stipulate that "for the purpose of promoting national integration, it shall be the role of the State to secure full residence rights for every citizen in all parts of the Federation."[12] This provision becomes difficult in being implemented in various states of the region. Consequently, indigenes of the states in the region and other citizens of Nigeria residing within the region are constantly struggling for citizen rights and privileges, where the indigenes believe the rights and privileges are reserved for them within their domains.[13] This sets a fertile ground for the endless myriad of problems in the region.

There has been a wave of north-south migration from the northernmost part of the country into the north central region. This migration is basically a movement of the Hausa/Fulani ethnic nationalities. These immigrants into the region not only seek means of livelihood, but seek to assert themselves (in the context of one Nigeria) on the indigenes of the region. Hence, there has been a perception of extra-territoriality which must be confronted by irredentism, leading to reoccurring bloodshed and damage of property in the region.

Socio-culturally, the north central region is made up of diverse ethnic groups which have not been able to harness their diversity for progress. Rather, these groups found themselves in constant competition, which is problematic for the society. Equally, the social conditions within the region provide a fertile ground for the preponderance of problems. These conditions include: high level of poverty, high population density, religious antagonisms, inadequate social and infrastructural facilities, high level of illiteracy and unemployment, et cetera. The failure of government and religious and traditional institutions to properly manage these social conditions of the region has become a recipe for the identified problems to persist.

IGWEBUIKE PHILOSOPHY, STRATEGIC RELIGIOUS ACTION AND THE THEORY OF CHANGE

After defining *Igwebuike* as a philosophy of harmonization and complementation that understands the world immanent realities to be related to one another in the most natural, mutual, harmonious and compatible ways possible,[14] we will now focus our attention on the strategic religious action that is incumbent towards contextualizing the theory of change. We begin our discourse by asking: What is the theory of change?

The theory of change as the name suggests, is a hypothesis of how we think **change** occurs. So essentially, it is a comprehensive description and illustration of how and why a desired change is expected to happen in a particular context.[15] Therefore, in the context of this study, the theory of change can be said to be a paradigm which promotes social change in the society, albeit positive. The theory explains the linkages in an initiative by explaining the processes of change.

This link shows why an outcome, step or action is a prerequisite for another.[16] In other words, the theory suggests why a particular action is necessary for a particular result to be achieved.

Using the theory of change, the strategic religious action I will humbly suggest is **inter-religious dialogue,** using the tool of *Igwebuike*. Inter-religious dialogue is necessary for social order and human and societal development. The role religion plays in the society cannot be overemphasized. Religion has become the way of life for many people. Religion appeals to their consciences and determines who they relate with, how they interact with their environment and what awaits them in the world and beyond. The connection people have with their religion is as strong as glue, that anything which seeks to undermine their belief or relationship with their religion, whether perceived or real, is considered an affront that must be confronted immediately. Hence, religion has become a tool for conflict, progress and propaganda.[17]

With the place religion has taken in the society, a strategy of inter-religious dialogue is *sine qua non* for finding solutions to the problems bedeviling the human society. Without regard to extremists' perspectives on some religions, all religions seek a good society (put in other word, life) for their respective followers. When inter-religious dialogue is adopted, a better understanding of various religions and the complementary roles they play in the development of the society and enhancement of human existence will be put in place. This is necessary for the prevention of religious extremism, violence and intolerance, which have often resulted in religious tensions, violent conflicts and killings.[18]

Through inter-religious dialogue, religious leaders will be given additional roles to their primary role of evangelism. They will be able to play mediatory roles in issues of human society and not just that of the religious realm. With that, religious institutions and leaders will play complementary roles to the efforts of government, civil society organizations and traditional institutions as they seek to develop the society and enhance peaceful co-existence.

EVIDENCE-BASED OUTCOME

Essentially, inter-religious dialogue will enable inter-religious relationship. This will bring the various people in the society into a common front for peaceful co-existence.

Inter-religious dialogue has played vital roles in conflict resolution and sustaining peace, even in the north central region of Nigeria. This was the case in the Yelwa-Shendam religious conflict of the early 2000s in Plateau State.[19] In the June, 2018 violent ethno-religious conflict in Riyom, Barkin Ladi and Jos South Local Government Areas,[20] where some victims of armed attack were saved by an Imam, due to the relationship that had existed between him and the people of the community.

CONCLUSION

In the context of this study, we have employed the use of the word, *Igwebuike*, as a philosophy of harmonization and complementation, because when human beings come together in solidarity and complementarity, they are powerful and can constitute an insurmountable force or strength, and at this level, no task (even the complexity of inter-religious dialogue) is beyond their collective capability. Although inter-religious dialogue has empirically played cogent roles in addressing human problems, it has not been given a proper place to flourish as it has not been formerly adopted as a strategic action. The government of the United States, through its Embassies, has been making efforts to encourage the adoption of inter-religious dialogue, with the commemoration of World Religions Day. When inter-religious dialogue is adopted as a strategic action, many problems bedeviling the society can be solved and future ones prevented. Once again, my humble submission in this study is that traditional African values, in relation to *Igwebuike* philosophy, strategic religious action and the theory of change (collectively speaking) are ***sine qua non*** for prosecuting the problems in question. In addition, it is important to note that inter-religious dialogue is very necessary for social order, human and societal development, and *Igwebuike* philosophy is the right tool to achieve this onerous task.

ENDNOTES

1   Article 18 of the Universal Declaration of Human Rights on Freedom of Religion or Belief (FoRB) specifically focuses on women and youth.

2   *Ibid*

3   In the context of this study, the theory of change can be said to be a paradigm which promotes social change in the society, albeit positive. The theory further explains the processes of change.

4   Kanu, I. A., Igwebuike as the consummate foundation of African bioethical principles. A paper presented at the International Conference on Law, Education and Humanities. 25th -26th November 2015 University of Paris, France, 2015a.

5   Kanu, I. A., Igwebuike as an ontological precondition for African ethics. International Conference of the Society for Research and Academic Excellence. University of Nigeria, Nsukka. 14th -16th September, 2015b.

6   *Ibid*.

7   Bazza, M. B., A special submission made to: *The Joint Initiative for Strategic Religious Action* (JISRA) as a member of the Nigeria Input Team on 24th July, 2020.

8   *Ibid*.

9   *Ibid*.

10   The 1999 Constitution of the Federal Republic of Nigeria (as amended), Section 147 (2).

11   The 1999 Constitution of the Federal Republic of Nigeria (as amended), Section 15 (3b).

12   *Ibid*.

13   This is the author's interpretation of Section 15 (3b) of the 1999 Constitution as amended.

14   Kanu, I. A., Igwebuike as the consummate foundation of African bioethical principles. A paper presented at the International Conference on Law, Education and Humanities. 25th -26th November 2015 University of Paris, France, 2015a.

15   *The Joint Initiative for Strategic Religious Action* (JISRA) Theory of Change (both Narrative and Visual), 2020.

16   Bazza, M. B., A special submission made to: *The Joint Initiative for Strategic Religious Action* (JISRA) as a member of the Nigeria Input Team on 24th July, 2020.

17   *Ibid.*

18   *Ibid.*

19   A Research Interview on the Berom-Fulani Ethnic Conflicts, 2001-2018, with H. Salleh, Kurra Falls, Gashish, Plateau State. Salleh expressed how Imam Abubakar saved Christians by hiding them in his house when Muslim Gun men stormed the communities in Gashish District on 23rd June 2018. The report was captured by many Media outlets and the Imam was given an award and subsequently honoured by the United States of America Embassy here in Nigeria in the year 2019.

20   Emmanuel Innocent, "Imam Ashafa and Pastor James Wuye: Bringing Peace to Warring Nigerian Communities". Premium Times, April 9th 2020, Retrieved July 24th, 2020. https://crcc.usc.edu/imam-ashafa-and-pastor-james-wuye-bringing-peace-to-warring-nigerian-communities/

BIBLIOGRAPHY

Akanni, A.A. (2014), 'History of Terrorism, Youth Psychology and Unemployment in Nigeria' in Journal of Pan African Studies, Vol.7, No. 3.

Article 18 of the Universal Declaration of Human Rights on Freedom of Religion or Belief (FoRB)

Augustine, Saint. 'Just-war Theory', available at http://www.mtholyoke.edu/-jasingle/justwar.html

Bandura, A. (1973), Aggression: A Social Learning Analysis. England Cliffs, NJ: Press.

Bazza, M. B., A special submission made to: *The Joint Initiative for Strategic Religious Action* (JISRA) as a member of the Nigeria Input Team on 24th July, 2020.

Centre for Defense Information,(2003), A Brief History of Terrorism. Available at http://www.cdi.org/friendlyversion/printversion.cmf?documentID=1502.

Chalianda, G. & Blin, A. (2007), (eds.) The History of Terrorism. (Schneider, E., Pulver, K. & Browner, J. trans.), Berkeley, University of California Press.

Dollard, J., Doob, L., Mowver, O., & Sears, R. (1939), Frustration–Aggression. New Haven, C.T. University Press.

Ebun-Amun, C. (2010), 'Bombing as Nigeria's new Sub-Culture?' The Nigerian Tribune, May 11.

Emmanuel Innocent, "Imam Ashafa and Pastor James Wuye: Bringing Peace to Warring Nigerian Communities". Premium Times, April 9th 2020, Retrieved July 24th, 2020. https://crcc.usc.edu/imam-ashafa-and-pastor-james-wuye-bringing-peace-to-warring-nigerian-communities/

Fiala, A. (2002), 'Terrorism and the philosophy of History: Liberalism, Realism and Supreme Emergency Exemption' in Essays in Philosophy, A Biannual Journal, Vol.3, Special Issue.

Frey, R.G. & Morris, C.H. (1991), Violence, Terrorism and Justice. Cambridge University Press, New York.

Hegel, G.W.F. (1967), The Phenomenology of the Mind. (J.B. Baillie, trans.), New York: Harper & Row Publishers.

Ikime, O. (1985). In Search of Nigerians: Changing Patterns of intergroup relations in an evolving nation-state. Presidential Inaugural Lecture, 30th Congress of the H.S.N., University of Nigeria Nsukka.

Kamal, M. (2008) 'The Meaning of Terrorism: A Philosophical Inqury' in National Centre of Excellence for Islamic Studies NCEIS Research Papers, Vol.1, No.1 University of Melbourne.

Kanu, I. A. *Igwebuike* as an Igbo-African hermeneutics of globalisation. *IGWEBUIKE: An African Journal of Arts and Humanities*, Vol. 2 No.1. pp. 61-66. 2016

Kanu, I. A. *Igwebuike* as the consummate foundation of African Bioethical principles. *An African journal of Arts and Humanities* Vol.2 No1 June, pp.23-40. 2016

Kanu, I. A. *Igwebuike* as an expressive modality of being in African ontology. *Journal of Environmental and Construction Management. 6. 3.* pp.12-21. 2016

Kanu, I. A. African traditional folktales as an integrated classroom. *Sub-Saharan African Journal of Contemporary Education Research.* Vol.3 No. 6. pp. 107-118. 2016

Kanu, I. A. *Igwebuike* as an Igbo-African philosophy for Christian-Muslim relations in Northern Nigeria. In Mahmoud Misaeli (Ed.). *Spirituality and Global Ethics* (pp. 300-310). United Kingdom: Cambridge Scholars. 2017

Kanu, I. A. *Igwebuike* as an Igbo-African philosophy for the protection of the environment. *Nightingale International Journal of Humanities and Social Sciences.* Vol. 3. No. 4. pp. 28-38. 2017

Kanu, I. A. *Igwebuike* as the hermeneutic of individuality and communality in African ontology. *NAJOP: Nasara Journal of Philosophy.* Vol. 2. No. 1. pp. 162-179. 2017

Kanu, I. A. *Igwebuike* and question of superiority in the scientific community of knowledge. *Igwebuike: An African Journal of Arts and Humanities.* Vol.3 No1. pp. 131-138. 2017

Kanu, I. A. *Igwebuike as a philosophical attribute of Africa in portraying the image of life*. A paper presented at the 2017 Oracle of Wisdom International Conference by the Department of Philosophy, Tansian University, Umunya, Anambra State, 27-29 April. 2017

Kanu, I. A. *Igwebuike* as a complementary approach to the issue of girl-child education. *Nightingale International Journal of Contemporary Education and Research*. Vol. 3. No. 6. pp. 11-17. 2017

Kanu, I. A. *Igwebuike* as a wholistic response to the problem of evil and human suffering. *Igwebuike: An African Journal of Arts and Humanities*. Vol. 3 No 2, March. 2017

Kanu, I. A. *Igwebuike* as an Igbo-African modality of peace and conflict resolution. *Journal of African Traditional Religion and Philosophy Scholars. Vol. 1. No. 1. pp. 31-40.* 2017

Kanu, I. A. *Igwebuike* and the logic (Nka) of African philosophy. *Igwebuike: An African Journal of Arts and Humanities*. 3. 1. pp. 1-13. 2017

Kanu, I. A. *Igwebuike* philosophy and human rights violation in Africa. *IGWEBUIKE: An African Journal of Arts and Humanities*. Vol. 3. No. 7. pp. 117-136. 2017

Kanu, I. A. *Igwebuike* as a hermeneutic of personal autonomy in African ontology. *Journal of African Traditional Religion and Philosophy Scholars. Vol. 2. No. 1. pp. 14-22.* 2017

Kanu, I. A. African philosophy, globalization and the priority of 'otherness'. *Journal of African Studies and Sustainable Development*. Vol. 1. No. 1. pp. 40-57. 2018

Kanu, I. A. *African traditional philosophy of education: Essays in Igwebuike philosophy*. Germany: Lambert Publications. 2018

Kanu, I. A. Igbo-African Gods and Goddesses. *Nnadiebube Journal of Philosophy*. Vol. 2. No. 2. pp. 118-146. 2018

Kanu, I. A. *Igwe Bu Ike* as an Igbo-African hermeneutics of national development. *Igbo Studies Review. No. 6.* pp. 59-83. 2018

Kanu, I. A. *Igwebuike* as an African integrative and progressive anthropology. *NAJOP: Nasara Journal of Philosophy*. Vol. 2. No. 1. pp. 151-161. 2018

Kanu, I. A. New Africanism: *Igwebuike* as a philosophical Attribute of Africa in portraying the Image of Life. In Mahmoud Misaeli, Sanni Yaya and Rico Sneller (Eds.). *African Perspectives on Global on Global Development* (pp. 92-103). United Kingdom: Cambridge Scholars Publishing. 2018

Micewski, E.R. (2006), 'Terror and Terrorism: A History of Ideas and Philosophical-Ethical Reflections' in Cultic Studies Review, Vol.5,No.2.

Primoratz, I. (2004), Terrorism: Philosophical Issues. Palgrave Macmillan, New York.

Roberts, A. (2008), The 'war on Terror' in historical perspective. In T.G. Mahnken & J.A. Maiolo (eds.), Strategic Studies: A Reader. New York: Routledge.

Rootberg, R. (2002), The New Nature of Nation-State Failure. The Washington Quarterly 25 (3)

Rootberg, R. (2003), State Failure and State Weakness in a time of Terror. Washington DC. Brooklyn Institution Press.

The Joint Initiative for Strategic Religious Action (JISRA) Theory of Change (both Narrative and Visual), 2020

Zoro, S. (2011). The North: Development and Discontent. The African Report 35:10-11.

IGWEBUIKE PHILOSOPHY AND LEADERSHIP STYLES

OMOJOLA Immaculata Olu, (SSMA), PhD
Department of Business Administration and Management
Villanova Polytechnic, Imesi Ile, Osun State
omojolassma@yahoo.co.uk

EXECUTIVE SUMMARY

This paper discusses Igwebuike philosophy and leadership styles. It is an attempt to see how this philosophy can be applied to leadership styles or how a connection can be drawn between the two terms. Igwebuike philosophy, according the author, means "'number is strength' or 'number is power;' that is, when human beings come together in solidarity and complementarity, they are powerful and can constitute an insurmountable force." Leadership has been defined by various authors in various ways. However, it has been agreed by many scholars that leadership involves people, unequal distribution of power, ability to influence, and values. Authoritarian, democratic and laissez-faire leadership styles were discussed as a concise presentation of all leadership styles. Phenomenological method of research was used for the purpose of this study. It was discovered that democratic or participative leadership style correlates with what the author of Igwebuike philosophy has in mind. The discussion also disclosed that both terms have number of people, involvement, goals and values in common. It was then recommended that Igwebuike philosophy should be a guide to leaders as they endeavour to know what to do and how to do it for the realization of organizational goals.

Keywords: Igwebuike Philosophy, Leadership styles, Kanu Ikechukwu Anthony, Authoritarian, Democratic, laissez-faire, Goals and Involvement

INTRODUCTION

Leadership is an act of giving directives to people in an organization for the accomplishment of organizational goals. It takes into cognizance some skills to guide individuals, lead a group and facilitate a team work through influences. A leader is one who constantly makes positive statements of ethics. Leadership has been defined by various scholars in various ways. Some, in an attempt to arrive at a good definition, describe leaders and their functions, while some

157

pay attention to traits or qualities. For example, Maxwell (2001) claims that "A good leader is a guy who can step on your toes without messing up your shine"(p.72), and Akindutire (2004) opines that a leader is a person who can help a group to achieve goals with as little fraction as possible, have a sense of unity and provide an opportunity for self-realization. "Leadership is a process whereby an individual influences a group of individuals to achieve a common goal" (Northhouse 2007, p. 122).

In the view of Lunnernburg and Ornstern (2008), "Leadership is not about who is smarter or tougher but about qualities we all have or can develop" (p. 84). Considering the input of (Zeichik 2012), "Leadership is inspiring others to pursue your vision within the parameters you set, to the extent that it becomes a shared vision and a shared success." (p. 3) Miguel (2017), while quoting Maxwell, says "A leader is one who knows the way, goes the way, and shows the way;" (p. 64), and Jack Welch offered, "Before you are a leader, success is all about growing yourself. When you become a leader, success is all about growing others." (p. 64)

Recently, Ward (2020) stresses that, "A simple definition is that leadership is the art of motivating a group of people to act toward achieving a common goal. This can mean directing workers and colleagues with a strategy to meet the company's needs." (p. 9) She further says that a leader is the inspiration for and director of the action. It is the person in the group that possesses the combination of personality and leadership skills to make others want to follow their directions.

In all these definitions, it can be deduced that leadership deals with people, motivation, influence, organizational goals and values. Also, nearly all these authors are of the opinion that leaders are made not born. To Jago (1992), "good leaders are made not born" (p. 7). If you have the desire and willpower, you can become an effective leader. Good leaders develop through a never-ending process of self-study, education, training and experience. It is surprising to the researcher that the even the definition given by Lunnernburg and Ornstern that pays attention to "qualities we all have or can develop" (p. 84) ended with leaders are made not born. The researcher is of the opinion that "have" in this definition is referring to inborn traits, while "can develop" is about learning. Some of the arguments of these authors can be summarized as follows: Stoner, Freeman and Gilbert (2002) say that what is to be leant are - motivation, a clear idea of what you need to improve and consistent practice, because to them, leadership works through emotions, and the most important quality of a leader is supervisory ability. Akindutire (2004), who also shares the same view, arrives at the conclusion that the major attribute of a leader is communication skills.

Jago (1982) later makes a distinction between the terms - a born leader and a made leader in this claim. "Leaders carry out this process (desire and willpower) by applying their knowledge and skills. This is called process leadership. However, we know that we have traits that can influence our actions. This is called "trait leadership," in that it was once common to believe that leaders were born rather than made." (p. 8) Ward (2020) is not taking a stand; instead, he agrees with the fact that leaders are born and that leaders can be made through constant practice. "While there are people who seem to be naturally endowed with more leadership abilities than others, anyone can learn to become a leader by improving particular skills." (p. 18). In line with this, Luenendonk (2016) associates certain traits to democratic leadership style especially. "There are certain traits that make being a democratic leader easier. If you possess the below four traits and you enhance these qualities, you can begin your journey towards democratic leadership." (p. 6) The four characteristics are intelligence, honesty, creativity and fairness.

The researcher stands with the views of Jago, Luenendonk and Ward, because in some cases, issues that might have caused a lot of problem can just be addressed by a leader without noise. If traits are not recognized, why do we prefer a particular person for a specific office? Or why do people appointed unopposed? Traits are inborn and traits of a particular trade or profession can be developed for effectiveness. Psychologists talk about enneagram-personality in sum total of the general characteristics which distinguish one individual from another. This is an attempt to showcase individual traits and what they can be used for. In the work of Anifaloba (1997), type three has been identified as the administrator and type eight, the boss. Both administrator and boss are terms that are common to leadership. Therefore, people of particular traits have been identified to be more effective in these areas. Through acquisition of knowledge and experiences, though, leaders can emerge and be successful. While leadership is learned, their (leaders) knowledge can be subjective to traits and qualities, such as background, values and character. Both knowledge and skills are relevant to leaders' achievements and exceptionality.

LEADERSHIP STYLES

Leadership style is a way and manner with which a superior gives directives and supervision for the execution of plans, through motivation, for the attainment of organizational goals. In general, twelve types of leadership styles can be identified for organizational improvement as follows:

1. Autocraticleadership style is centered on the boss. In this leadership, the leader holds all authority and responsibility without consulting their subjects.
2. Democratic leadership style: subordinates are involved in making decisions; headship is centered on subordinate's contributions.
3. Strategic leadership style which is geared towards a wider audience at all levels for creation of better performance.
4. Transformational leadership motivates others to do more than originally intended and often even more than they thought possible. They set more challenging expectations and typically achieve higher performance.

5. Team leadership: working with the heart and minds of all workers is the focus. It also recognizes that team work may not always contain trusting cooperative relationship.

6. Cross-cultural leadership normally exists where various cultures are included. This leadership has also industrialized as a way to recognize front runners who work in the contemporary globalized market.

7. Facilitative leadership that is too dependent on measurement and outcome, not a skill, although it takes much skill to master.

8. Laissez-Faire leadership style gives authority to employees or subordinates to work as they choose with minimal or no interferences.

9. Transactional leadership maintains or continues the status quo. It is the leadership that comprises an exchange process, whereby followers get immediate, tangible reward for carrying out the leader's orders.

10. Coaching leadership encompasses teaching and supervising followers. A coaching leader is highly operational in a setting where result or performance required improvement.

11. Charismatic leadership manifests a leader's revolutionary power. Charisma does not mean sheer behavioural change.

12. Visionary leadership is about leaders who recognize that the methods, steps and processes of leadership are all obtained with and through people.

All these leadership styles have been summarized by Stonner et al (2012) as authoritarian, consultative and participative, in which consultative and participative styles have been used interchangeably by many authors. Similarly, Lunnernburg and Ornstern (2008) and Akindutire (2004) present the summary of all the leadership styles as autocratic, democratic and laissez-faire. For the purpose of this work, authoritarian /autocratic, democratic/ consultative/ participative and laissez-faire leadership styles will be discussed to arrive at how they can be linked with *Igwebuike* philosophy.

AUTHORITARIAN OR AUTOCRATIC LEADERSHIP STYLE

Authoritarian leadership style involves formulation of policies by the leader. He is also responsible for stating implementation format. He controls and directs all activities without any meaningful input from his subjects. Leaders using this type of style will quickly punish any subordinate that is not working at their pace, because their attention is always on task and output, and not on employees' welfare. Authoritarian leaders are often referred to as "autocratic," and they are termed powerful because they always accompany their commands with threats or intimidations.

This type of leadership style has a lot of negative effects both on employee and the organizational growth. Employee will lack creativity and sense of responsibility, especially when the leader is not available, which will eventually tell on the organization. It is becoming an obsolete style of leadership, but can be used in some cases as Janse (2018) opines, "In teams where consensus is not easily reached because of a high diversity of team members or a group that is only briefly going to be working together, the authoritarian leader sees quickly what needs to be done and who is best suited for this" (p. 9).

DEMOCRATIC OR PARTICIPATIVE LEADERSHIP STYLE

Democratic or participative leadership style has been presented by authors as also consultative. This is defined by Gastil (2018) as "Distributing responsibility among the membership, empowering group members, and aiding the group's decision-making process." (p. 8) The democratic style of leadership encompasses the notion that everyone, by virtue of their human status, should play a part in the group's decisions. However, the democratic style of leadership still requires guidance and control by a specific leader. Leaders may even ask subordinates to vote before a decision is accepted. Therefore, majority carries the vote. Gastil further says that the democratic or participative leadership style places significant responsibility on leaders and their staff. This is true for all organizations, from private enterprises and government agencies to educational institutions and nonprofit entities. Democratic leaders build their employee and expect staff who report to them to have detailed experience and to display self-assurance. Leaders of this type must possess the following qualities: honesty and integrity, confidence, inspire others, commitment and passion, good communicator, decision making, capabilities, accountability, delegation and empowerment, creativity or innovation, empathy, resilience, emotional intelligence, humility, transparency, vision and pPurpose (Hassan, 2020). Kanu (2017) presents these qualities as: listening, empathy, healing, awareness, persuasion, foresight, stewardship and commitment to growth of people.

This type of leadership style is relevant in all cases as it makes both the leader and subordinates to have the same focus. It is a leadership style that has benefits in creating a sense of value and job fulfilment for employees, because their opinions and efforts are relevant in the decision-making process of the organization. This is in line with the opinion of Kanu (2017), who says that, "In every circumstance, the good of those led is placed over the self-interest of the leader. This is the leadership that promotes the valuing and development of people, the building of community, and the promotion shared power" (p. 8).

This will also encourage staff to stay with the organization for a long time to see that organizational goals are realized. Consultative leadership style is task-oriented, and focuses on the end result almost as much the leader seeks the opinion and viewpoints of his subordinates, before taking final decisions. It is a tactful way of asking for the opinion of subjects by the leader. This definition is not far from what democratic and consultative leadership styles stand for.

LAISSEZ-FAIRE LEADERSHIP STYLE

Laissez-faire leadership style is also referred to as free rein leadership style. Leaders in this regard allow followers to have complete freedom to make decisions concerning the completion of their work. It permits followers a self-rule, while at the same time offering guidance and support when requested. The laissez-faire leader provides followers with all materials necessary to accomplish their goals, but does not directly participate in decision making, unless the followers request his assistance.

In the description of universal teachers, laissez-faire leadership style is "no leadership at all" (p. 4), because the leader uses his/her power very little, if at all, giving subordinates a high degree of independence in their operations. Such leaders depend largely on subordinates to set their own goals and the means of achieving them, and they see their role as one of aiding the operations of followers by furnishing them with information and acting primarily as a contact with the group's external environment.

However, leaders are encouraged to learn all leadership styles and apply them to situations in their organizations. Whichever style a leader adopts, his/her intellectual capacity helps to conceptualize solutions and to acquire knowledge to do the job. Stoner et al (2002) feel that a manager's style must address situation, while paying attention to organizational size, specific work, time and environmental factors. (p. 471). It is to be noted, therefore, that the most popular and prevalent of all leadership styles is the democratic style. It has more advantages than disadvantages. It is very easy to practice, makes problem solving easy, working together increases the knowledge of members and encourages team spirit that brings about subordinates believing their leaders. In any organization, what subordinates consider the greatness attribute of a leader is credibility or trustworthiness. They want to say from time to time that, 'my boss has won my trust!'

IGWEBUIKE PHILOSOPHY

According to Kanu (2019)

> 'Igwebuike' is an Igbo word that is characterized by three simple words. On his terms, the three words involved: *Igwe* is a noun which means number or population, usually a huge number or population. *Bu* is a verb, which means *is*. *Ike* is another verb, which means *strength* or *power*. Thus, put together, it means 'number is strength' or 'number is power', that is, when human beings come together in solidarity and complementarity, they are powerful or can constitute an insurmountable force. (p. 1).

Kanu (2017) further explains this in this assertion. It (Igwebuike philosophy) "is anchored on the African worldview, which is characterized by a common origin, common world-view, common language, shared culture, shared race, colour and habits, common historical experience and a common destiny. Life is a life of sharedness." (p. 17). In the researcher's assessment of this philosophy, it pays attention to togetherness, collegiality, closeness and sharing. In its merit, it focuses on people, and that no member of the same group can exist or function well without support from others. It also gives encouragements to people to stay and work together in unity for progress (Kanu, 2016).

IGWEBUIKE PHILOSOPHY AND LEADERSHIP STYLES

In an attempt to draw a line between the *Igwebuike* philosophy and leadership styles, the summary of leadership styles presented in this work will be compared. Among the three styles discussed as a compressed form of all leadership styles - authoritarian, democratic and laissez-faire, the democratic or participative leadership style fits in properly to what the author of *Igwebuike* philosophy has in mind. The democratic leadership style involves people, as leadership generally stresses on staff strength in organizations. *Igwebuike* philosophy also involves large numbers of people. The philosophy is about sharing - "common origin, common world-view, common language, shared culture, shared race, colour and habits, common historical experience and a common destiny. Life is a life of sharedness" (p. 17), while democratic or participative leadership style emphasizes people or personnel working together irrespective of colour, origin or race. One is qualified to participate in decision making by virtue of only being a human person. It boils down to a democratic leader having mutual respect for his subordinates and allowing a free flow of ideas. On this, Kanu (2017) asserts that "*Igwebuike* posits that the level of the leader's impact is dependent on the level of connection he is able to have with his people" (p. 7).

Another common factor of these terms is focusing on a common goal or goals. Any group of people that have agreed to relate together in that regard must work towards a collective target. While the *Igwebuike* philosophy put emphasis on 'number is strength' or 'number is power'; that is, when human beings come together in solidarity and complementarity, they are powerful and can constitute an insurmountable force; it is about what they can achieve together (Kanu, 2015 & 2018). Any organization without a focus or output will not last, and it is this output or productivity that a democratic leader stands to gain in any organization, be it for-profit or non-profit organization. Leaders alone cannot improve quality; employees must be encouraged to take ownership of their work. The best way to achieve this is to make them part and parcel of the organization through participation in decision making. If this not done, they become negative about the organization and sell it to outsiders. This negative thought might quickly put down whatever business it may be and vice versa.

RECOMMENDATIONS

Based on the discussions above, it is recommended that leaders should carry their subordinates along in decision making, as the democratic leadership style involves people and the *Igwebuike* philosophy advocates for large numbers of people in leadership. A democratic leader should keep in mind that working together for the attainment of organizational goals, in the spirit of delegation of duty, will reduce stress and improve productivity.

It is also recommended that formation and in-service training for staff should be paramount in the mind of a democratic leader to enable them to be committed to duty. Leaders should keep in mind that regular formation is a better and lasting form of motivation for staff, since *Igwebuike* philosophy is about life of 'sharedness.'

This recommendation can be concluded by saying that the *Igwebuike* philosophy can give any leader a clue to what is expected to be done from time to time, which means, a leader must know what he should be, know and do for the attainment of organizational goals, since according to Kanu (2017), "the success of any organization, religious or secular, state or nation is highly dependent on the quality of leadership. Where there is no good leadership, there can't be unity, peace and progress" (p. 3).

CONCLUSION

This paper has discussed how the *Igwebuike* philosophy is relevant to leadership styles. Among the three leadership styles discussed as a condensed form of other styles - authoritarian, democratic and laissez-faire - only the democratic style matches what *Igwebuike* philosophy advocates in the life of 'sharedness.' Leadership definitions capture the essentials of being able and prepared to inspire others, which is based on ideas from the leader and the subordinates. Ability to communicate these ideas properly to subordinates and properly implement them is the responsibility of the leader.

Although the performances of a leader will be influenced by his values, background, knowledge and experiences, good leaders, however, will continue to work and study to improve their leadership skills, not rely on already gained knowledge. The two terms, *Igwebuike* philosophy and leadership styles, have, to a very great extent, large number of people, goals or productivity and involvement in common. In conclusion, Irabor (2019) reviewed Kanu's essay on inclusive leadership and *Igwebuike* philosophy. He came up with the fact that this philosophy could still "inform the grooming of a leader that will explore the principles of solidarity and complementarity within the whole" (p. 2).

REFERENCES

Akindutire I. O. (2004). *Administration of Higher Education.* Lagos. Sunray Press.

Anifaloba P.J (1997). *Removing the Plank with Enneagram- Knowing Yourself And Understanding Others Better.* Nigeria. Claverianum Press.

Gastil, J. (2018) "A Definition and Illustration of Democratic Leadership". New York: McGraw-Hill.

Hasan S. Top 15 Leadership Qualities That Make Good Leaders (2020). Retrieved (28/4/2020) from https://blog.taskque.com/characteristics-good-leaders.

Kanu, I.A (2017). *Igwebuike* Philosophy and the Issue of National Development in African Journal of Arts and Humanities Vol. 3 No 6,

Kanu, I.A (2017). *Igwebuike* as an Igbo-African Philosophy of Inclusive Leadership. A paper presented at the Second African Philosophy World Conference held at the University of Calabar, Cross Rivers State, Department of Philosophy, Conversational School of Philosophy, from October 12th to 14th 2017.

Kanu, I. A. (2018). *Igwe Bu Ike* as an Igbo-African Hermeneutics of National Development. *Igbo Studies Review. No. 6.* pp. 59-83.

Kanu, I. A. (2018). Igwebuike as an African Integrative and Progressive Anthropology. *NAJOP: Nasara Journal of Philosophy.* Vol. 2. No. 1. pp. 151-161.

Kanu, I. A. (2018). New Africanism: *Igwebuike* as a philosophical Attribute of Africa in portraying the Image of Life. In Mahmoud Misaeli, Sanni Yaya and Rico Sneller (Eds.). *African Perspectives on Global on Global Development* (pp. 92-103). United Kingdom: Cambridge Scholars Publishing.

Kanu, I. A. (2019). *Igwebuike* Research Methodology: A New Trend for Scientific and Wholistic Investigation. *IGWEBUIKE: An African Journal of Arts and Humanities* (IAAJAH). *5. 4.* pp. *95-105.*

Kanu, I. A. (2019). Igwebuikeconomics: The Igbo Apprenticeship for Wealth Creation. *IGWEBUIKE: An African Journal of Arts and Humanities. 5. 4.* pp. *56-70.*

Kanu, I. A. (2019). Igwebuikecracy: The Igbo-African Participatory Socio-Political System of Governance. *TOLLE LEGE: An Augustinian Journal of the Philosophy and Theology. 1. 1.* pp. 34-45.

Kanu, I. A. (2019). On the origin and principles of *Igwebuike* philosophy. *International Journal of Religion and Human Relations*. Vol. 11. No. 1. pp. 159-176.

Kanu, I. A. (2019b). An *Igwebuike* approach to the study of African traditional naming ceremony and baptism. *International Journal of Religion and Human Relations*. Vol. 11. No. 1. pp. 25-50.

Kanu, I. A. *Igwebuike* as an Igbo-African hermeneutics of globalisation. *IGWEBUIKE: An African Journal of Arts and Humanities*, Vol. 2 No.1. pp. 61-66. 2016

Kanu, I. A. *Igwebuike* as the consummate foundation of African Bioethical principles. *An African journal of Arts and Humanities* Vol.2 No1 June, pp.23-40. 2016

Kanu, I. A. *Igwebuike* as an expressive modality of being in African ontology. *Journal of Environmental and Construction Management. 6. 3.* pp.12-21. 2016

Kanu, I. A. African traditional folktales as an integrated classroom. *Sub-Saharan African Journal of Contemporary Education Research.* Vol.3 No. 6. pp. 107-118. 2016

Kanu, I. A. *Igwebuike* as an Igbo-African philosophy for Christian-Muslim relations in Northern Nigeria. In Mahmoud Misaeli (Ed.). *Spirituality and Global Ethics* (pp. 300-310). United Kingdom: Cambridge Scholars. 2017

Kanu, I. A. *Igwebuike* as an Igbo-African philosophy for the protection of the environment. *Nightingale International Journal of Humanities and Social Sciences.* Vol. 3. No. 4. pp. 28-38. 2017

Kanu, I. A. *Igwebuike* as the hermeneutic of individuality and communality in African ontology. *NAJOP: Nasara Journal of Philosophy.* Vol. 2. No. 1. pp. 162-179. 2017

Kanu, I. A. *Igwebuike* as a complementary approach to the issue of girl-child education. *Nightingale International Journal of Contemporary Education and Research.* Vol. 3. No. 6. pp. 11-17. 2017

Kanu, I. A. *Igwebuike* as a wholistic response to the problem of evil and human suffering. *Igwebuike: An African Journal of Arts and Humanities.* Vol. 3 No 2, March. 2017

Kanu, I. A. *Igwebuike* as an Igbo-African modality of peace and conflict resolution. *Journal of African Traditional Religion and Philosophy Scholars. Vol. 1. No. 1. pp. 31-40.* 2017

Kanu, I. A. *Igwebuike* and the logic (Nka) of African philosophy. *Igwebuike: An African Journal of Arts and Humanities.* 3. 1. pp. 1-13. 2017

Kanu, I. A. *Igwebuike* philosophy and human rights violation in Africa. *IGWEBUIKE: An African Journal of Arts and Humanities.* Vol. 3. No. 7. pp. 117-136. 2017

Kanu, I. A. *Igwebuike* as a hermeneutic of personal autonomy in African ontology. *Journal of African Traditional Religion and Philosophy Scholars.* Vol. 2. No. 1. pp. 14-22. 2017

Kanu, I. A. *African traditional philosophy of education: Essays in Igwebuike philosophy.* Germany: Lambert Publications. 2018

Kanu, I. A. New Africanism: *Igwebuike* as a philosophical Attribute of Africa in portraying the Image of Life. In Mahmoud Misaeli, Sanni Yaya and Rico Sneller (Eds.). *African Perspectives on Global on Global Development* (pp. 92-103). United Kingdom: Cambridge Scholars Publishing. 2018

Irabor, Benson Peter. (2019) A Review of Kanu Ikechukwu Anthony's "*Igwebuike* as an Igbo-African Philosophy of Inclusive Leadership. *IGWEBUIKE: An African Journal of Arts and Humanities Vol. 5 No 7, September 2019. pp 168*

Jago, A.G. (1982). Leadership: Perspectives in theory and research. Management Science, 28(3), 315-336.

Janse, B. (2018). Authoritarian Leadership. Retrieved [22/4/2020] from ToolsHero: https://www.toolshero.com/leadership/authoritarian-leadership/

Luenendonk, M. (2016). Democratic Leadership Guide: Definition, Qualities, Pros & Cons, Examples. Retrieved (28/4/2020) from https://www.cleverism.com/democratic-leadership-guide/

Lunnernburg F.C and Ornstern A.C (2008). Educational Administration: Concept and Practices. USA. Wadsworth: Cengage Learning.

Maxwell J.C. (2001). The Power of Leadership. Nigeria: Joint Heir Publications Ltd.

Miguel M. M. Integrity and Leadership Defined in The Journal of Government Financial Management. Volume: 66. Issue: 4 Publication date: Winter 2017. Page number: 52. www.questia.com

Northhouse, G (2007). Leadership Theory and Practice. (3rd Ed.). Thousand Oaks, CA: Sage Publications.

Stoner J.A.F, Freeman R.E and Gilbert D.R (2002). Management Sixth Ed. New Delhi: Asoke K. Ghosh.

Universal Teachers Publication. (2017). Leadership Styles: Consultative Leadership, Free Rein Leadership. http://www.universalteacherpublications.com/mba/free-project/p1/page5.htm

Ward S. (2020). The Definition of Leadership. Retrieved (28/4/2020) from https://www.thebalancesmb.com/leadership-definition-2948275

IMPACT OF MODERN CONFLICT MANAGEMENT MANCHANISM ON IGWEBUIKE PHILOSOPHY

Francis N. C. Iwuh
Mdibbo Adama University of Technology
Yola, Adamawa State
nduemerem16@yahoo.com

EXECUTIVE SUMMARY

The presence of the colonizers has created a new form of conflict in Africa. There was an established, recognized and effective system of resolving conflict prior to the advent of the colonial masters. The presence of modern conflict management has posed a great challenge to the existing traditional method. The work adopted a descriptive method to study the impact of modern conflict resolution on Igwebuike philosophy. The study is necessitated by the experimentation of the novel model of conflict resolution in the same environment and space, where the traditional conflict resolution once blossomed. This research work will attract the attention of policy makers, traditional rulers and political leaders in deciding the best method to resolve conflict. It has also exposed the deficiency and corruption inherent in modern conflict resolution. Thus, in the healing process, modern methods only rub and never massage the broken bones of conflict in Igwebuike philosophy of peace and conflict resolution.

Keywords: Igwebuike, Philosophy, Conflict, Management, Kanu Ikechukwu Anthony, Resolution, Modern

INTRODUCTION

Africa, just like other societies, was developing at her own pace with well-established mechanisms of managing conflicts before the colonial masters came and sewed their own western adjudication system that are alien to Africans. With the advent of colonialism, African values, norms and beliefs, which provided the normative and undergirding framework for conflict management, were severely weakened, undermined and disregarded. However, the resilience of African justice systems across African states illustrates that they still manage to occupy a central place in the world of dispute resolution in Africa. While in Europe, for instance, the police are a means of crime detection, several African societies relied on oath taking, divination and blood covenant in pre-colonial times. Traditional African methods of resolving conflict were geared towards restoring peace, and not necessarily in punishing the offenders. Emphasis was not on punishment but on reconciliation and restoration of social harmony among the disputants in conflict. Thus, Western justice systems thrived on commissions of inquiries, constitution and court system of lawyers and judges. Africans used council of elders, king's court, people's assemblies, etc., for dispute management and justice dispensation.

A very important reason for being aware of our tradition is so that we may draw lessons from them for the solutions to current problems. It is obvious that the Western approaches to conflict resolution have failed here in Nigeria in bringing back peace, and people even believe that the ongoing conflicts in the country are due to these Western systems of adjudication (Charles, 2016 p. 4). Traditional conflict resolution mechanisms may not have outlived their usefulness, especially when compared to modern reality, for pre-colonial Igbo society was embedded in the tradition and culture of the people.

There have been numerous conflicts in the history of Igbo people of eastern Nigeria. These conflicts can be due to many factors, such as; ethnic rivalry, religious violence, dispute over ownership of land, boundary issues, as well as political elections. Through the barometer of *Igwebuike* philosophy, this paper tends to study the impact of modern conflict management mechanism, using some of the basic features of *Igwebuike* philosophy of peace and conflict resolution to draw the conclusion that modern conflict management in Igbo land has actually been a resounding failure.

"MODERN" CONCEPTUALIZED

In peace studies, the term modern is used to differentiate with what is traditional. While the traditional refers to the indigenous or rural community which upholds and demonstrates the customs and norms of African society, modern refers to other societies outside Africa, and especially the European societies. We must understand here that the nature and functions of customs and norms in modern society quite differed from those of the African traditional societies. The modern world is also a world of competing interests, ideas, values, views, ideologies, religions and cultures – a world full of conflicting interests on all levels, between individuals and groups of people within their societies, between all sectors of societies, as well as between economies, nations, states, and so forth. Different conflict methods are used to manage and increase cooperation, promote reconciliation and strengthen relationships in the modern world. Modern here refers to the Western world as opposed to the African continent.

Modern can also be applied to those things that exist in the present age, especially in contrast to those of a former age or an age long past. Hence, modern, in this case, can mean the conflict management method used presently as opposed to the traditional methods that have been in existence since time immemorial in Africa. The use of modern model of conflict management is relatively new in the African society. However, before the introduction of a new method by alien cultures, the traditional methods of settling disputes varied from one society to the other. These methods were essentially based on each society's way of life. The introduction had a lot of imposition and condemnation of the original pattern of conflict resolution. Worthy of note here is that the experimentation of the novel model of conflict resolution was in the same environment and space, where the traditional conflict resolution once blossomed. The environment and space were the same, but the principles and practitioners of the conflict resolution were quite different. Even the result was proportionately different. It is, however, important to emphasize the point that the environment of conflict situation largely depends on the applicability of what method is in vogue. Environmental setting, therefore, is very necessary a determining factor in the desirability and adaptation of a specific method to use in the resolution of a particular conflict.

CONFLICT DEFINED

Etymologically, conflict is a word that is derived from the Latin word, *"confligere"*, which means to "strike together". Conflict means to strike, to fight, to struggle or battle, to clash, confrontation, a controversy or quarrel, active opposition, strife or incompatibility, to meet in opposition or hostility, to contend, to go contrary or to be at variance. Nwolise (2003) agrees with these, as he describes conflict as a clash, confrontation, battle or struggle. From the definitions above, conflict is all about disagreement on issues or things. It is disagreement in opinions between people or groups, due to differences in personal attitudes, beliefs, values or needs. For Charles (2016), "Conflict can be defined as the manifestation of a hostile attitude in the face of conflicting interests between individuals, groups or states. The conflicting interests can be over resources, identity, power, status or values" (p.1). It is generally seen as a struggle between two or more people over the same scarce resources at the same time. Ezenwoko and Osagie (2014) assert that, conflicts are generally accepted to be an inevitable phenomenon in the lives of men (p. 136). It cannot be completely separated from the inter-relationships that exist among individuals and communities. It is often argued that because human beings are by nature competitive and aggressive, there will always be conflicts amongst them. Conflict is, therefore, a natural occurrence among human beings.

Peace scholars generally agree that there must be more than one party to have a conflict and that the time factor is important. One cannot avoid conflict in families, at work or even when walking on the road. To this effect, Zartman (1997) posits that, "Conflict is an inevitable aspect of human interaction, unavoidable concomitant of choices and decisions." Peace scholars can go on defining conflict, but the truth is as Faleti (2014) observed, "Conflict is a fluid and definitely elastic concept which can be twisted into different shapes and has become an issue over which scholars find themselves in sharp disagreement with their colleagues" (p.36). This is true, owing to the fact that as he (Faleti 2014) observed, conflict can be constructive or destructive. Constructively, conflict can be used to explore different solutions to a problem and stimulate creativity, while, destructively, conflict can hinder progress, and cause hatred and division in the society (p.36). It has been demonstrated that continuous interaction among the individuals and communities cannot always be peaceful.

CAUSES OF CONFLICT

1. Competition for inadequate resources

Competition is the major source of conflict, because it drives people into struggling for limited resources, and people put in all their energy to get what they need. The conflict that occurs as a result of inadequate resources may assume a destructive dimension when what is available is not judiciously distributed. Those that are relatively deprived would always struggle to improve their lot. It is a situation of survival of the fittest.

2. Contradicting value systems

Another factor which may bring about conflict is contradicting value systems, such as the religious belief, ideological positions and general world view of the interacting parties. Values are beliefs or principles which are important to people. Conflict arises when one person's value system contradict another person's value system. Value system conflict is the most difficult conflict to resolve, because people will always hold on tenaciously to their position, believing that their opinion is better than that of others.

3. Group and individuals needs

Needs here range from psychological, political, economic to social needs of man. These are things that are fundamentally of utmost importance to people; they must be satisfied as soon as the purchasing power is available. These needs could be love, belonging, association, power etc. Therefore, needs have the potential of generating conflict, when perceived and expressed differently by people or group.

4. Manipulation of information

Manipulation of information can cause conflict in any community, relationship or workplace. When the flow of information is distorted or the content changed, conflict is bound to arise. Distortion of information comes in the process of passing information, from the sender to the receiver. As information move from one channel to the other, distortion sets in. distortion could either occur in packaging or in understanding of the message.

5. Perception

Lastly, perception has been discovered to cause conflict. Perception refers to how we see, understand or interpret the situations of things around us. What we see is sometimes different from what it really is, or from the way others see, understand or interpret them. You do not judge a book by its cover.

CONFLICT MANAGEMENT

Conflict managements are broad terms for methods and mechanisms used to avoid, minimize and manage conflicts between different parties (Niklas and Mikael, 2005). Wallensteen (2002) differentiates between conflict management and conflict resolution, saying that, conflict management typically focuses on the armed aspects of conflict: bringing the fighting to an end, limiting the spread of the conflict and, containing it;conflict resolution is more ambitious, as it expects the parties to face jointly their incompatibility and find a way to live with it or dissolve it. A number of scholars, especially from non-Western societies, have argued that conflict management is a successful tool for resolving conflicts over a longer time period, and that it creates the foundation for effective conflict resolution. This is contrasted with a more Western argument that the importance of conflict management lies in its ability to solve short-term conflicts. Both of these views are entirely accurate, and compatible, and there might just be a cultural difference in our focus (Niklas et al, 2005). Both of these views can, and should, be incorporated in a theoretical framework for conflict management and resolution, since they entail no inherent contradiction. They are in fact often applied in different stages of a conflict and address fundamentally different issues. Nevertheless, a number of Western scholars claim that the difference is one of long-term versus short-term perspectives and that it is a question of either resolving the underlying problem or managing the current problem.

Therefore, management measures are applied in later phases when a conflict is manifest, but before violence has occurred. Conflict resolution could, on the other hand, be applied in the de-escalation phase after a violent conflict has occurred. Nevertheless, resolution can be applied in all phases as soon as the conflict is manifest. Thus, traditional peace scholars use conflict resolution for African method and conflict management for modern method, because in the traditional method, conflicts are often rooted out. Practitioners try to dig out the root cause of every conflict, while such cannot be said of the modern method. Modern practitioners manage conflict; they try to reduce the effect of conflict to the barest minimum.

IKECHUKWU ANTHONY KANU

THE PRACTICE OF MODERN CONFLICT MANAGEMENT IN IGWEBUIKE PHILOSOPHY

Prior to the advent of modern culture, Igbo people had a well laid down, though undocumented, traditional process of conflict resolution. Charles (2016) asserts that "Each people, race, or identity group in the world had (and have) their own ways of doing things especially as it concerns social control and conflict resolution, (p.7). The big questions have always been, why the imposition of an alien method of managing conflict on African society? What is wrong with the traditional method? Peace scholars have debated and argued over the most appropriate mechanisms for managing conflicts in Africa. Some scholars believe that the application of Western methods in resolving conflicts in local communities may have some limited usefulness. Others, however, believe that the use of traditional mechanisms of conflict resolution would be most appropriate in addressing issues that are emanating from a socio-economic and political setting that is not completely modern. Yet, others think that a successful tackling of the conflict challenges that abound in Igbo-land would require a new and novel thinking that would accommodate both mechanisms by according preference to one or the other where it is most suitable (Charles, 2016 p.4). Chris (2014) disagrees with Charles, saying, "To a great extent, the Igbo people do not believe in the modern conflict management process, they believe in using the past history to settle conflict. They believe that to settle dispute amicably no side suffers any adverse effect, they go home happy."

Interestingly, the pre-colonial Igbo society was a decentralized society and decisions were taken at family, clan and age grade levels. Council of elders, usually made up of the most elderly and senior members of the community, exists to decide individual and community disputes. Dispute resolution is seen closely as a system of justice, to which the community, rather than individual leaders, is at the centre (Shedrack, 2014, p.98). Therefore, the council of elders is the highest judicial institution in Igbo land. Sadly enough, today, the council of elders who were once seen as custodians of wisdom and people of impeccable character are gradually being overshadowed in the administration of justice in the land to an alien system. Charles (2016) strongly believes that African value systems and conflict transformation systems are a viable means of resolving African conflicts today. The use of modern methods of conflict management, more often than not, has been a resounding failure in Igbo society.

Now, using the *Igwebuike* philosophy of peace and conflict resolution as a standard of Igbo conflict resolution, let us discuss the impact of modern conflict management. According to Kanu, "*Igwebuike* is an Igbo word; one of the major dialects in Africa. It is a principle that is at the heart of African thought, and in fact, the modality of being in African ontology" (2017, p. 6). He went on to say that it can be employed as a word or used as a sentence: as a word, it is written as *Igwebuike*, and as a sentence, it is written as, Igwe bu ike, with the component words enjoying some independence in terms of space. The three words involved: '*Igwe*' is a noun which means 'number' or 'population,' usually a huge number or population. '*Bu*' is a verb, which means 'is.' '*Ike*' is another verb, which means 'strength' or 'power' (Kanu,

2016). Thus, put together, it means 'number is strength' or 'number is power;' that is, when human beings come together in solidarity and complementarity, they are powerful or can constitute an insurmountable force. Its English equivalents are 'complementarity', 'solidarity' and 'harmony'. The preferred concept, however, is 'complementarity' (Kanu, 2017, p. 6).

At first contact with *Igwebuike*, one can comfortably say that modern conflict management mechanism has failed. *Igwebuike* as a concept thrives on complementarity, "to be with others". The modern method breeds more conflict than resolution; this is true because man is a social being created to be with others. On this point, Kanu (2017), the founding father of *Igwebuike* African Philosophy, avers that,

> As an indigenous African philosophy, *Igwebuike* gives an understanding of the human person as a being who is in relation with the other in the world. It establishes that there exists a common link between human persons and that it is through this relationship that every other human person realizes himself or herself. It is the foundation of openness, availability, affirmation of the other, freedom from threat based on the ability or good in others (p. 6).

The Western world, with its individualistic ideology, does not encourage community living, this "to be with others". Thus, the force on Africans to accept their method of conflict resolution creates more complex conflict, of identity, culture, tradition and personality. Again, modern method uses force to enforce judgment. They often use the police, and in some cases army, to enforce whatever judgment that has been reached in the law court. Funny enough, conflict always arises when modern method tries to enforce judgment. This is totally absent in traditional method. Compliance to decision reached is a collective responsibility in traditional conflict resolution. This is supported by the first basic features of *Igwebuike* philosophy of peace and conflict resolution, which states that, "Conflict is not viewed as a problem between the disputants but as a problem of the entire community. Conflict, therefore, attracts the attention of the community." Going further, Kanu (2017) elaborates on the fifth basic feature of *Igwebuike* philosophy of peace and conflict resolution, saying, "There is a high degree of public participation. There are no secret trails in African traditional legal system. Since the problem between the disputants is seen as a community problem, in restoring harmony, there must be a general satisfaction among the public regarding the procedure and outcome of the case (p. 9)." To this end, conflict between/among members of the community is viewed as a community conflict. The seventh and eighth basic features of *Igwebuike* philosophy of peace and conflict resolution holds that, "Decisions are reached through agreement rather than force....The enforcement of a decision is reached through social pressure rather than the police or military" (Kanu, 2017, p.9). So, acceptance of the judgment is seen there and then through demonstrative action of reconciliation. Reconciliation is at the heart of Igbo conflict resolution. The institutions that resolve conflict in Igbo traditional society speak with truth and integrity to the conscience of the parties in conflict; a soft word, no doubt turns away anger, and in African traditional societies, words have power. Moreover, the words of elders are anchored on wisdom. This was captured beautifully well in the third basic feature of *Igwebuike* philosophy of peace and conflict resolution by Kanu (2017, p.9) in these words: "The emphasis is on reconciliation and restoring social harmony. It purpose is, therefore, aimed at rebuilding broken relationships and restoring the community."

It must be made clear here, that every effort to manage conflicts through administrative and bureaucratic machinery in Igbo land, coupled with theories and methods crafted in Euro-American institutions, has failed to yield practical results in many conflict situations. To this, Kariuki (2015) opines that,

> Modernity has had its fare share of negative impacts on African justice systems. In pre-colonial period, elders were the rich and wealthiest people as they had land and livestock. Their wealth and respect enabled them to be independent during dispute resolution processes. However, in modern societies, younger people have accumulated wealth and in most cases, older people rely on the younger people. This has enabled dispute resolution by elders to be affected by bribery, corruption and favoritism... Apart from corruption and bribery, modernity and westernization have broken down the close social ties and social capital between families and kinsmen (pp.12-13)."

The presence of modern conflict management has posed a great challenge to the existing traditional method. Being a method that is corrupt and manipulative, people guilty,, especially those who are easily run to them for settlement, knowing that they can get their way to "a favourable judgment."

Hence, Nwolise (2004) posits that African traditional societies are known to hold secrets of peacemaking and peace building locked in their culture formed from customs and norms, before the coming of the colonial masters disrupted them. The processes of conflict resolution, such as mediation, counseling, conciliation, informal tribunals, arbitration of several types and criminal and civil justice system may not achieve the desired result. Over the centuries, African societies have built a wealth of experience as well as specific mechanisms and institutions to prevent conflicts, peacefully resolve conflicts once they arise and work through reconciliation processes. Even with modernization, these traditional institutions still hold sway, keeping the heart of the society in harmony. Inasmuch as modern adjudication system is being practiced, traditional methods of resolving conflicts are still alive in our communities.

CONCLUSION

Modern conflict management might have helped in the process of conflict resolution, but it has not resolved conflicts. It may be a means but not an end to conflict resolution in African society. So, forcing this method on Africans has never worked and will not still work. Africans should be allowed to continue with the traditional method which has always been in existence, tested and trusted to resolve conflict in our society. Since it has come to stay, modern conflict management mechanism should assist traditional conflict resolution in resolving conflicts, and not the other way round. Through the *Igwebuike* barometer, we have discovered that modern method caused more conflict than resolving it, since it does not foster community living, "the being with the other." The end product is not to make peace but to create enemies, as the judgment pronounced in modern conflict method breeds hatred, disunity and rivalry.

Civilization brought a cultural conflict between the African and the modern cultures. The modern culture was viewed as superior and dominant, thus subjugating African cultures. Cultural imperialism was extended to the world of dispute resolution. Therefore, modernized system of justice is retributive in nature by emphasizing a winner-loser paradigm in dispute resolution that does not resolve the underlying causes of the conflict. The adoption of the modernized justice system in Igbo land has made many traditional societies to revert to their own traditional dispute resolution by elders. The traditional method of resolving conflict is the best form of conflict management for the African people, since it digs deep into the root causes of the conflict to ensuring that peace is given a chance to reign once more through reconciliation.

REFERENCES

Charles, M.O. (2016). *Tiv and Igbo Conflict Management Machanism: A Comparative Study*, Port Harcourt, Centre for Conflict and Gender Studies (CCGS), 5(7), 22-29.

Chris, D. (2014). *African Traditional Procedures of settling Dispute: A Case Study between the People of Ihiagwa*. Owerri, Donasco the Casino United.

Ezenwoko, F.A. and Osagie I. J. (2014).*Conflict and Conflict Resolution in Pre-colonial Igbo Society of Nigeria*. Benin City, University of Benin.

Faleti, A.S. (2014). "Theories of Social Conflict" in Shedrack G.B. (ed.), *Introduction to Peace and Conflict Studies in West Africa*. Ibadan, Spectrum Books Limited.

Kanu I. A. (2015b). *A hermeneutic approach to African traditional religion, theology and philosophy*. Nigeria: Augustinian Publications.

Kanu, I. A. (2015a). *African philosophy: An ontologico-existential hermeneutic approach to classical and contemporary issues*. Nigeria: Augustinian Publications.

Kanu, A. I. (2016). Igwebuike as an Igbo-African hermeneutic of globalization. *IGWEBUIKE: An African Journal of Arts and Humanities. 2. 1.pp.* 1-7.

Kanu, A.I. (2017). *Igwebuike as an Igbo-African Modality of Peace and Conflict Resolution*, A paper presented at the 2017 Igbo Studies Association International Conference held at Great Wood Hotel, Owerri, Imo State, pp.1-10.

Kanu I. A. (2017). Igwebuikeconomics: Towards an inclusive economy for economic development. *Igwebuike: An African Journal of Arts and Humanities. Vol. 3. No. 6.* 113-140.

Kanu I. A. (2017). Sources of *Igwebuike* Philosophy. *International Journal of Religion and Human Relations.* 9. 1. pp. 1-23.

Kanu, A. I. (2016a). *Igwebuike* as a trend in African philosophy. *IGWEBUIKE: An African Journal of Arts and Humanities. 2. 1.* 97-101.

Kanu, A. I. (2017c). *Igwebuike* as an Igbo-African philosophy of inclusive leadership. *Igwebuike: An African Journal of Arts and Humanities.* Vol. 3 No 7. pp. 165-183.

Kanu, A. I. (2017d). *Igwebuike* philosophy and the issue of national development. *Igwebuike: An African Journal of Arts and Humanities.* Vol. 3 No 6. pp. 16-50.

Kanu, A. I. (2017f). *Igwebuike* as an Igbo-African Ethic of Reciprocity. *IGWEBUIKE: An African Journal of Arts and Humanities. 3. 2. pp.* 153-160.

Kanu, I. A. (2016a). *Igwebuike* as an Igbo-African Hermeneutics of Globalisation. *IGWEBUIKE: An African Journal of Arts and Humanities,* Vol. 2 No.1. pp. 61-66.

Kanu, I. A. (2016a). *Igwebuike* as the consummate foundation of African Bioethical principles. *An African journal of Arts and Humanities* Vol.2 No1 June, pp.23-40.

Kanu, I. A. (2016b) *Igwebuike* as an Expressive Modality of Being in African ontology. *Journal of Environmental and Construction Management. 6. 3.* pp.12-21.

Kanu, I. A. (2017). *Igwebuike* as an Igbo-African Philosophy for Christian-Muslim Relations in Northern Nigeria. In Mahmoud Misaeli (Ed.). *Spirituality and Global Ethics* (pp. 300-310). United Kingdom: Cambridge Scholars.

Kanu, I. A. (2019). *Igwebuike* research methodology: A new trend for scientific and wholistic investigation. *IGWEBUIKE: An African Journal of Arts and Humanities* (IAAJAH). 5. 4. pp. *95-105.*

Kanu, I. A. (2018). *Igwe Bu Ike* as an Igbo-African hermeneutics of national development. *Igbo Studies Review. No. 6.* pp. 59-83.

Kanu, I. A. (2018). *Igwebuike* as an African integrative and progressive anthropology. *NAJOP: Nasara Journal of Philosophy.* Vol. 2. No. 1. pp. 151-161.

Kanu, I. A. (2018). New Africanism: *Igwebuike* as a philosophical Attribute of Africa in portraying the Image of Life. In Mahmoud Misaeli, Sanni Yaya and Rico Sneller (Eds.). *African Perspectives on Global on Global Development* (pp. 92-103). United Kingdom: Cambridge Scholars Publishing.

Kanu, I. A. (2019). *Igwebuikeconomics*: The Igbo apprenticeship for wealth creation. *IGWEBUIKE: An African Journal of Arts and Humanities* (IAAJAH). *5. 4.* pp. *56-70.*

Kanu, I. A. (2019). *Igwebuikecracy*: The Igbo-African participatory cocio-political system of governance. *TOLLE LEGE: An Augustinian Journal of the Philosophy and Theology. 1. 1.* pp. 34-45.

Karuiki, F. (2015). Conflict Resolution by Elders in Africa: Successes, Challenges and opportunities. Kenya, Karuiki Muigua & Co.

Niklas, L.P. S. and Mikael, S. W. (2005). Central Asia-Caucasus Institute & Silk Road Studies Program.

Nwolise O.B.C. (2003). War-Making, peace-making and conflict resolution in Africa, *A guide to peace education and peace promotion strategies in Africa*, 2.H.B. Harunah, O.B.C Nwolise, and D. Oluyemi-Kusa. Eds. Lagos, African Refugee Foundation (AREF).

Nwolise O.B.C. (2004). Traditional Approaches to Conflict Resolution Among the Igbo People of Nigeria: Reinforcing the Need for Africa to Rediscover its Roots. *AMANI.*

Shedrack, G.B. (2014). "The Methods of Conflict Resolution and Transformation." in Shedrack G.B. (ed.), *Introduction to Peace and Conflict Studies in West Africa.* Ibadan, Spectrum Books Limited.

Wallensteen, P. (2002). *Understanding Conflict Resolution: War, Peace and the Global System.* London, Thousand Oaks, CA; & New Delhi: Sage Publications.

Zartman, I.W. (1997). *Governance as Conflict Management: Politics and Violence in West Africa.* Washington D.C., Brookings Institution Press.

IGWEBUIKE AND COMMUNICATION IN NOLLYWOOD: A QUALITATIVE REVIEW

Justine John Dyikuk
University of Jos, Plateau State
justinejohndyikuk@gmail.com

EXECUTIVE SUMMARY

The current digital society has affected almost every sector of life. The Nigerian movie industry, which suffered the onslaught of colonialism, is not left out. Nollywood is tossed about by the desire to be truly African, on the one hand, and the aspiration to be at par with Hollywood and Bollywood, on the other. This qualitative review entitled "Igwebuike and Communication in Nollywood: A Qualitative Review" investigated the matter, using the Homophily Principle of communication as theoretical framework. It found undue Western influence, negative narratives and inability to explore *Igwebuike* as the communalistic philosophy of Igbo people in home movies. It recommended promotion of African heritage, transmission of culture and civilization, promotion of community life, decolonizing the film industry and entrenchment of a valuable digital culture as possible panacea. The study concluded that, given its place in global reckoning, Nollywood has the capacity to overtake other prominent industries in the world towards providing a classroom of entertainment and education for second generation Igbos and other Africans in the diaspora.

Keywords: Communalism, Communication, Film, Igwebuike, Nollywood, Kanu Ikechukwu Anthony.

INTRODUCTION

Culture and communication are critical elements of the Nigerian movie industry. This is because most contents of cinematic platforms are laced with African flavour. From typical village square scenes to settings of royalty in the Igwe, Emir or Oba's palace, the film industry in Africa is Africanised. This Africanisation speaks to the heart of culture and communication. While communication transmits culture, culture is handed over to unborn generations through effective and efficient communication. This brings to the fore the *Igwebuike* philosophy of the Igbos of South Eastern Nigeria, which communicates the communalistic behaviour, ethos, beliefs, culture, tradition and norms of the people. The already-vibrant movie industry in Nigeria is a handy platform for the romance between *Igwebuike* rendering and communication. As the philosophy which encapsulates the way of life and values of the Igbos, *Igwebuike* pushes the frontiers of family system, kindred and a strong sense of fellow-feeling.

Because the movie industry in Nigeria has journeyed through an amateur screen to a golden goose on a global spotlight (Dyikuk, 2015), it serves as a vehicle for transmitting various values which are dear to the people. One of such values is *Igwebuike* which connotes communal living and peaceful existence in Igbo societies. Igbo films, which are an irresistible recipe on the Nollywood menu, are replete with scenes which express Africanism, care for one another and common solidarity. Despite the lofty place it occupies on the movie screen in Nigeria, some critics, like Johnson (2000), are of the opinion that Igbo and English movies are culturally confusing. Perhaps this is because, for instance, a film could begin with Emeka (Not real name), in the village, as a local champion who speaks using idiomatic expressions and end with him, in Lagos, as a "White Man" who appears in a suit and dazzles everyone with big grammar (British accent). Unfortunately, despite few instances where culture is infused in scenes, the film industry in Nigeria has not paid enough attention on promoting values, customs and traditions. Copying Western values has also been an albatross of the industry.

To this end, this study aims at:

1. Appraising the place of communication and culture in Nollywood, despite Western influence
2. Accounting for Nollywood through a historical sketch
3. Doing a critical review of *Igwebuike* in Nollywood
4. Assessing elements of communication in Nollywood
5. Making case for communicating an *Igwebuikenised* cinema in Nigeria

CONCEPTUAL SPADEWORK

a. ***Igwebuike***: As a composite metaphorical *Igwebuike* Igbo word, *Igwebuike* is a combination of three words - *Igwe bu ike,* which means: "*Igwe* is a noun which means number or population, usually a huge number or population. *Bu* is a verb, which means *is*. *Ike* is another verb, which means *strength* or *power*. Thus, put together, it means 'number is strength' or 'number is power', that is, when human beings come together in solidarity and complementarity, they are powerful or can constitute an insurmountable force or strength, and at this level, no task is beyond their collective capability" (Kanu, 2017b, pp.69-70).

b. **Communication:** Various types of communication include: verbal, nonverbal and written communication (Go, Monachello, Baum, 1996 & Dyikuk, 2017b). Also, "Expressive or informal communication occurs when information is not directly related to role performance" (Mohamad, 2008,p.9). In this article, we would understand communication as showcasing *Igwebuike* (African values) in Nigerian films.

c. **Nollywood:** This is the Nigerian film industry which traces its roots to 1992, in Onitsha, when Kenneth Nnebue produced the movie *Living in Bondage* 1 & 11 - an Igbo-language film with English subtitles. Experts cite this as the beginning of commercial film production in Nigeria (Mordi & Onu, 1999).

THEORETICAL FRAMEWORK

The study adopts the Homophily Principle of communication as theoretical framework. This principle, which speaks to the heart of the degree of difference on any attribute or group of attributes between a sender and a receiver, holds that for any change agent, such as films makers, cinematographers, videographers, communication scholars, journalists, teachers and other professionals, to succeed in influencing a receiver of communication, namely audiences and viewers, both the agent and the receiver must have the same attributes. These attributes could mean the same culture, norms, education, socialization process and socio-cultural, religious and political values (Mgbejeme, 2009).

The choice of the Homophily Principle of communication as theoretical framework for the study is informed by Pan-Africanism, which seeks a decolonization of the cinematic platform towards raising African scholars and films makers who are in touch with their roots and share the same vision, passion, values and norms with their people. The principle argues that it is when films makers, cinematographers, videographers, communication scholars, journalists, teachers and other experts in the Nigerian film industry Africanise the screen that their audiences would better appreciate watching Nollywood. A Nollywood inspired by *Igwebuike*, especially African communalism, is key to effective education and entertainment which the movie industry desires to achieve.

LITERATURE REVIEW AND DISCUSSION

Igwebuike Rendering: An Overview

Igwebuike is an Igbo-African philosophy of complementarity. *Igwebuike* explains how the ethic of reciprocity is at the heart of African philosophy and religion (Kanu, 2017d). *Igwebuike* philosophy aligns with its inner principles of inclusiveness, complementarity and solidarity (Kanu, 2017b). The Igbos believe that "No people can rise to an influential position in the community of nations without a distinct and efficient nationality" (Kanu, 2017e, p.36). This is because of the high sense of community over the individual. "Igwebuike rests on the African principles of solidarity and complementarity. It argues that 'to be' is to live in solidarity and complementarity, and to live outside the parameters of solidarity and complementarity is to suffer alienation" (Kanu, 2016, p.110-111).

Explaining this further, Kanu opines that the African worldview:

> is ruled by the spirit of complementarity which seeks the conglomeration, the unification, the summation of fragmented thoughts, opinions and other individualized and fragmented thoughts and ideas. It believes essentially that the whole is greater than the corresponding parts. It is also a view that maintains that by the coming together of the individual or parts, a viable and sustainable whole will emerge, and by this, the parts will get to the brim purpose of their existence (2017c, p.14).

The extended family system is tied to faith in the Supreme Being and the deities, as well as in ethos of the people. "Because their existence and action, in the midst of communication, are limited by time, place, perception and knowledge, their being is existentially complimentary. Hence they are naturally candidates for company and co-operations" (Kanu, 2018, pp.18-19). In Africa, the individual is connected to the divine through interaction with the deities and ancestors who are believed to intercede for the living. This reveals a collegiality that is tied to faith and morals which further provide "dos" and "don'ts" as ethical codes that guide personal and interpersonal communication.

NOLLYWOOD: A HISTORICAL SKETCH

The first Nigerian films by two filmmakers, Ola Balogun and Hubert Ogunde were produced in the 1960s, but the high cost of production put them out of market (Adesokan, 2006). By this time, the stage had been set for television broadcasting in the country. The 1970s saw the emergence of the first Nigerian feature, *Kongi's Harvest,* written by Wole Soyinka and directed by Ossie Davis. When state-owned stations began broadcasting in the 1980s, theatre productions which were circulated in video format took centre stage in Lagos. Through his NEK Video Links, Kenneth Nncbuc produced two Yoruba movies namely *Aje Ni IyaMi* (1989) and *Ina Ote* (1990). From that time on, an amateur video trade production (Cinema of Nigeria) began. However, it was his movie, *Living in Bondage* 1 & 11 - an Igbo-language film with English subtitles which was produced in Onitsha in 1992 (Mordi & Onu, 1999) that experts hold as the beginning of Nollywood and commercial film production in Nigeria.

When Nnebue's two movies *Glamour Girls* 1 & 2 (1994) and *True Confession* (1995) hit the new movie industry (Shaka, 2003), lack of equipment, piracy and harsh economic policies by International Monetary Fund (IMF) and Structural Adjustment Programme (SAP) frustrated the industry (Haynes, 1995). In his submission, Uchenna (2009) explains that what we know today as Nollywood passed through four periods of development, namely; the colonial period

(1903-1960), independence period (1960-1972), Indigenization Decree period (1972-1992) and Nollywood period (1992 till date). He further maintained that the history of film in Nigeria from 1903 to 1992 is related to the crucial stages of Nigeria's history. As it stands today, the Nigerian film industry (Nollywood) ranks among the top three filmmaking industries in the world, in terms of the quantity of productions, popularity amongst Nigerians and the transnational audiences (Hanmakyugh, 2019).

IGWEBUIKE AND COMMUNICATION IN NOLLYWOOD: AN INVESTIGATION

Identities based on religion, ethnicity, regionalism and communalism, which are essentially "given" rather than "chosen" have existed since the creation of Nigeria (Jega, 2001). For the Igbos of Eastern Nigeria, *Igwebuike* explains their identity. This identity further reveals who they are and their ultimate destiny. Their identity is communal in nature. Accordingly, "These common history, culture, and customs are what this thesis describes as 'communalism' in terms of the nature of the Igbo and African cultures. It embodies the substance of the beingness of Africans or the Africanness of Africans as a matter of fact, their existence and the quiditas of their characteristics" (Uwah, 2009, p.11). This is where Igwebuike comes in.

Igwebuike captures the communalistic nature of Igbo societies. The anthropological depictions of Africans, especially Igbo philosophy and thought, are seen in their communalism which buttresses, more or less, the aesthetic cultural elements of these films (Uwah, 2009). Experts on African film think that "Communalism captures the eco-system that operates in African cosmology which serves as a core attribute of most Nollywood filmic story lines" (Uwah, 2009,p.54). It is essential to understand that the notion of being in existence is founded on communalism, whereby, every being is considered to be related to one another (Uwah, 2009). To this end, the concept of God in African communalism is revealed by the names given to Him in African languages (Uwah, 2011).

For Moemeka (1997, p.181), "Just as the communalistic culture demands that the younger generation must respect, listen to, and learn from the elders, so it demands from the elders appropriate action to provide conducive learning experiences for the younger generation." Communication is always a question of attitude towards one's neighbour closely tied to communication rules designed to ensure communal social order. He contends that in both verbal and non-verbal, communalistic acts are engaged in in order to confirm, solidify and promote social order (Moemeka, 1998).

Igwebuike is conveyed through effective communication. Perhaps, this is why to maintain cohesion in African communalistic societies, there is a "belief in a kind of power communication [vital force] between the 'spirit world' and the 'human world', whereby activities in one realm affects those in the other realm" (Uwah, 2011,p.94). The Igbo communication style is learned within the primary socialization process of the Igbo ethnic group. They also use their communication styles for code switching, engaging in conversations with their co-ethnic membership as well as interacting with family members in their ancestral home (Onuzulike, 2018).

That second generation Igbos are able to learn Igbo traditional culture directly from their home-land through Nollywood (Onuzulike, 2018) demonstrates the relevance of Igwebuike to the cinematic platform. Movies such as My Best Friend (2003), Oil Village (2001), Widow (2007), Last Ofala (2002), Fool at 40 (2006) showcase the concept of communalism (Uwah, 2009). Film as a means of communication is a potent tool for image making, cultural diplomacy, propaganda, education, information and entertainment (Hanmakyugh, 2019). Today, "One impressive aspect of Nollywood in all of these is in the representation of religio-cultural rituals as a major aspect of communalism" (Uwah, 2011,p.86). Culture is the bedrock of Nollywood's thematic film expositions. One can, therefore, conclude that Nollywood is Nigeria's cultural ambassador. Although Nollywood films are quite potent in celebrating and promoting Nigerian cultures, some of these films have come under thematic criticisms as they glamourize negative ritual themes in the name of culture (Hanmakyugh, 2019).

RECOMMENDATIONS: TOWARDS COMMUNICATING AN *IGWEBUIKENISED* NOLLYWOOD

1. **Promotion of African Heritage:** Even as it seeks to mirror society, Nollywood should promote local content, which includes rich artifacts, customs/cultural images and idioms. By the same token, African drama and cinema should be at the forefront of promoting African (Nigerian) identity (Dyikuk, 2015) to the world through *Igwebuike* and all it encapsulates. That way, Nigerians abroad and successive generations would be able to remember their rich heritage.

2. **Transmission of Culture and Civilization:** This study argues that *Igwebuike* should promote an African civilization through culture. Lovers of sports, movies, documentaries and other genres of television in the country should take advantage of what digital television offers to not only have a good time in terms of recreation but also learn new cultures and civilization (Dyikuk & Chinda, 2017) which are capable of building bridges of peace amongst various people across the country and the African continent.

3. **Promotion of Community Life:** *Igwebuike* stands for community life and sharing. As such, Nigerian films should be "deeply rooted in Nigerian cultural traditions and social texts, which focus on Nigerian community life" (Onuzulike, 2009,p.176). This is in agreement with the submission of another film scholar who explained that "One impressive aspect of Nollywood in all of these is in the representation of cultural rituals as a major aspect of communalism" (Uwah, 2009, p.25). Interestingly, the works of experts on communication and African communalism, like Moemeka (1997), lend credence to Igbo style of communication which promotes community life, sharing and a strong sense of fellow-feeling.

4. **Decolonizing the Film Industry:** Because Africa has been misunderstood and misrepresented by the West, it behooves scholars and film experts to use Nollywood as a platform for decolonisation. "By understanding the interactivity between Africans and their environment as communalistic people, one discovers the errors of the colonialists who rejected what they did not understand of the people's cultures and [mis]represented them as barbaric and paganistic" (Uwah, 2009, p.25). Promoting *Igwebiuke* worldwide may serve as the desired recipe that would checkmate the incursion of Western values in the local film industry.

5. **Entrenching a Valuable Digital Culture:** Because "the world has evolved a fascinating digital culture" (Dyikuk & Chinda, 2017,p.41), it is crucial for film makers to seize the opportunity to promote good homegrown movies which teach morals and values from an African perspective. For example, the criticism that the ongoing Big Brother Naija which seems to showcase Western values is receiving could be addressed by using the platform to entrench African values. Besides, Nollywood can help the diaspora community or second generation Igbos to be in touch with their roots.

CONCLUSION

We saw that although culture and communication are important elements of the Nigerian movie industry, the *Igwebuike* philosophy, which aligns with the principles of inclusiveness, complementarity and solidarity, has not been given a pride of place on the screen. This is why the author employed the Homophily Principle of communication as theoretical framework to demonstrate that film makers, cinematographers, videographers, communication scholars and journalists in Nigeria have the capacity to change the narrative towards giving *Igwebuike* philosophy, with its ingredients of culture, norms, education, socialization process and socio-cultural, religious and political values, its rightful place in home movies.

Given its place in global reckoning, Nollywood could overtake Hollywood and Bollywood if experts insist on infusing African values, like *Igwebuike*, into film production. This way, Africans in the diaspora, particularly second generation Igbos, will benefit more. In conclusion, to effectively and efficiently communicate an *Igwebuikenised* Nollywood, promotion of African heritage, transmission of culture and civilization, promotion of community life, decolonizing the film industry and entrenchment of valuable digital culture must be given high premium.

REFERENCES

Adesokan, A. (2006). *New Nigerian Cinema: An interview with Akin Adesokan* - www.indiana. edu. Accessed on 8/19/2020.

Dyikuk, J. J. & Chinda, F. E. (2017). Digital Terrestrial Television: A Critical Assessment of the Adventures and Misadventures of Nigeria's Digital Switch Over. *International Journal of Applied Research and Technology. 6(12)*: [40 – 49].

Dyikuk, J.J (2015). The Nollywood Narrative: Africa's Golden Goose on a

Global Spotlight? Global Advanced Research Journal of Social Science (GARJSS) Vol. 4(X).

Dyikuk, J.J (2017). Scrutinizing organisational communication through work-environment, power and politics in Nigeria. International Journal of Advanced Research and Publications (IJARP). Vol. 1 Is. 2. [45-53].

Go, F. M., Monachello, M. L., & Baum, T. (1996). *Human resource management in the hospitality industry.* NY: John Wiley & Sons, Inc.

Hanmakyugh, T.T (2019). Ritual culture phenomenon in Igbo films: A study of *Money is Money. EJOTMAS: EKPOMA Journal of Theatre and Media Arts.* Vol. 7 Nos. 1-2. [376-385]

Jega, A. 2001. Identity Transformation and Identity Politics Under Structural Adjustment in Nigeria. Stockholm: *Nordiska Afrikaininstitutet* and Centre for Research and Documentation.

Johnson, D. (2000). *'Culture and Art in Hausa Video Films'* In Haynes, J (ed) *Nigerian Video Films.* Ohio: University Centre for International Studies.

Kanu, I.A (2016). Igwebuike as a trend in African philosophy. *An African Journal of Arts and Humanities.* A Publication of Tansian University, Department of Philosophy and Religious Studies. Vol. 2 No 1.[108-113].

Kanu, I.A (2017a) Igwebuike as a wholistic response to the problem of evil and human suffering. *Igwebuike: An African Journal of Arts and Humanities.* A Publication of Tansian University, Department of Philosophy and Religious Studies. Vol. 3 No 2. [63-75].

Kanu, I.A (2017b). Igwebuike as an igbo-african philosophy of inclusive leadership. *Igwebuike: An African Journal of Arts and Humanities.* A Publication of Tansian University, Department of Philosophy and Religious Studies. Vol. 3 No 7. [165-183].

Kanu, I.A (2017c). Igwebuike and the logic (*Nka*) of African philosophy. *An African Journal of Arts and Humanities.* A Publication of Tansian University, Department of Philosophy and Religious Studies. Vol. 3 No. 1 [9-18].

Kanu, I.A (2017d). Igwebuike as an Igbo-African ethic of reciprocity. *An African Journal of Arts and Humanities*. A Publication of Tansian University, Department of Philosophy and Religious Studies. Vol. 3 No 2. [153-160].

Kanu, I.A (2017e). Igwebuike philosophy and the issue of national development. *An African Journal of Arts and Humanities*. A Publication of Tansian University, Department of Philosophy and Religious Studies. Vol. 3 No 6. [16-50].

Kanu, I.A (2018.) Igwebuike and being in Igbo ontology. *Igwebuike: An African Journal of Arts and Humanities*. A Publication of Tansian University, Department of Philosophy and Religious Studies. Vol. 4 No 5. [12-21].

Mgbejume, O. (2009). Communication and society: Some basic issues. Jos: Motion picture academy.

Moemeka, A. (1998). "Communalism as a Fundamental Dimension of Culture" in Journal of Communication. Blackwell Publishing. [118 – 138].

Moemeka, A. (1997). Communalistic societies: Community and self-respect as African values. In C. Christians & M. Traber (Eds.), Communication Ethics and Universal Values (pp. 170–193). Thousand Oaks, CA: Sage.

Mohamad, S. F (2008). "Effects of communication on turnover intention: A case of hotel employees in Malaysia". *GraduateTheses and Dissertations*. Paper 11164.

Mordi, V & Onu, C (1992). Living in Bondage 1 & 2. Prod. Nnebue, K. With Kenneth Okonkwo, NnennaNwabueze, Francis Agu, and Kanayo O. Kanayo. Nek Video Links Production.

Onuzulike, U (2018). The Igbo Communication Style: Conceptualizing Ethnic Communication Theory. DO - 10.1007/978-3-319-75447-5_4.

Onuzulike, U. (2009). Nollywood: Nigerian Videoēlms as a Cultural and Technological Hybridity. International Journal of Intercultural Communication Studies, 18(1), 176–187.

Onuzulike, U. (2018). Explicating Communication Styles in the Diaspora: The Case of Young Igbo-Americans. In W. Jia (Ed.), Intercultural Communication: Adapting to Emerging Global Realities: A reader (2nd ed., pp. xxx–xxx). San Diego, CA: Cognella Publisher.

Shaka, F. 2003. *'Rethinking the Nigerian Video Film Industry: Technological Fascination and the Domestication Game.'*In F. Ogunleye (Ed), *African Video Film Today.* Manzini, Swaziland: Academic publishers.

IKECHUKWU ANTHONY KANU

Uchenna, O. (2009). *Nollywood: The Emergence of the Nigerian Video Film Industry and its Representation of Nigerian Culture.* [Online] A Master's Thesis submitted to the Faculty of Clark University: Worcester, Massachusetts.

Uwah, I. E (2009). From rituals to films: A case study of the visual rhetoric of Igbo culture in Nollywood films. PhD thesis, Faculty of Humanities, Dublin City University, Ireland.

Uwah, I. E (2011). The representation of African traditional religion and culture in Nigeria popular films. *Politics and Religion* 1/Vol. V. UDK: 316.72:[791.23:2(669) ; 791.232(669).

THE IMPACT OF IGWEBUIKE IDEOLOGY ON PEACE BUILDING IN AFRICAN

Okafor, Emmanuel Ikenna (Ph.D)
Department of Christian Religious Studies,
Peaceland College of Education, Enugu
&

Ude, Chizoba Chilotaram
Department of Social Studies Education,
Institute of Ecumenical Education, Thinkers Corner, Enugu
&

Okolo, Rosemary Ngozi (Ph.D)
Department of Religion and Cultural Studies,
University of Nigeria, Nsukka
&

Amaechi-Ani, Nneka Nkiru.
Department of Social Studies Education,
Institute of Ecumenical Education, Thinkers Corner, Enugu
agbudugbu@gmail.com

EXECUTIVE SUMMARY

African continent had perceived group soldering as the greatest strategies to tackle difficult and tedious challenges that torment human society. It is an ideology that rose from the natural and spontaneous communalistic spirit in the people's collective relationships. Igwebuike is an Igbo Language which literally means large number is strength. It is a concept that has been developed by Prof. Kanu Ikechukwu Anthony within the context of the underlying principle of African philosophy, religion and culture. The basic ideology there is that united majority is aviable machinery in solving group or members' problems. This paper therefore aims at re-focusing on how Igwebuike as an ideology can be adopted in Africa to provide lasting peace in Africa and among African states and people. The research observes that serious concern is not given to the Igwebuike ideology on the area of peace build. Attention was very much on application of the ideology for economic gains, group opposition attacks and for political gains. The research recommends that earnest concern should be given to this ideology throughout Africa with the use of age –grade system, communal worship system, women folk, kinship system, to mention but a few. The research adopted historical and sociological approaches. Data were sourced from both primary and secondary means. Data were analyzed with phenomenological method of data analysis.0

Keywords: *Igwebuike* ideology, Kanu Ikechukwu Anthony, Peace–building and African people

INTRODUCTION

The impact of *Igwebuike* ideology overwhelmly occupies the African perception of peace-building. For the sake of peace-building in Africa, Late Dr. Nnamdi Azikiwe had made serious effort to unite African nations; the evidence can be derived from his establishment of a newspaper industry with the name, West African Pilot, and the establishment of a financial institution known as African Continental Bank. Before his death, he was popularly known as the Zik of African. Zik's initiative motivated the name given to one of the old generation's banks as United Bank for African-UBA.

At the face of confusions that triggered Nigerian civil war some Nigerians including Dr Nnamdi Azikiwe still advised for one Nigeria. Today, against the creation of another country out from Nigeria, some still advocate for one Nigeria with good political restructuring. The country's academic system teaches unity in diversity in the area of social studies. In the researcher's council area, during a serious political tussle, a prominent politician in the local government area in the person of Rt. Hon. Dr. Festus Uzor stated thus: "No Ezeagu man is more Ezeagu than the other. You are… because we are… You cannot be… if we are …" He is stressing here that the office occupied by one politician in Ezeagu Local Government Area is made possible because majority of Ezeagu politicians supported the person therefore when the same majority stand behind someone, he or she alone should not counter.

Igwebuike captures and communicates the Igbo-African world. *Igwebuike* is the form and symbolic of the Igbo-African mental being and the gateway to Igbo-African philosophy. Beyond the literal understanding of *Igwebuike* (*Igwe*- number; *bu*-is; *ike*-strength) as "there is strength in number", it captures the Igbo philosophy of relationality, complementarity and interconnectedness of reality (Kanu 2014; 2015; 2016; 2017; 2018; 2019). It concatenates Igbo forms, symbolism, signs, media, meaning, anthropologies, universal cosmic truths, functions, semantic powers, physics, phenomena, faculties, and Igbo environ-mentalities, and symbolizes the propositional powers of Igbo knowledge, perception, identity, phenomenalism, physics, metaphysics, logic, history of analytic character, speculative mindset and positive provisions for definitions of facts (Kanu 2020). In a nutshell the views and actions stated above, rally round the idea in the Igbo word *Igwebuike*. Larger group alliance is always strength and powerful. An Igbo adage states thus: *Ofu onye siere oha, oha e richee ya, ma na oha siere ofu onye, o ma richee ya*. This means that if an individual prepares meal of any quantity for a large united group, the group will consume it all, but when the group prepares any quantity of food for the individual, he cannot finish it.

In view of the above, it could be ascertained that this *Igwebuike* ideology has serious impact on the African people's security and peace-building in virtually all the ramifications of their lives, be it political, economic, social, education, religion, health and so on. Mrs Ajayi Marian (personal communication, 7 April 2020) states that most African comm.unities from history believed in team work. They did group farming, group hunting etc. What Mrs Ajayi says is true, because today, for example, in the hunting games, when a group march to the bush, with their individual guns, dogs etc, they threaten the bush, making every animal there uncomfortable. After the game, many animals are caught. This is just a sample of how united majority can subdue any obstacle that arises. When united group spirit is well developed, there is no doubt, the group can move mountains in return, such unity sustains peace among them and fosters security.

Igwebuike ideology is not relatively far from African communalism but the only demarcation is that communalism can exist between independent individual communalist relationships, but *Igwebuike* sees the group mission as supreme to individual Interest: Most African states were able to gain political, economic and even religious independence because of their formidable united majority (*Igwebuike)* spirit. The Igbo/Ibibio women that confronted the ruling muscles of the colonialists in the so called Aba women riot, was made possible on the basis of *Igwebuike* ideology which had impacted lasting peace among the local women and families in the zone. Among the findings of the research is that with effective actualization of the idea of group soldering so many problems can be tackled to their barest minimum. That notwithstanding, the same *Igwebuike* ideology can be used for negative intention or goals, for example, the mob actions, team armed robbery et cetera. The paper intends to re-echo how *Igwebuike* as an ideology would be implemented in Africa, its communities and nations, to provide lasting peace in Africa, its nations, and peoples. The research also discovers that much more serious concern is not given to the *Igwebuike* ideology on the area of peace building. The ideology is mostly applied for selfish economic gains, group opposition attack and counter attacks, political gains, selfish social solidity, etc. It is recommended in this research that more serious concern should be attached to *Igwebuike* ideology throughout Africa with the use of traditional machineries such as age-grade system, communal worship system, the Masquerading society, the title institutions, family institution, and other modern machineries like the youth clubs and associations, neighborhood watch teams, elders forum, town union, Christian and Muslim Associations, Government and Non-governmental Organization et cetera. The methodologies used in this research are both historical and sociological approaches. Data used were generated from primary and secondary stocks. The method of data analysis was phenomenological analytical method. *Igwebuike* ideology is synonymous with the broom bunch as an adage or concept. Individual sticks that make up the broom bunch can easily be broken, but to break the broom bunch is definitely difficult. The broom exhibits its strength in its bunch than when it is separated from the bunch. The broom sticks in a bunch are peaceful, that is why they have agreed to be tied together as one entity. This is the basis on which *Igwebuike* as an ideology champions all ramifications of human welfare in typical African society.

CLARIFICATION OF CONCEPTS

The concepts or terms that fundamentally call for explanations are: *Igwebuike* ideology, peace-building, and African (People). *Igwebuike* as a word finds its origin in Igbo ecolingual base. *Igwebuike* links itself with terms like communalism, cooperative movement and even united majority. Though slight differences might exist between these three terms but the variation seems to be insignificant. Akukwe (1996) Opines that cooperative comes from the Latin word co-operate, i.e. to work together. According to Akukwe, the idea of men working together is as old as man himself because of his social nature. Because of his inherent limitations, man needs the co-operation of his fellow human beings to develop his physical, intellectual and spiritual potentialities (Akukwe, 1996). According to Summers (2001), communal is perceived as that shared by a group, especially a group of people who live together, or that which involves people from many different races, religions, or language groups. This adjective communal, forms the basis of the term communalism. Majority on the other hand, links itself with number. Most of the people or things in a particular group (Summers, 2001). The *Igwe* in the word connotes majority/large in number, the '*bu*' means is in English Language. It is just a verb that shows the attribute of the suffix to the prefix '*Ike*' which means strength/power in English Language. While communalism emphasizes on sharing things in common, cooperative/cooperation focuses on the unity to achieve specific goal(s). When these three basic strands of thought are merged together, the concept of *Igwebuike* becomes comprehensible.

Peace-building has peace as the head word. Peace in the lay man view might imply or mean happiness. But peace connotes, no war, agreement, no noise, calmness, etc (Summers, 2001). Peace-building, simply means the art of structuring, sustaining a condition of calmness, noiselessness, agreement in positive mindedness, no war, no conflict, no violence etc. African people as we all know, are one of the peoples that make up one of the continents of the world, dominated with the people with dark or black identification. Mr. Onwuka Francis (personal communication, 13 March 2020) points out that what aboriginals of Igbo nation commonly call or presume Africans to be is the people with black hair-*Ndi Isi Oji*. Summers (2001) adds that the word "African interprets someone from Africa. Mr. Gabriel Patrick (personal communication 6 April, 2020) points that Africa as an area is in most cases presented as a sunny zone. What Patrick stresses could be truly acceptable because Africa has the highest geographical coverage where the sun radiates the ultra violet rays heavily. Dr. Obiora Aniebo, a Geographer/Geo-Physicist (Personal Communication, 8 May, 2020) opines that the ultra-violet rays discharge greater heat within Africa as a geographical region more than other regions across the globe. Therefore we conceptually agree that Africa is sunny, more so, it is the indigenous region of the people who are more or less black or dark in complexion, with black hair color.

IMPACT OF IGWEBUIKE IDEOLOGY IN PEACE-BUILDING

In discussing *Igwebuike* as an idea, it is pertinent to stress here that peace-building in any given society, runs the holistic gamut of the people's livelihood ranging from economic, social, political, religious, and health welfare. It is on this background that this research would examine the import of *Igwebuike* ideology in peace-building among African States. It is also envisaged that this examination will arouse the interest of African people to understand that the idea of *Igwebuike* has recommendable relevance in sustaining peace among African States, countries or nations. Be that as it may, human livelihood is similar to the local stove phenomena where when there is absence of or exclusion of one of the three stands of the stove it incapacitates the firmness of the local stove. In regard to this, we can testify that when an aspect of people's welfare is in shambles, no matter how less important it may appear, it affects the peaceful sustainability, growth and progress of the people. Therefore this paper cut across peace-building in every affair of African people for actualizing central hallmark for general peace building in Africa. At this point, let us turn to examine them one after the other.

IMPORT OF *IGWEBUIKE* IDEOLOGY ON ECONOMIC PEACE

At the family level, economic peace helps to curb so many risks that could introduce violence of various forms, poverty etc. Ezeador and Ezeani (2019:60) buttress that:

> ... one of the traditional means of socialization of children is through trading. However, the introduction of young girls into street trading increased vulnerabilities of the girls to sexual harassment. Sexual abuse of young girl in Nigeria is linked with child labour ... poverty and inaccessible to funds for parents to take care of their wards has contributed to child sexual abuse.

On this realm, *Igwebuike* ideology becomes very pivotal. Instead of families engaging their children especially the girls in child labour because of poverty and inaccessibility to funds for parents to take care of their children to degenerate families expected standard, the concept of *Igwebuike* comes into place to salvage such ugly situation. Families became can collectively agree to engage on a particular source of income where both parents and wards should be involved in a risk free manner for the economic growth of the entire family. Their collective input can be on farm work and other mini businesses where parents and older siblings will have monitoring eye to one another. In this team work, everyone covers a particular vacuum in the business to enable the agreed enterprise to flourish. A group soldering of this nature tackles poverty and reduces other risks or dangers that could develop due to economic under development, and incapacitations. Okafor and Amechi –Ani (2019:309) maintain that:

> *Aziza* as a concept in Africa runs a whole garmut of the world–view of oneness, togetherness, communalism, patriotism, and synergy. The physical structure of the Aziza is that it is made up of individual palm frond sticks. These sticks can stand individually, but each individual stick cannot function on its own. Nevertheless, when they are tied together, they serve the purpose for which they are made or more. This had been the principle that had held African fore –bears together, and had aided their ability to achieve the much they could achieve before the advent of Western and Arabian culture.

What Okafor and Amaechi-Ani points out her echoes the replica of what the Igbo meant by *Igwebuike*. The *Aziza* symbol which they used as a principle is a masterpiece to understanding of the ideology *Igwebuike*. When people are consistently binded together for economic reasons and every member of the united economics front is economically comfortable peace is automatically built among the members. In a situation of this kind, one would not be wrong to say that such group has built economic peace. On a similar vein, Okafor (2019:90-91) elaborates thus:

> Economic factor appears to be the most common factor responsible for migration. Man always tries as much as possible to make ends meet. Human ends invariably differ from one person to another. In some cases, means of economic survival can be conceived in a given society with very limited areas of human endeavour, hence, people with higher ends struggles to source out other areas of economic engagements in order to actualize other life dreams. When these areas of endeavour are not found within the immediate environment, people begin to think of other places or settings where they can find the opportunities for wealth acquisition. In so doing, people migrate beyond their immediate environment.

This migration peculiar with people that source for economic interest has been classified as both permanent and temporary (Anigbo, 1992). No matter the class or condition for migration, for that of economic reason, migrants see group migration as a formidable mechanism for great economic achievement. The commonest team migration observable with the south-eastern part of Nigeria is the Ebonyi State (hired labourers) farmers migrants. They move in groups of two, three, four and five team partnership. Whatever farm work each team charges, they complete it in no distant time. As they do it, they attract more jobs for themselves, meanwhile they make enough money each annual farming season. Different ethnic groups, communities, villages, nations, and state indigenes who find themselves in foreign soils synergized and formed associations that principally assist their members in pursuing social and economic gains. For the fact that these group soldiering expeditions sustain the peoples' economic lives, they are bound to build peace both in Diaspora and at home to enable them keep acquiring more wealth and create a conducive atmosphere to enjoy the wealth.

Having seen that their coming together enhances opportunities of sustaining available economic tempo among them, they ought to keep the flag flying. With financial strength groups can sponsor community development project thereby extending economic development in various communities, local government areas, states and so on. With sustainable economic development definitely there are greater chances of building a durable peace in the continent- Africa.

Economic impact of Igwebuike ideology has not be exhausted. Let us x-ray the ideology in the involvement of women in traditional Igbo economy in the area of salt production and pollution of laid down traditional religious taboos. On this circumstance. Njoko (2008:17) maintains that:

> The salt lakes had their deities and were hedged around with many taboos. For example, menstruating women and one who had fornicated without atoning for it could not fetch water from the lake. Contravention of any of the taboos incurred the dreadful wrath of the deities. The women producers formed themselves into a guild. All these devices were aimed at achieving a set of purposes to restrict entry into the industry, exclude men from participation and protect the lakes from misuse and defilement. Salt seems to have been the mainstay of Uburu and Okposi Economy. It was marked throughout Igboland and even beyond

A critical look at the management of the salt industry by the Uburu and Okposi people demonstrates an exact presentation of *Igwebuike* ideology in an economic scene. The producers of the salt from the lake were predominantly women. They were challenged with a problem of tradition order promulgated by deities. But they were able to sustain the industry by forming a guild to deprive others, including men, the chance of entering the lake in order to protect the lake and allow their salt business to progress. This guild without any doubt had handled future war at the lake, foster calmness, order, noiselessness among other things because of the cooperation, oneness, togetherness and synergy that they were able to maintain. By doing this, they succeeded in building peace in their channel of economic sustainability. The earnings from the industry contribute immensely to the family up keep. As far as their families are well taken care of economically, with the spirit of togetherness and cooperation, peace will prevail. This peace motivated character would be extended to the larger or wider society, making the society peaceful. Apart from industrial woman group and other sorts of groups already discussed as integrals in the *Igwebuike* ideology, it will not be an over-statement to identify the same ideology in age grade system, kinship system, *Umuada, Umunyedi* etc as it affects the economic well being of the members and the society at large. The age set association, the kinship members, Umuada, Nwunyedi folks cetera have been active in economic assistance to members and their different communities. The age grade contributes immensely to the economy of the traditional African society. They can donate money to assist members and non-members. In some cases they sponsor skill acquisition programs, administer cooperative bodies etc. The Kinship, *Umuada*, and *Nwunyedi* institutions do related functions of the age grades.

Mr. Festus Ozor Egwu (personal communication, 20 April, 2020) narrated some experiences where a member of their kinship was attacked by a conflagration which destroyed his large rice farm in Anambra East area, he stated that their kinship on the hearing the incidence started with compulsory material contribution to their affected kinsman. As the Kinsmen were donating money and material things, the next farming season, according the informant, the *Umuada* folk mobilized themselves to assist the victim with two local week days free labour in which the victim was mandated not to offer food to the *Umuada*.

Considering the economic supports given to humanity with the believe in the *Igwebuike* ideology, everyone would embrace peace. The ideology would bring peace since it is used to make whoever that is in agony to be liberated or alleviated.

IMPORT OF *IGWEBUIKE* IDEOLOGY ON POLITICAL PEACE

Politically, the ideology helps to sustain peace. Orji and Olali in Okafor (2020) stress that traditional institutions are symbols of indigenous people's rights, privileges, laws, customs and traditions which include but not limited to parameter rules and their councils. The traditional institution in Nigeria context is inclusive of chiefs-in- council, elders in council, title holders who may be appointed based on their contributions to growth and development of their communities (Okafor, 2020:251. The act of producing these traditional leaders is often time an arduous task. Anigbo (1987: 176) uses references to Ibagwa-Aka to emphasize on this difficulty thus:

> The chieftaincy dispute in Ibagwa Aka centers on an issue as to which of two individuals should be the acknowledged representative of one town and be recognized as such both internally and externally such an individual is known by various names, Viz: a "chief," "natural ruler" "traditional ruler," "traditional head of autonomous Igbo village community".

In the struggle for such political leadership, taking the Igbo traditional political system as a masterpiece, it had been the *Igwebuike* ideology that settles it and still encourages peace-building. Majority side will always carry the vote. When an aspirant sees that majority of his people do not want him or her in certain leadership position in the village, community, etc he/she is left with no option than to accept defeat, without raising any dust. *Igwebuike* ideology responds to democratic representation for the people. Ijeoma (1988) opines that;

> Democracy therefore as an institutional arrangement and a method of making decisions endeavours to ensure that the society thereby arrives at an orderly, stable and legitimate government which would guarantee the presentation of rights and freedom with which men are endowed to. It is therefore my

contention that any methods through which men are able to institute an orderly, stable legitimate government to the satisfaction and happiness of the greatest number in democracy.

With this ideology, the political terrain historically and traditional was peaceful, orderly and stable. It had aided peace building among African States. Complete adherence to *Igwebuike* ideology on political matters will encourage peace-building because it restores political peace and stability

RELEVANCE OF *IGWEBUIKE* IDEOLOGY IN MAINTAINING SOCIAL PEACE

On the aspect of social group soldiering, Ikeyi (2004:210) explains thus:

> Although all of us probably would be able to identify and describe the various small groups we belong to, we might find it difficult to follow the same process with the large groups that affect us. As patrons or employees of large organization and governments, we function as part of large groups at all time. Thus, sociologists must study large groups as well as small groups in order to understand the workings of society.

In fact, all groups must not be at equal sizes to acquire the *Igwebuike* ideology. Groups differ probably as a result of circumstances, objective, natural scope and so on. When we listen to our social media, we hear about several groups showcasing their relevance in one way or the other. The actions of different groups tend to inform us that a united group is strength. Today the Academic Staff Union of Universities is embarking on an industrial action since March. The individual in this body cannot achieve any goal if left to pursue his welfare independently. But as far as the individuals in that platform have organized themselves in pursuance of everybody's interest, a lot of their welfare would be looked into. Other groups that make corrections on the affairs of the state also help to ensure decorum in numerous situations. When these groups follow legal measures to exist, they will diplomatically achieve some of their interests, meanwhile encouraging peace-building in the society.

Traditionally, certain united groups are known as agents of peace-building in the society. They include the masquerading society, the kinship, the *Umuada* and *Nwunyedi* folks, the age grade teams, the village associations or union etc. Occasions where a member of the society defaults the norms of the community considering the gender or sex of the offender, and the degree of the offence, one or more of these s are mobilized to visit and punish the offender. In some cases evil doers are ostracized or excommunicated.

In the olden days when Western education was introduced in the hinterland, the village unions or associations formed tax force teams to generate money that was used to finance school programs in the rural areas. The most intelligent pupils were sponsored in continuing their secondary school studies. Some village unions sent their intelligent sons to the university within Nigeria or even Overseas. All these are in the spirit of the ideology of *Igwebuike*. More so, this spirit of livelihood among the aboriginals encourages peace-building. Mr. Boniface Ejike (personal communication 14 November 2020) avers that in the year 1981, a member of his age grade, by name Emmanuel Ozo happened to beat his aunty and was stupidly disturbing the entire village. On a masquerading festival, the kinsmen, masquerade cult and his age set visited him in his father's house and was terribly dealt with. He continued that after beating the young Emmanuel with so many strokes of cane, he was coerced to finish 20 liters of water before he can be allowed to go for the day. According to Mr. Boniface, from that day henceforth, Mr. Emma really amended his ways. The Mr. Emma in question according to him is presently among those who advocate for peace in their community. *Igwebuike* ideology plays a vital role in the security of lives and properties. Today, towns and villages form their government through which they inaugurate vigilante or neighbourhood watch groups authorized by the national government in form of community policing to secure lives and properties. All these collective efforts are known as *Igwebuike*, and offers social peace among dwellers of several communities.

RELEVANCE OF *IGWEBUIKE* IDEOLOGY IN BUILDING RELIGIOUS PEACE

Traditionally, religion has been the filament that sustains life of community norms, customs, values and taboos. It is the deities that execute and monitor crimes. Though individuals have their personal objects that represent numerous gods for them but spiritual regard becomes so efficacious when a large group of people install shrines and the spirits that they will honour in worship. These deities, shrines, gods install by the people remain the intermediary between the people and the Almighty God. The groups unanimously promulgate righteous, unrighteous and forbidden actions the god of the land now do the policing role on the laid down rules agreed by the group. This group religious tenets are the yardsticks for maintenance of law and order in the traditional society. It is this background that when people remember the spiritual implications of committing certain abominations, they will rethink, thereby making the adherent to experience religious peace. Religions in return attracts peace to other spheres of life. Religious peace makes better transcendent connection which more people are committed to it. The holy bible states that when two or three are gathered, I am in their midst. The more people gather together as a religious community, the more they see themselves as brothers and sisters living peacefully. Problems come in when critics and misconceptions emanate from two or more religions or denominations. On this note ecumenism now forms a basis to harmonize the *Igwebuike* ideology that will foster religious peace among the hostile groups. At anytime an African man feels he is having some distant relationship with God it gives him so much worry, in order to assure close contact with the supernatural they pledge, vow and sacrifice. Most of these pledges and vows are made by individuals in the midst of the a worshipping community. To this end Okafor (2019:74) asserts that

The African man engages in religious pledges and vows to enable him be psychologically and spiritually balanced. God is the sole arbiter and controller of man and his activities here on earth. Based on this, he continuously makes pledges and vows because of the problem that assails his feelings.

As far as these pledges and vows are made amidst the group, the group led by the officiating priests must acknowledge the fulfillment of those pledges and vows made. It is culturally believed that they are undergoing covenants of peace reminding every member of the group that curses befall whoever makes troubles among them. In order to lay more emphases on the religious collective commitment among Africans, Nwokike (2005:8) uses the Awha people's belief in the worship of the earth goddess thus:

> This is Ani Awha, representing the earth which gives yam and every food crop: the earth on which plants grow: the earth on which animal grow: and the mother earth which eats up a dead animal or tree. In Awha, when libations are poured even in simple prayer Ani Awha is called upon together with the ancestors to come and take control of each situation to bring peace, prosperity and good health.

Even though Africans felt they have secured religious peace still supplicate for general peace-building and prosperity of the entire community as a group. In most cases, collective religious activities of a group are often time used to build peace among nations, families, communities etc.

IMPORTANCE OF *IGWEBUIKE* IDEOLOGY IN RESTORING HEALTH PEACE

Unhealthy conditions absolutely hinder peace of mind of the affected persons and relations. Health itself is a condition of being sick or not being sick. The health of an individual influences to a large extent, the life of the person. To the traditional Igbo, the summumbonum or highest value is life (*Ndu*). This is made manifest in their names e.g. *Ndubisi*-life is of supreme importance, *Nduka* – life is greater, *Ndukaku* – life is greater than wealth, *Nduamaka* – life is good (Madu,2004:23). Onunwa in Madu (2004) points that health is for more social that biological. It does not entirely mean an absence of physical ailments. That there is a clear unitary concept of psychosomatic interrelations is an apparent reciprocity between the mind and matters. Health and life intermingle. We cannot virtually say that one is sick, there are undesirable conditions that can make one unhealthy in absence of sickness. Take for example when very young lady loses her husband at the very early stage of the marriage. Condition of this nature gives both the deceased age grade, *Umuada*, *Nwunyedi* and the kinship members serious concerns. Even the widow's maiden home members are also worried. These groups rally around the widow for assistance with the intention to think out ways to secure her life and longitivity of her stay in the deceased husband's home. Similar concern is applicable to a widower.

Then when someone is sick the African people reaction will easily reflect message on how sacred life is being regarded. The traditional societies that make up Nigeria using Igbo ethnic group as a specimen, had deep respect for the sacredness of life and dignity of human person. African traditional societies had a lot of cultural values such as philosophical thoughts and proverbs, community life, hospitality, sense of human relations and industry, respect for authority and elders, sense of the sacred and of religion that were deep, sense of time and the respect for the sacredness of life (Ele, 2019). In African, a patient is assisted by a lot of groups of which some of them he is a member. For the treatment, ideas flow from every corner. Some people have reconciled their differences because of illness. The African man, especially the Igbo believe that enmity does not extend to illness or death. It is the idea of *Igwebuike* that arouses the motivation to care for the sick or afflicted because it is a reciprocal relationship. If it is discovered that an individual is reluctant over other people's life and health consequently he will be left alone when he faces the same problem. In that regard group attention to health relatively becomes compulsory thereby establishes the desire for peace building in the society.

RECOMMENDATIONS:

The study recommends that:

1. The traditional agents of peace building e.g. the masquerading cult, age-grade system, *Umuada* and *Nwunyedi* folks, etc. should be encouraged as far as they conform with the civil rules.
2. Members of the civil society should always try to align with group cooperative movement with the positive intention to improve the living standard of the populace.
3. Individuals with financial prowess should form groups for still acquisition who will be training successive groups on different skill especially in rural and semi-urban settings. This will help to improve inter-personal relationships among the citizenry.
4. Religious sentiment should not be allowed to counter the insisting *Igwebuike* system of living in African states. Religion should be kept far from the people's togetherness.
5. Government, Non-governmental organizations, agencies etc can assist the society by embarking on sensitization programmes to improve more on the *Igwebuike* ideology as a veritable source of peace building in African society.

CONCLUSION

Igwebuike is a wonderful ideology which the society does not assimilate as valuable formation that is capable of building peace in the society. African fore-bears had used it to maintain peace to a reasonable degree, through the masquerade society, age-grade, *Umunna* – kinsmen/

kindred, *Umuada, Ndi Nwumjed,* the youth organizations, the family etc. It was an ideology used in the decades back for the maintenance and construction of roads, markets, public squares, installation of pipe-borne water, electrification of communities, building of schools, sign boards, reconciliation of warning individuals, families and communities.

In some cases the ideology might not fight for peace to exist. It is noteworthy that there are so many areas of the people's lives that it is adopted in which it enhances and promotes peace building. Generally speaking, as far as the ideology is able to promote economic peace, political peace, and social peace, religious peace and otherwise, it has automatically portrayed in earnest, central peace for all and sundry.

REFERENCES

Akukwe, F.N (1996). *Community development cooperatives and democracy. A guide for social workers.* Onitsha: Veritas Printing & Publishing co. Ltd

Amgbo O.A.C (1987), *Commensality and Human Relationship among the Igbo.* Enugu: Chuka Printing Company limited.

Anigbo, O.A.C (1992). *Igbo elite and Western Europe*: Onitsha: Africana-Fep Publishers Limited.

Ele, C.O (2019), "The sacredness of human life in contemporary Nigeria: Violation and solutions" in E.J.O Ndubisi (ed) *Oracle of Wisdom Journal of Philosophy and Public Affairs,* Vol 3, No 1 PP 23-36.

Ezeador C.N and Ezeani, K.D. (2019). "Engaging women in peace keeping: An alternative way to curbing sexual violence in women" in J.O. Ndubisi (ed) *Oracle of Wisdom Journal of Philosophy and Public Affairs* Vol. 3 (1) PP 57-64,

Ijeoma, B.I. (1988). *Afrocracy: Basis for national stability: Partless democracy.* Benin: Idodo Umeh Publishers Limited.

Ikeyi, J.O. (2004). *Sociology: An introductory text.* Enugu: Zik Chuks Nigeria.

Kanu, A. I. (2016a). *Igwebuike* as a trend in African philosophy. *IGWEBUIKE: An African Journal of Arts and Humanities. 2. 1.* 97-101.

Kanu, A. I. (2017c). *Igwebuike* as an Igbo-African philosophy of inclusive leadership. *Igwebuike: An African Journal of Arts and Humanities.* Vol. 3 No 7. pp. 165-183.

Kanu, A. I. (2017d). *Igwebuike* philosophy and the issue of national development. *Igwebuike: An African Journal of Arts and Humanities.* Vol. 3 No 6. pp. 16-50.

Kanu, A. I. (2017f). *Igwebuike* as an Igbo-African Ethic of Reciprocity. *IGWEBUIKE: An African Journal of Arts and Humanities. 3. 2. pp.* 153-160.

Kanu, I. A. (2012). The problem of being in metaphysics. *African Research Review: An International Multi-Disciplinary Journal.* Vol.6. No.2. April. pp. 113-122.

Kanu, I. A. (2012). The problem of personal identity in metaphysics. *International Journal of Arts and Humanities.* Vol.1. No.2. pp.1-13.

Kanu, I. A. (2012a). The concept of life and person in African anthropology. In E. Ezenweke and I. A. Kanu (Eds.). *Issues in African traditional religion and philosophy* (pp. 61-71). Nigeria: Augustinian.

Kanu, I. A. (2012b). Towards an Igbo Christology. In E. Ezenweke and I. A. Kanu (Eds.). *Issues in African traditional religion and philosophy* (pp. 75-98). Nigeria: Augustinian.

Kanu, I. A. (2013). African identity and the emergence of globalization. *American International Journal of Contemporary Research.* Vol. 3. No. 6. pp. 34-42.

Kanu, I. A. (2013). African Identity and the Emergence of Globalization. *American International Journal of Contemporary Research.* Vol. 3. No. 6. pp. 34-42.

Kanu, I. A. (2013). Globalisation, globalism and African philosophy. C. Umezinwa (Ed.). *African philosophy: A pragmatic approach to African probems* (pp. 151-165). Germany: Lambert.

Kanu, I. A. (2013). On the sources of African philosophy. *Filosofia Theoretica: Journal of African Philosophy, Culture and Religion, Vol. 2. No. 1.* pp. 337-356.

Kanu, I. A. (2013). The dimensions of African cosmology. *Filosofia Theoretica: Journal of African Philosophy, Culture and Religion, Vol. 2. No. 2.* pp. 533-555.

Kanu, I. A. (2014). A historiography of African philosophy. *Global Journal for Research Analysis. Volume. 3. Issue. 8.* pp. 188-190.

Kanu, I. A. (2014). Being and the categories of being in Igbo philosophy. *African Journal of Humanities. Volume 1. Issue 1.* pp. 144-159.

Kanu, I. A. (2016a). *Igwebuike* as the consummate foundation of African Bioethical principles. *An African journal of Arts and Humanities* Vol.2 No1 June, pp.23-40.

Kanu, I. A. (2016b) *Igwebuike* as an Expressive Modality of Being in African ontology. *Journal of Environmental and Construction Management. 6. 3.* pp.12-21.

Kanu, I. A. (2017). *Igwebuike* as an Igbo-African Philosophy for Christian-Muslim Relations in Northern Nigeria. In Mahmoud Misaeli (Ed.). *Spirituality and Global Ethics* (pp. 300-310). United Kingdom: Cambridge Scholars.

Kanu, I. A. (2017). *Igwebuike* as an Igbo-African Philosophy for the Protection of the Environment. *Nightingale International Journal of Humanities and Social Sciences.* Vol. 3. No. 4. pp. 28-38.

Kanu, I. A. (2017). *Igwebuike* as the Hermeneutic of Individuality and Communality in African Ontology. *NAJOP: Nasara Journal of Philosophy.* Vol. 2. No. 1. pp. 162-179.

Kanu, I. A. (2017a). *Igwebuike* and Question of Superiority in the Scientific Community of Knowledge. *Igwebuike: An African Journal of Arts and Humanities.* Vol.3 No1. pp. 131-138.

Kanu, I. A. (2017b). *Igwebuike* as a Complementary Approach to the Issue of Girl-Child Education. *Nightingale International Journal of Contemporary Education and Research.* Vol. 3. No. 6. pp. 11-17.

Kanu, I. A. (2018). *Igwe Bu Ike* as an Igbo-African Hermeneutics of National Development. *Igbo Studies Review. No. 6.* pp. 59-83.

Kanu, I. A. (2018). Igwebuike as an African Integrative and Progressive Anthropology. *NAJOP: Nasara Journal of Philosophy.* Vol. 2. No. 1. pp. 151-161.

Madu, J.E. (2004). *Honesty to African cultural heritage.* Onitsha: Coskan Associates.

Njoku, O.N (2008). "Women in traditional economy" (ed) E.J, Otagburuagu and A.E Afigbo, *New Brides More Hopes: Igbo Women in Socio-Economic Change.* PP 104-135, Enugu: Global Publishers Nigeria Limited.

Nwokike, J.C (2005*). Pottery and cultural life of Awka people plus art history* 1&2. Enugu: De-Adroit Innovation

Okafor, E. I and Amaechi-Ani (2019). "*Aziza* as a concept and principle. A basis for a formidable African society" (Ed) E. Nwabueze. *New Frontiers in Contemporary African Studies.* Pp 309-318 Enugu: Abic Publishers Limited.

Okafor, E.I (2019). "Migration as a pattern of life: implications on the religion-traditional identity of Africans" (Ed) I.A. Kanu. *Journal of African Studies and Sustainable Development*. Vol. 2 No. 7, pp 87-100. Yola: Altograde Nigeria Limited.

Okafor, E.I (2019). "Pledges and vows to deities in African Traditional Religion: Implications to the practitioners and the society: An Igbo example" in E. Nwabueze (e.d) *lkoro Journal of Contemporary African Studies* Vol 13 No. 2 pp 70-84, Nsukka: Institute of African Studies.

Okafor, E.I (2020) "Influence of criminal and violent minded Interests on Nigeria traditional institutions: The question of morality in a populous religious society". (Ed) F.O. Orabueze. *Ogbazuluobodo University of Nigeria Journal of Multidisciplinary Studies* vol. 1 No. 02 pp 247-256, Enugu: Timex

Summers, D. (2001). *Longman dictionary of contemporary English*, England: Parson Education Ltd

ABOUT THE AUTHOR

Ikechukwu Anthony KANU, O.S.A is a Friar of the Order of Saint Augustine, Province of Nigeria. He is Professor of African Philosophy and Religion, Tansian University, and a Tenured Professor of Orthodox Studies at The University of America, San Francisco, USA. The former Rector of Villanova Polytechnic, Imesi Ile, Osun State and currently an Adjunct Professor to the University of Jos, Plateau State, Veritas University Abuja and Saint Albert the Great Major Seminary, Abeokuta. He is the President of the Association for the Promotion of African Studies (APAS) and the Global President of the World Cultural Studies Research Association (WCRA).

Printed in the United States
by Baker & Taylor Publisher Services